Bondage to the Dead

Modern Jewish History

Henry L. Feingold, *Series Editor*

Detail of Warsaw Ghetto monument, fortieth anniversary of Warsaw Ghetto Uprising, April 1983. Courtesy of the author.

For Jo— best 9/9 7
All the best

Bondage to the Dead

Poland and the Memory of the Holocaust

Michael C. Steinlauf

Syracuse University Press

Some of the material used in this book was previously published in "Poland" by Michael Steinlauf in *The World Reacts to the Holocaust*, edited by David S. Wyman (Baltimore: Johns Hopkins Univ. Press, 1996). Used with permission.

Permission to reprint the poem "I did not manage to save . . ." by Jerzy Ficowski from *A Reading of Ashes* published by the Menard Press, London, is gratefully acknowledged.

The paper used in this publication meets the minimum requirements of American National Standard for Information Sciences—Permanence of Paper for Printed Library Materials, ANSI Z39.48-1984. ∞

Library of Congress Cataloging-in-Publication Data
Steinlauf, Michael.
    Bondage to the dead: Poland and the memory of the Holocaust / Michael Steinlauf.
        p.   cm. — (Modern Jewish history)
    ISBN 0-8156-2729-7 (alk. paper). — ISBN 0-8156-0403-3 (pbk. : alk. paper)
    1. Jews—Persecutions—Poland. 2. Holocaust, Jewish (1939–1945)—Poland.
    3. Holocaust survivors—Poland. 4. Poland—Ethnic relations. I. Title.
    II. Series.
DS135.P6S76 1996
940.53'18'0943—dc20   96-9714

Contents

Illustrations

Preface

Tracing the development of the Polish reaction to the Holocaust in the decades after World War II is both extremely important and extremely difficult. It is important, first of all, because of geography. In 1939, Poland was the center of the European Jewish world. It was the site of the largest Jewish population in Europe, the heirs to a highly developed civilization rooted for nearly a thousand years in Polish soil. The destruction of the Jews of Poland accounted for more than half of all the victims of the Holocaust. At the same time, and hardly coincidentally, here most of the ghettos were established, and here the death camps stood: Chełmno, Treblinka, Sobibór, Majdanek, Bełżec, Auschwitz-Birkenau. Here the railroad tracks converged, bringing Jews from the remotest corners of Europe to feed the Nazi death machine. At the most fundamental level, therefore, Poland was the arena within which the encounter between murderers and victims, Germans and Jews, that we have come to call the Holocaust played itself out. This event did not directly involve Poles. Poles found themselves, rather, witnesses to the Holocaust, from beginning to end. To witness murder on such a scale, at such close range, for such a long time, cannot lead to simple responses. To inquire about Polish reaction to the Holocaust is to investigate the effects of a mass psychic and moral trauma unprecedented in history.

Superimposed upon this paradigm are the many things that made

Poles more than just witnesses to the Holocaust. In relation to the Germans they were also victims, indeed, after the Jews and the Gypsies, the most relentlessly tormented national group in Hitler's Europe. Publicly at least, Polish memory of the war years has been preoccupied with issues of Polish survival, martyrdom, and resistance. In relation to the Jews, although Poles collectively were powerless to affect their fate as a whole, this was not the case on an individual level. Individual Poles could and did help save, or destroy, individual Jews. Although most Poles did neither, doing nothing was itself, for each individual, the product of a choice.

Such moral and psychological complications become even denser when we situate the war years amid the complexities of recent Polish history. Chief among these is the development in Poland of modern anti-Semitism, which was particularly influential just before the war and played a substantial role in Polish politics and society during and after the war. Anti-Semitism, as not only Poles have pointed out, is hardly identical with mass murder, but when we examine Polish responses to the Holocaust, Polish anti-Semitism, in its numerous historical contexts and functions, is a crucial complication.

To this must be added the factor that more than any other has crippled the way Poles recall not just the Holocaust, but all of their history: Poland's incorporation, for over four decades, into the Soviet empire. In Poland, as elsewhere in Eastern Europe, postwar rulers, whose central legitimation was the alleged historical inevitability of the communist system, worked especially hard to rewrite history books, redesign school curriculums, reeducate youth to believe that all of history was no more than a prelude to, the "prehistory" of, the Communist seizure of power. Within this carefully crafted narrative, uses for the Holocaust were also found. The fate of the Jews became an object lesson in the horror of this prehistory, and another proof that the only alternative to "progress" was "barbarism." But discussion of the Holocaust, like so much of postwar Polish discourse, evolved in an atmosphere so politically charged, so constricted by labyrinthine political manipulation, that what counted as a rule was not what was said but who said it and what forces they represented. Meanwhile, collective psychic and moral dilemmas that the war had seared into Polish consciousness, problems that, as nowhere else in postwar Europe, cried out for an airing, for a long and necessarily painful public exploration, were instead driven underground to fester.

Although this situation, its causes, and its consequences are the subject of this book, one consequence should be touched on here: the difficulty of writing such an book. Nearly every issue that will be examined in the following pages is controversial. This applies not only to postwar responses to the Holocaust but also to Polish Jewish relations throughout history and, above all, just before and during World War II. Half a century after these events, not only their meaning but the events themselves are still hotly disputed, even by historians. It would be naive to ignore the identity of the disputants. In most cases the sides are clear: Poles versus Jews, both sides often having experienced the events in question. The truth may lie "in between," but it may with equal likelihood lie with one or another of the "sides," or somewhere else entirely. Given all this, what remains is to make one's way as best one can through a forbidding terrain using all the skills, both professional and human, at one's disposal. For the record, because in this field particularly such things matter: I am a French-born son of Polish Jewish Holocaust survivors, raised and educated in the United States, who has spent considerable time in Poland since the early 1980s. I pride myself on being perceived as "pro-Jewish" among Poles and "pro-Polish" among Jews. Preparing to write this book, I was drawn to the opening words of Emmanuel Ringelblum's study, *Polish-Jewish Relations During the Second World War*, a work that the archivist of the Warsaw Ghetto wrote in hiding after the ghetto's destruction, just before his capture and murder by the Germans. Ringelblum, his wife and son, and thirty-one other Jews were hidden by a Pole, who was killed along with them, and were also betrayed by a Pole.

When a *sofer*—a Jewish scribe—sets out to copy the Torah, he must, according to religious law, take a ritual bath in order to purify himself of all uncleanness and impurity. This scribe takes up his pen with a trembling heart, because the smallest mistake in transcription means the destruction of the whole work. It is with this feeling of fearfulness that I have begun this work.[1]

Half a century later and worlds removed from the hell in which these words were written, the subject before us remains disturbing and important enough that recalling these words seems an appropriate way to begin.[2]

Acknowledgments

Preliminary research for this book was funded in part by a grant from IREX. I would like to thank Jerzy Halbersztadt for his extraordinary involvement in this project from beginning to end, including providing me with a significant portion of my documentation. Ewa Koźmińska-Frejlak also assisted with documentation. Stefan Wilkanowicz made available to me important bibliographical materials. Monika Adamczyk-Garbowska, Alina Cała, Jerzy Halbersztadt, Czesław Miłosz, Rafael Scharf, and Paweł Śpiewak made invaluable criticisms of the manuscript. I also owe the aforementioned, along with Helena Datner-Śpiewak, Konstanty Gebert, Jan Jagielski, Jerzy Jedlicki, Ninel Kos, Monika and Stanisław Krajewski, Hanna Krall, Gayle Wimmer, Andrzej Wróblewski (may his memory be a blessing), Ryszarda Zachariasz, and numerous other Poles and Polish Jews a great debt of gratitude for innumerable hours of talk dedicated to illuminating this anguished tangle.

This book is my gift to them, a small attempt to reciprocate for all I have received.

Last but hardly least, to Meri and Zevi, who kept me company and kept me sane.

Michael C. Steinlauf is Senior Research Fellow at the YIVO Institute for Jewish Research in New York. He was born in Paris and grew up in Brooklyn, New York; his parents were Holocaust survivors from Poland. A Fulbright Fellow in 1983–84, he was one of the first students since the war permitted to study Jewish history in Poland. Fluent in Polish and Yiddish, he has returned to Poland on numerous other occasions, among them on behalf of the United States Holocaust Memorial Museum. He has published widely on the cultural history of East European Jews and Polish-Jewish relations, and has taught at the University of Michigan at Ann Arbor, Brandeis University, Gratz College, and Franklin and Marshall College.

Bondage to the Dead

1

Poles and Jews Before the Holocaust

In the Polish Commonwealth (to 1795)

The Jewish connection to Poland is as old as Polish history: the earliest known reference to Poland is from the pen of a Spanish Jew who in the tenth century accompanied an Arab official on a diplomatic mission to Eastern Europe.[1] The earliest records of Jewish settlement in Poland date from the late twelfth century. This is also the date of several hundred silver coins with Hebrew letters, presumably struck by Jewish minters in the employ of Polish princes. Although historians have at various times emphasized non-Western sources of Jewish migration to Poland, today there is agreement that it was primarily Western European in origin. Its key period was the fourteenth and fifteenth centuries, when economic, political, and social dislocation combined with persecution to drive thousands of Jews eastwards from northeastern France and Germany. This was a migration, in other words, of Ashkenazi Jews (*Ashkenaz* being the Hebrew name for Germany), who brought with them a well-developed culture based in Hebrew texts as well as in a young and particularly flexible vernacular language, Yiddish. During the centuries when the remaining Jewish communities of Western Europe suffered the turmoil that prepared them for the problematic gifts of Emancipation, Ashkenazic civilization sank deep roots in the East.[2]

In Polish historiography, the century and a half from 1500 to 1650 is known as the Golden Age. It was a period when Polish kings ruled a vast Polish-Lithuanian Commonwealth [*Rzeczpospolita Obojge Narodów*] that stretched from the Oder River to the Dnieper, from the Baltic to the Black Sea.[3] At a time when its western neighbors were caught up in fratricidal religious strife, and both to the east and to the west, experienced the birth pangs of new absolutist states, the Polish Commonwealth presented a striking contrast: a land of great ethnic and religious diversity, multiple centers of authority, and comparative stability. Besides Jews, the Commonwealth was home to German Lutherans, Polish Calvinists, Arians, and Anabaptists; Armenians, Greeks, and Scots; Tatar and Turkish Moslems; and Eastern Orthodox communities, many frequently themselves in the throes of schism. The Church, which saw itself as Rome's last defense against "eastern," that is, Russian, "barbarism," was a relatively youthful institution still somewhat unsure of itself. Polish religious tolerance, guaranteed in the Confederation of Warsaw of 1573, a document unparalleled in the West at this time, was in practice less a question of principle than survival: religious uniformity could simply not be enforced.[4] Regardless, and most important for our purposes, this is the frequently cited historical underpinning of a key ingredient of modern Polish self-perception: the conviction that Poles are at heart a very tolerant people.[5]

Political authority too tended toward comparatively democratic, decentralized forms. Beginning in 1573, Polish kings were elected by a parliament of representatives of the noble estate [*szlachta*]. Membership in the *szlachta*, which constituted 10 percent of the population (a high proportion by Western European standards of the time), was hereditary, but was not entirely closed to those of common birth; non-Poles and even converted Jews were accepted into its ranks. Increasingly, the king's authority was circumscribed by the power of a nobility based in huge landed estates, disposing of private towns and even private armies. The grain trade was the system's lifeblood: shipped down the Vistula River to the Baltic port of Danzig (Gdańsk), Polish grain fed Western Europe and enriched Polish landowners. Poland of the Golden

Age was often called a "noblemen's paradise." It also provided a particularly favorable environment for its numerous ethnic-religious communities not just to practice their way of life in relative tranquility, but to enjoy as well considerable autonomy in the administration of their affairs.

All this may suggest why Jews found the Polish Commonwealth during this period a rather hospitable place to live. At first they settled in the western Polish lands, primarily in the crown cities. Here, granted charters of privileges much more favorable than those in Western Europe, Jews filled trade and financial functions like those they had for centuries in the West. But the cities held antagonists: German merchants, Polish and German artisans organized in guilds decrying Jewish competition; Church authorities denouncing Jewish influence on Christian souls. Not as lethal as their Western European counterparts, such antagonisms nevertheless made attacks on the Jewish quarter by artisans' apprentices and seminary students, as well as temporary orders of expulsion from various cities, a not uncommon feature of life in fifteenth-century Poland. Beginning in the sixteenth century, Jews increasingly linked their economic fate to the dynamic *szlachta*, who, over the next century and a half, expanded their power particularly in the eastern borderlands, the *kresy*, as the Poles called them. These ethnically mixed territories that lay on the shifting eastern frontier of the Commonwealth today make up Lithuania, Belarus, a bit of eastern Poland, and most of Ukraine. Jews served the *szlachta* as lessees and managers of the new properties. In so doing, while colonizing the eastern frontier for the *szlachta*, they founded or expanded towns that often acquired large Jewish majorities. These towns, which Jews called *shtetlekh* (sing. *shtetl*), particularly common in the east but widespread throughout the Commonwealth, became the characteristic form of Jewish settlement until late in the nineteenth century, when the largest cities again began to attract great numbers of Jews.

In the economy of agrarian Poland, the *shtetl* played a fundamental role. While the lord reigned in his nearby manor, and peasants toiled in the lord's fields that surrounded their tiny villages, the *shtetl's* marketplace, ringed with stores and workshops, and weekly filled with peasant wagons, functioned as the sole commercial center for the entire region, the only place to sell produce or livestock, purchase nails or matches, mend or buy a pot or fur coat or pair of boots. Here the Jews had no economic competitors, and were relatively free, so long as they continued to pay taxes to the *shtetl's* lord, to organize their communal life as they saw fit. A traditional community council [*kehilla*] collected taxes for the landowner and for its own purposes, thereby maintaining a cemetery, synagogue, study houses, civil court, ritual slaughterhouse, bathhouse, poorhouse, and similar institutions along with their functionaries. Numerous voluntary societies [*khevres*] provided a host of other services. From the cutting of one's fingernails to the regulation of weights and measures to the chanting of daily prayers, Jewish life was lived under the sign of Jewish law and custom. Although many aspects of this life were common to Jewish communities throughout medieval Europe, in Poland Jews were enabled to create a particularly coherent culture, one characterized by what Abraham Heschel has called "the highest degree of inwardness."[6] Moreover, beginning in the Golden Age and lasting nearly to the end of the Commonwealth, Polish Jews developed an intercommunal structure unprecedented in the Diaspora: a hierarchy of regional and provincial councils overseen by two supreme deliberative and judicial bodies that constituted a kind of "national" Jewish government.[7] In the sixteenth and seventeenth centuries, Jews compared communal life in Poland to that in the Land of Israel in Second Temple times, while in Polish popular discourse the expression "Poland, paradise of the Jews" joined "noblemen's paradise" as a term with strongly ironic connotations.

The Golden Age ended in the second half of the seventeenth century as the Commonwealth was laid waste by invasions of Swedes, Prussians, Tatars, Russians, and Cossacks. The Cossack armies in particular, filled with Ukrainian Orthodox peasants eager for revenge against their Polish Catholic and Jewish colonizers, were responsible for slaughter that imprinted itself for centuries in both Polish and Jewish historical memory.[8] In the aftermath of several decades of violence, the Polish grain trade failed to revive. Increasingly, the Commonwealth's virtues of multiplicity and decentralization proved its undoing: royal authority disintegrated;

szlachta families, often in alliance with foreign powers, plotted and waged war against each other; cities fell into decay; and a once free peasantry found itself bound to the land in serfdom. This decomposition led, by the end of the eighteenth century, to the partition of the Commonwealth among its three newly powerful neighbors, and to the disappearance of Poland as a political entity.

The trauma of the Cossack massacres, however, did little to arrest the continuous development of Jewish communities. If the old cities declined, Jews rooted themselves ever more firmly in the *shtetlekh* and reaffirmed their economic alliance with the *szlachta*. If grain no longer functioned as an economic mainstay, Jewish merchants moved to lumber and furs, while shopkeepers and artisans developed new products and services. By the mid-eighteenth century, when there were about 750,000 Jews living in the Commonwealth, one quarter of all the Jews in the world lived in Polish *shtetlekh*.[9] Jews had become a fixture of the Polish landscape, as familiar an element of the natural order as the peasant village or the landowner's manor. Indeed, one popular *szlachta* conception identified this tripartite division of the social world with the races descended from the sons of Noah: the peasant as Ham, the landowner as Japhet, the Jew as Shem.

Although individual relations varied greatly, on the whole relations between Jews and Poles were free of violence. This is hardly to say that Poles and Jews "knew each other." Side by side with a host of personal contacts between individual Poles and Jews, contacts that were often not without a measure of respect and even affection, was a system of powerfully rooted stereotypes. For the peasant, the Jew was associated with the character traits typical of the preindustrial conception of trade: craftiness, deceit, and miserliness. He was also an object of mystery, the possessor of secret lore, an alien being who, as the Church never let the peasant forget, had rejected the true faith and was implicated in the murder of God. Yet counterbalancing such fears was the Jew's role as an object of laughter: perceived as sober, chaste, nonviolent and therefore unmanly, ridiculous in dress, speech, and customs. For the *szlachta*, little was fearful about the Jew. The landowner's Jewish agent was often a trusted adviser; indeed, every noble was said to "have his Jew." But the mass of Jews in the landowner's eyes was con-

Partition of Poland

temptible and ludicrous. By the nineteenth century, the comic stereotype of the dancing little Jew [*żydek*, pronounced "zhidek"], clutching his belly, stroking his beard and babbling gibberish had become a fixture of the popular imagination, a kind of Polish Black Sambo.[10] For his part, the Jew, outwardly subservient, was inwardly contemptuous of both the *poyer* (peasant) and the *porets* (noble), though his attitude toward the *porets* was colored by awe as well. For the Jew, both peasant and noble, each in his own way, manifested those characteristics of brutality, ignorance, and loutishness that were the antithesis of the Jewish ethos; they were, in a word, *goyim* (gentiles).

Under Three Empires (1795–1918)

For more than one hundred years, while "Polish" continued to designate a language and increasingly a modern national and cultural identity, the geographic term "Poland" remained a historical curiosity. The Commonwealth was partitioned among its three neighboring empires. Prussia took the western areas, Austria the southern province called Galicia, while the lion's share, central Poland along with most of the eastern borderlands, went to Russia.[11] For the Prussians and the Austrians, their new Polish provinces were agricultural hinterlands. By the end of the nineteenth century, Poles in both areas were reaping some of the economic and social benefits of the West, though Bismarck and Franz-Joseph pursued very different nationality policies: in Germany, a campaign aimed at Germanizing the Poles [*Kulturkampf*]; in Galicia after 1867, the development of a haven for Polish nationalism, and freedom for the *szlachta*, still ensconced in their traditional estates, to run the province. In the huge territories they had annexed, the czars at first pursued policies that varied geographically. The *kresy*, where a Polish minority of city dwellers and *szlachta* lived in a sea of Lithuanian, Belorussian, and Ukrainian peasant villages and Jewish towns, were to russify and merge with the Great Russian heartland. Central Poland (so-called Congress Poland, after the Congress of Vienna in 1815 that had drawn its boundaries), most of whose population was ethnically Polish, was at first permitted a degree of autonomy.

Not content with limited autonomy as the western showpiece

Congress of Vienna 1815

of the czars, however, and nurtured by the memory of Tadeusz Kościuszko's last stand against the Russians in 1794, the *szlachta* dreamed of freedom, not only at home but also throughout Europe. Their ethos led them to become a vanguard in the republican struggles that transformed the European political system during the nineteenth century. They fought the old order in Polish legions organized under Napoleon, and a generation later as defenders of the revolutionary cause in Italy, Hungary, and elsewhere in the Springtime of Nations of 1848. They also mounted two doomed insurrections against the Russians, in 1831 and 1863. "Poland is a symbol," declared the Danish Jewish critic George Brandes in 1885, "a symbol of all which the best of the human race have loved, and for which they have fought. Everywhere in Europe where there has been any fighting for freedom in this century, the Poles have taken part in it, on all battlefields, on all barricades. . . . Conversely, it may also be said that everywhere [in Europe] where there is any fighting for freedom, there is fighting for Poland."[12] Freedom fighting bore a price. In the aftermath of the second uprising against the czars, the very name Poland was replaced by the designation Vistulaland, *szlachta* property was expropriated, and, with few exceptions, Polish speech was banned from public use. Polish national consciousness was cultivated above all in the Church, which during this period, particularly at the parish level, also provided important material aid to the insurrectionists, and thereby solidified an intimate alliance with the Polish national cause.

For Polish Jews in the nineteenth century, as for Poles, much depended on who their new masters were.[13] In Prussian Poland, given the sudden opportunity to "westernize," many Jews moved to the larger German cities and were soon indistinguishable from their German co-religionists. In Galicia, by the end of the nineteenth century, Jewish life fell into two different patterns. In Kraków, Lwów, and other large cities, an educated, emancipated Jewish bourgeoisie had begun to enter Austrian politics; in the countryside, where the *szlachta* still ruled as in the days of the Commonwealth, masses of Jews continued to live a traditional life in cramped, economically marginal *shtetlekh*.

In Russia the situation was more problematic. For centuries the czars had refused to admit the "enemies of Christ" into their realms;

Jews in Russia 19ᵗ c. ——

with the partitions, they suddenly found themselves ruling over
nearly a million Jews. Their instinctive response was to isolate
them from the Great Russian masses; this response was the origin
of the Pale of Settlement, essentially the areas of conquered Poland
where the Jews were settled and to which they were now confined. What to do with the Jews beyond locking them up was a
question the czars never consistently resolved. Czarist attempts to
force reforms of Jewish society were often indistinguishable from
punitive decrees. Even an occasional carrot, such as access to universities or permission to reside in Moscow or St. Petersburg, was
invariably succeeded by the stick. After 1881, there were no more
carrots. Used as scapegoats for everything from peasant drunken-
ness to the revolutionary movement, Jews were subjected to ever
new restrictions, expelled from villages and cities, and murdered
in pogroms fomented, beginning early in the twentieth century,
by groups with government connections.

Throughout the nineteenth century, as with their other subject
minorities, the czars attempted to undermine Jewish communal
autonomy. Jewish communities found numerous ways to circum-
vent such decrees; bribing corrupt officials was one of the most
popular. More important, even under siege, traditional Jewish society manifested signs of considerable inner strength and even
renewal. Indeed, these phenomena characterized Jewish communities both in the Russian "prison house of nations" and in Galicia under "enlightened" Habsburg rule. We may point first of all
to extraordinary biologic vitality. During the ninety years from 1820
to 1910, while the population of the Russian Empire rose from 46
to 131 million, the number of Jews increased from 1.6 to 5.6 million.[14] This gives a higher rate of growth than the general population even without the 2 million Jews who migrated westward
during the last decades of this period. When these are added the
result is a rate of growth 70 percent higher than that of the general
population. In Galicia, the Jewish growth rate was even higher.

Second, the nineteenth century witnessed the conquest of Eastern European Jewish communities by a powerful revivalist religious
movement. Hasidism originated in the Ukraine in the eighteenth
century, and after a bitter struggle with prevailing orthodoxy, institutionalized itself in Congress Poland, much of the eastern bor-

derlands, and Galicia as the dominant form of Judaism. With its populist spirit, passionate optimism, and crusading combativeness, Hasidism swept Eastern Europe precisely at the time when Western European Jews, unfortified by any comparable revival, were abandoning traditional lifeways for those of the modern citizen. With its network of charismatic leaders [*tsaddikim*] ensconced in "courts" visited by masses of pilgrims, its own houses of worship, schools, printing presses, and sources of income, Hasidism established vigorous new centers of communal authority to withstand the double assault of czarist autocracy and modern Western thought.

Nevertheless, even in the "backward East," secular ideas began to touch the Jews. The Jewish Enlightenment, or Haskalah, moving eastward from Germany in the late eighteenth century, gained a handful of disciples as a tiny western-oriented Jewish bourgeoisie began to develop in the larger towns. Eager for knowledge of the world, these Jews turned to non-Jewish languages, first German, then Russian in the *kresy* and Polish in Congress Poland and Galicia. Cultural contacts between Poles and modernizing Jews early established a characteristic pattern: Jewish attraction to the Polish freedom struggle, that is, to the noble *szlachta* ethos; Polish sympathy for the Jew seen as an ally of the Polish cause.[15] Berek Joselewicz, who formed a Jewish regiment that fought the Russians under Kościuszko, then joined the Polish legions and fell in battle at Kock defending Napoleon against the Austrians, became a legendary figure for generations of assimilating Jews and their Polish friends. Following in his footsteps, a small number of Jews fought beside their Polish comrades in the insurrections of 1831 and 1863. In 1863, in an act that would symbolize Polish-Jewish cooperation for generations to come, Ber Meisels, the orthodox chief rabbi of Warsaw, preached support for the Polish uprising.

This was a crucial period in the shaping of a distinctive Polish national identity. Polish romantic poets, above all the national bard Adam Mickiewicz, began to see in Polish history a mythic narrative of self-sacrifice at the vanguard of a universal struggle for freedom. Polish romantic messianism, which identified Poland as the "Christ of nations," could hardly avoid recognizing in the Jews a parallel tradition. While ultimately, this recognition inspired a

brief solidarity

capitalist development

kind of competitive messianism and even a "victimization envy" that would fuel Polish anti-Semitism,[16] for Mickiewicz, the Polish "Christ of nations" and his suffering "elder brother" were destined for a messianic alliance. Mickiewicz's epic, *Pan Tadeusz,* substantial portions of which Polish schoolchildren have memorized for generations, includes a tavernkeeper named Jankiel, the most well-known Jewish figure in Polish literature. At a gathering of *szlachta,* bearded Jankiel, a virtuoso on the hammered dulcimer [*cymbał*], performs a concert of Polish patriotic music that recalls his audience to their sacred national task. "For our freedom, and for yours," the universalistic slogan of the Polish insurrectionists, became the watchword too of Jewish solidarity with the Poles against a common oppressor.

After two failed uprisings, however, a new generation of Polish intelligentsia, the Positivists, reacted strongly against the past. Not the noble gesture, but the patient, rational development of industry and culture was to be the measure of the nation's progress. In the afterglow of Polish-Jewish insurrectionary solidarity, this period seemed at first also to bode well for Polish-Jewish relations. In contrast to Western Europe, where an energetic native bourgeoisie, anchored in long-established urban centers, had vanquished the landed nobility, in late-nineteenth-century Poland, Polish industrialists were relatively rare. Neither the *szlachta* nor the peasants, emancipated only during the 1860s, could spearhead the economic transformation of Poland; only Germans, and above all, Jews, Poland's traditional commercial "classes," possessed the economic and psychosocial requirements.[17] From the 1880s until World War I, while hundreds of thousands of Jews abandoned the *shtetlekh* for the largest cities, Warsaw became the commercial hub of the Russian Empire, while the textile mills of Łódź and Białystok produced much of its clothing. For the Positivists, at the dawn of this transformation, the Jewish banker or industrialist who was prepared to embrace "Polishness" could be seen as an ally of the Polish cause.

Yet in nineteenth-century Europe, capitalism was, to say the least, hardly an unmixed blessing. In the eyes of its numerous Polish critics, whose *szlachta* origins were never distant, capitalism seemed particularly ugly and disorienting, and inevitably un-Polish. In Poland, that is, the turmoil of capitalist development, nowhere in Europe a very pretty thing, became mired not only in class but also in national antagonisms, chief among them hostility to Jews. The rapid overturning of the feudal order was accompanied by a change in the Polish perception of the Jew; amid the atomization of urban life, the familiar stereotypes were swept away, and in their place emerged an unknown and potentially frightening personage, who continued, however, to live next door.

This transformation was much more than in the eye of the beholder. Beginning in the 1880s, the heirs of the Haskalah in the Russian Empire, profoundly discouraged by the prospects for Russian reform and surrounded by the stirrings of Polish and other national movements, embarked on the building of national consciousness among Jews. This project was to take many competing forms, including various kinds of Zionism, Diaspora nationalism, and Jewish socialism.[18] Whatever their ideology, however, so long as they had to respond to Eastern European realities, all these movements, even Zionism, found it necessary to make demands of the Diaspora. These demands included autonomous political activity in defense of Jewish interests (a struggle for minority as well as civil rights), a modern culture based in Jewish languages, and new relationships to non-Jewish peoples based on mutual respect. Underlying these demands and lending them historical force was the centuries-old experience of Jewish autonomy in the Polish lands. In their attitude toward the gentile world, many of the Jewish activists broke with deeply rooted stereotypes, and looked to their non-Jewish counterparts with admiration, often envy, and respect. More than one Jewish nationalist was raised on Adam Mickiewicz, Henryk Sienkiewicz, and other bards of Polish fighting prowess and national self-sacrifice.

But a Jewish national movement was totally unacceptable to Poles and was perceived as the final straw in growing Jewish intractability. By the turn of the century, much of the Polish intelligentsia's goodwill toward its Jewish neighbors had evaporated. Only a few Jews had decided to assimilate into Polish culture and become "good Poles." In the eastern borderlands, educated Jews had turned to Russian culture, in Prussian Poland to German culture, and both these groups were manipulated by czar and kaiser, respectively, against the Poles. Furthermore, as the Poles saw it, the vast majority of Jews remained outside any European culture; they were desperately poor, and clung to outlandish traditional attire and an offensive Germanic jargon. Worse yet, among the new generation of educated Jews, even as social assimilation continued uninterruptedly, the ideology of assimilation began to go out of fashion. An independent Jewish politics profoundly frightened Poles. Combined with the apparent economic power of the small Jewish oligarchy, such fears, cultivated whenever possible by the Russians, raised the specter of a "Judaeo-Polonia," a latter-day "paradise of the Jews" that was supposedly the Zionists' true aim: a Jewish state on Polish soil. In Poland, that is, that staple of European anti-Semitism, Jews as a "state within a state," rooted itself with particular tenacity. Finally, there was a new personal assertiveness among younger Jews. These were no longer the comical *żydki,* or even wise old patriarchs; in a world increasingly out of joint, here were Jews who didn't know their place.

These developments in the Polish perception of Jews coincided with the emergence of a polemic over the nature of Polish national identity that was to leave its mark on all of subsequent Polish history. It was triggered by a critique of the past, by the need to move out of what was perceived as a cul-de-sac of history, and led to a debate over the issue of who was a Pole. So long as "Polishness" was the exclusive property of the *szlachta,* the Polish national struggle, it was perceived, could not hope to advance beyond doomed insurrections. Did Polishness include the peasant, who in 1863 had not infrequently turned in his insurrectionist landlord to the Russians? Did it include women? Did it include non-Roman Catholics and those not of Polish ethnic stock? Did it, finally, include the Jews? In answer to such questions, two alternatives began to emerge.

The first, which we can term "pluralist," offerred a conception of Polishness reminiscent of what had been possible in the old Polish Commonwealth, where a gentleman might describe himself as "a canon of Kraków, a member of the Polish nation, of the Ruthenian [Ukrainian] people, of Jewish origin".[19] This "noble" notion of national identity assumed that Polishness designated a community of cultural and historical values that was inclusive and voluntary. It was a base from which a future campaign to create a "nationalities state" [*państwo narodowościowe*] could be launched,

Pluralism or
exclusivist

a struggle whose ideals would be both Polish and universal, part of a history of Polish freedom struggles whose motto had been "For your freedom, and for ours." By the century's end, such tendencies found a political home with the nondogmatic socialism of the Polish Socialist Party [Polska Partia Socjalistyczna, PPS], founded in 1897 by Józef Piłsudski. Here the old *szlachta* ethos cohabited with modern ideas of social justice. Closely associated with the *kresy*, Piłsudski and his comrades saw the Russians as the chief enemy and entertained notions of tactical alliances with the Austrians. The goal, above all, was an independent Polish state, and in this struggle, Jews, insofar as they considered themselves Polish patriots, were welcomed.

In direct opposition to the pluralist alternative was another set of notions that we can call "exclusivist," which found their political focus in the National Democratic Party [Narodowa Democracja, ND or Endecja], founded by Roman Dmowski and his associates also in the late 1890s. The Endecja (pronounced "endetsya") advocated what it called "integral nationalism," whereby membership in the Polish national community was narrowly defined and included ethnic Polish descent and the profession of Roman Catholicism. It dreamt not of a nationalities state but a nation state [*państwo narodowe*]. Strongest in German-occupied western Poland, the Endecja stressed bourgeois over *szlachta* values, realpolitik over insurrection, and envisioned compromise with the Russians but were unfailingly hostile to the Germans.

Using the popular contemporary language of social Darwinism, Endeks argued that a modern national existence demanded "national egoism" in a merciless struggle for survival against other peoples, chief among them the Jews. In the Middle Ages, at a time when a modern Polish nation had not yet existed, Jews had been invited to develop trade in the Polish lands. But now, according to the Endeks, as it stood on the threshold of a modern existence, the Polish nation, young and much too trusting, was confronted by an all too experienced and ruthless opponent. A modern nation cannot exist, they argued, without a commercial class. But the Jews, they claimed, controlled Poland's commerce, indeed *were* its commercial class. This reasoning tapped Polish envy at supposed Jewish quick-wittedness and business sense [*sprytność*], an envy well expressed in modern times in a popular couplet that was said to have been a Jewish boast to Poles: *Wasze ulice, nasze kamienice* (Your streets, [but] our apartment buildings).[20] The Jews, the Endeks concluded, had to be driven out of Polish commerce and industry and replaced by ethnic Poles. Endek ideologues, certainly, were well aware of the progress of modern anti-Semitic movements from France to Russia, and learned much from them. But what made Polish anti-Semitism different and gave it a unique logic was its insistence that it was simply the sign of a national conflict, of a struggle between two peoples contending for economic and political dominance in one land. Furthermore, the Endeks saw Poles as the underdogs. The rise of the Jewish national movement was taken as the perfect confirmation of this. Having already subjugated Poles economically, what could these Jews want, the Endeks argued, but political rule over Poles as well?

Although the conflict between Piłsudski's and Dmowski's followers was political, the struggle between the pluralist and exclusivist alternatives went considerably beyond the political arena. More even than a clash of ideas, it was a struggle between ways of being in the world. Pluralists, touched with a bit of messianic hope, heirs to a history of exemplary martyrdom, adopted a generous and tolerant stance toward the world. Exclusivists, caught up in immanence, read Polish history as a chronicle of victimization and insisted that Poles learn that they would always stand alone. The weakness in the pluralist stance was the risk of degenerating into empty posturing; by the same token, under certain circumstances—and the events of this century would provide them in great number—the exclusivist stance could easily slip into paranoia.

Between the World Wars (1918–1939)

Suddenly and unexpectedly, at the end of World War I, the three empires that had partitioned Poland collapsed, Germany and Austria defeated in war, Russia wracked by revolution. The new Polish state, cast into the twentieth century, like its neighboring "successor states," out of the wreckage of what had been the most destructive war in history and into an era of nearly continuous

The new Poland, post WW. I
2nd Polish Commonwealth

economic crisis, was also beset by its own unique problems.[21] After 123 years, "Poland" was scarcely an idea; the new country was a patchwork of regions with diverse economic, social and political traditions and needs. Polish industry, which had been based in Congress Poland and oriented to the Russian market, now had to compete in the West; it never regained its prewar vigor. Although most of the Polish population continued to live on the land, Polish agriculture was in permanent crisis. Peasant farms, already small, were continually shrinking, subdivided and parceled out from one generation to the next. Meanwhile, especially in the eastern parts of the country, the historical *kresy*, powerful *szlachta* families still ruled over giant estates and successfully resisted land reform for the entire interwar period. Among the results was a growing mass of impoverished landless peasants.

Then there was the problem of national minorities. Interwar Poland was only two-thirds ethnically Polish; the remainder of its population was Ukrainian, Jewish, Belorussian, and German, in that order; in most of the *kresy*, Poles were themselves a minority. Under such circumstances, civil harmony would have demanded some sort of pluralist approach to national issues. But despite dubbing the state the Second Commonwealth [*Rzeczpospolita*], it was the exclusivist, ethnically based notion of Polishness that proved increasingly influential and led to rising hostility to non-Poles. This hostility was also in part provoked by some of the minorities themselves, who allowed their demands to become the subject of political intrigue by Poland's powerful neighbors. With Ukrainian and Belorussian Soviet Socialist Republics across the border, Ukrainian and Belorussian activism in Poland, including terrorism, was encouraged by the Soviet Union, while in the 1930s, manipulation of ethnic Germans as well as Ukrainians became a weapon of Nazi foreign policy. But to view Jews in a comparable way required a rather exaggerated notion of the power of international Jewry, a notion that was a German specialty during this period, but hardly unknown in Poland.

These and other problems made the establishment of a stable constitutional government an impossible task. Indeed, for most of its existence, the Second Polish Commonwealth was not governed democratically, but ruled by Józef Piłsudski and his disciples. Piłsudski, who by the 1920s had broken with socialism and the PPS, proved himself a true son of the *szlachta,* a military leader who guided Poland to independence, then took his army east into the *kresy* and engaged the Soviets, Ukrainians, and Lithuanians on the field of battle. Abandoning the government in 1922 to parliamentary rule, Piłsudski's charisma was powerful enough for him to seize power from an ineffectual government in 1926, then rule the country until his death nine years later, all the while maintaining great popularity. In an age that produced monstrous despotisms all over Europe, the Marshal, as he preferred to be called, created a comparatively inoffensive "nonparty" regime under the name *Sanacja,* implying moral cleansing. He managed to be a dictator without being either a Fascist or an anti-Semite, and to hold the line against the more aggressive manifestations of Endek nationalism. The clique of military men who succeeded him for the remaining four years of Polish independence was much less successful at this.

Despite enormous changes in the situation of Polish Jews during the twenty years of the Second Commonwealth, their demographic and economic profile remained exceptional.[22] In a country that was nearly three-quarters rural, Jews were increasingly a big-city population: although one-third continued to live in the *shtetlekh,* and one-quarter in the countryside, nearly half of all Jews lived in cities with populations of over twenty thousand. While the Jewish share in the total population was 10 percent, in the largest cities it was 30 percent. Although Jewish population growth in this period was surpassed by that of the Poles, the number of Jews, unlike elsewhere in Central Europe, continued to increase in absolute terms. Jews were vastly overrepresented in commerce and the professions. In 1921, more than 60 percent of those in commerce were Jews; in 1931, more than half the doctors in private practice and one-third of the lawyers were Jews. Although foreign investment and state-run enterprises had begun to displace Jewish-owned industry, on the eve of World War II Jewish firms still employed more than 40 percent of the Polish labor force, while certain industries, textiles and food most notably, were predominantly in Jewish hands. While such statistics were grist for anti-Semitic propagandists; most Jews were hardly well-off professionals or captains of industry. Typically, Jews were small shopkeepers and artisans: tailors, shoemakers, bakers, living on the edge of survival.[23]

In the Minorities Treaty, which Poland, along with other successor states, had been required to sign at the Paris Peace Conference, Jews were granted civil and some minority rights. Secular Jewish leaders hailed the treaty as the "magna carta" for Jewish national autonomy in Poland.[24] Such hopes proved illusory, for successive Polish governments, including the Sanacja, in practice consistently rejected claims based on Jewish national rights. Thus, while government-supported Jewish schools were stipulated in the Minorities Treaty, Polish governments refused to finance them and denied them accreditation. Nevertheless, regardless of official attitudes and even as Jews were becoming fully literate in Polish and in certain circles even abandoning Yiddish, they were increasingly using the notion of Jewish nationality to define themselves.[25] This transformation was a result of both negative and positive factors, of defensive withdrawal but also expansive hopes. It was a reaction, on one hand, to increasing Polish hostility to Jews, even to assimilating Jews. But the new Jewish identity was also shaped by the opportunity to develop Jewish culture and institutions under conditions that were vastly more promising than anything that had been possible under the czars.

In an ideological age, one measure of the Jewish world that emerged in interwar Poland was the range of its political life. Jewish voters now cast ballots in three different sorts of elections: to the national Polish parliament, to their local city or town council, and to the local *kehilla*. More than a dozen Jewish political parties competed for this Jewish vote. The most successful, particularly in national elections, were the General Zionists. Aspiring both to a Jewish homeland in Palestine and to the leadership of the Jewish community of Poland, the General Zionists waged a militant parliamentary struggle for Jewish national rights and "national dignity." Although the Zionist movement included a religious wing, most Orthodox Jews were represented by the anti-Zionist Agudat Yisrael, the second most popular Jewish party at the national level and the dominant force in *kehilla* politics. The Agudah maintained a traditional Jewish stance of moderation and pursued a policy of private intercession with the government; after Piłsudski took power it was the only Jewish party that joined the governing coalition. On the Left, the anti-Zionist Bund had the overwhelming allegiance of Jewish workers, most organized in Bundist labor unions. Boycotting the national elections as a bourgeois sham, the Bund contended for influence on the local level and attempted to build bridges to the Polish Socialist Party.

The influence of the Jewish political parties far transcended conventional politics. Indeed, measured by their ability to effect political change, the parties were ultimately impotent.[26] But the Jewish parties and their activists were instrumental in elaborating a dense web of institutions and organizations that affected every aspect of Jewish life. For example, Zionists supported a school system in which Hebrew was the primary language of instruction, Bundists and their allies one with Yiddish as the language of instruction. But the most popular system of Jewish education was the network of schools maintained by the Agudah, which included, for the first time, elementary schools for girls as well as, equally unprecedented, a spacious modern rabbinical seminary, Yeshivat Hakhmei Lublin.[27] Similarly, about a dozen youth groups generally linked to Zionist and Socialist parties recruited members throughout Poland. Fixtures of the largest cities and the smallest *shtetlekh* alike were the libraries and clubs where such *bavustzinike* (socially conscious) young people gathered to study, debate, and socialize.[28] At the same time, Orthodox Jews continued to fill traditional study and prayer houses maintained by local *khevres* and hasidic sects. In Warsaw in the 1920s, according to official and doubtless incomplete statistics, there were 442 synagogues and prayer houses for a population of about 350,000 Jews.[29] Cooperatives, credit unions, orphanages, hospitals, newspapers, publishing houses, theater companies, orchestras, choirs, sports clubs, and cultural societies, many sponsored by political parties but many others independent, were the links in a far-flung network that defined what can best be described as the Jewish nationality of interwar Poland.

A result was a community whose influence radiated throughout the world. Even as Polish rabbis fought the flood of secular ideas and life-styles, Polish *yeshivot* (seminaries) attracted thousands of American students, while Polish graduates of these *yeshivot* went on to found new educational centers in Palestine, Western Europe, and the United States. Traditional religious scholarship published in Poland was distributed throughout the world; some publishers, such as the Rom printing house in Vilna, attained mythic reknown.[30] In the realm of secular culture a similar situation developed. The YIVO Institute, founded in Vilna in 1925, became the world center for the study of the Yiddish language and Eastern European Jewish civilization as a whole. Although Yiddish writers in Poland perenially lamented the loss of their readers to Polish, nevertheless, in relation to the vicissitudes of Yiddish elsewhere in the world, Poland remained the center of the Yiddish printed word. During the interwar period, between three and five Yiddish daily newspapers were available at Warsaw kiosks, while more than seventeen hundred different periodicals appeared.[31] Even the Yiddish writers who had permanently settled abroad, usually in New York, would frequently return to Poland and inevitably appear in the legendary quarters of the Yiddish Writers' and Journalists' Union in Warsaw, commonly known by its address, Tłomackie 13.[32] But with the rarest of exceptions, this address, along with the Jewish world it represented, was unknown to Poles, who commonly described Jewish society as an exotic "dark continent" that lay behind a "Chinese wall."

The relations between Poles and Polish Jews in the interwar period began badly and ended worse. On the day Polish independence was declared, anti-Jewish violence, hitherto rare in Poland, erupted throughout the country. In the eastern borderlands for the next three years, while numerous armies, paramilitary units, and bands of outlaws slaughtered each other as well as masses of civilians, Jewish life proved particularly cheap. Jews primarily fell victim to Ukrainian forces, but pogroms were also staged or abetted by Polish forces, particularly those commanded by Gen. Józef Haller. Typically, each side accused the Jews of aiding the other. Out of this turmoil arose a belief destined to play a fateful role during World War II and well beyond. Based partly on the anti-Semitic stereotype of the "commie Jew" and partly on the considerable Jewish involvement in the various "revolutionary" and "provisional" committees set up by the advancing Red Army, a conviction arose among Poles that the Jews as a whole were pro-Soviet. Accordingly, in one highly publicized incident during the Polish-Soviet War of 1919–20, Jewish officers in the Polish army were declared security risks and interned in a detention camp.[33]

In the meantime, responding to international outcry over the pogroms, the Polish government and press heatedly denied the involvement of Polish troops, and, launching another accusation that would recur for decades, charged that Polish Jewish activists in collusion with western Jews had organized an international propaganda campaign to besmirch Poland's honor. This accusation, in turn, was linked to Polish anger about the role of international Jewish delegations in drafting the Minorities Treaty. The Polish representatives to the Paris Peace Conference, primarily Endek activists, denounced the treaty as meddling in Polish internal affairs, and for many Poles it may have been difficult to understand, indeed, why Jews were content with civil rights in the West, but demanded additional national minority rights in Poland. The coda to these initial years came in November 1922 when the Polish parliament selected Gabriel Narutowicz as the first constitutionally elected president of Poland. Narutowicz, unfortunately, was chosen with the support of a bloc of Jewish and other minority representatives. Immediately dubbed "president of the Jews" in the Endek press, he was assassinated two days after his inauguration.

During subsequent years, and particularly after Piłsudski's coup, national passions abated somewhat. Yet anti-Semitic propagandists discovered new fields to conquer; much was made, for example, of alleged Jewish infiltration of Polish culture. By the 1930s, the eminent Polish poet of Jewish origin, Julian Tuwim (like Heinrich Heine in Germany a century earlier), was regularly attacked for polluting the national language. It became increasingly difficult for a Jew to become a "good Pole." Even those Jews ready and willing to assimilate, indeed even the handful of converts, found themselves isolated, spurned by Poles even as they were ostracized by Jews. Meanwhile, under constant pressure from the Endecja, the Sanacja regime, both formally and informally, adopted portions of the Endek program concerning Jews. It became virtually impossible for a Jew to hold a civil-service position; banks made it more difficult for Jewish businesses to qualify for loans;

new taxes hurt Jewish shopkeepers and artisans; quotas restricted Jewish enrollment at Polish universities.

As elsewhere in Europe, the 1930s brought economic catastrophe and an escalation of social conflict, which in Poland worsened the already volatile relations between Poles and Jews. Violence flared particularly in the *shtetlekh* and the universities. Endek agitators went out among the poorest peasants, announcing that the time had come not just to boycott Jewish merchants, but to expel them from their shops and stalls and take over. A result was bloodshed in numerous towns. Meanwhile, at the universities, right-wing nationalists became increasingly aggressive. Jewish students were required to occupy segregated seating in lecture halls (the so-called bench ghetto, which Jewish students protested by standing during lectures), while gangs of "gentlemen" hooligans armed with canes and razors assaulted their Jewish classmates on campuses and terrorized Jews in the streets and parks. Despite the traditional Endek aversion to Germany, some youths openly emulated the Nazis; one group, the National Radical Camp [Obóz Narodowo-Radykalny, ONR], adopted a Fascist program and split from the National Democrats. In response to anti-Semitic violence, Jewish unions and youth groups formed self-defense units that collected arms and resisted attacks. But such groups learned that, for a vastly outnumbered minority, violent resistance to violence, while psychologically satisfying, could be counterproductive, for it often provoked even greater violence.[34]

Many in Poland were upset by the violence, including the Church. In 1936, Cardinal August Hlond, the primate of Poland, issued a pastoral letter condemning hatred and violence against Jews. His statement was characteristic of the Church's position on the "Jewish question" before World War II. "One may love one's own nation more, but one may not hate anyone," he declared, "not even Jews." And he simultaneously gave his clear support to the "moral" struggle against what he termed Jewish atheism, Bolshevism, pornography, and fraud, as well as to nonviolent boycotts of Jewish businesses.[35] There were certainly also those, primarily in the intelligentsia and on the Left politically, who opposed the notion of any kind of struggle against the Jews. At its 1937 party congress, the Polish Socialist Party not only condemned anti-Semitism and Fascism but also resolved to support national rights for all minorities including the Jews. Indeed, the PPS and the Bund had developed something of a tradition of cooperation. Such politics, however, was the exception. By the 1930s, besides the PPS, only the tiny Democratic Party (Stronnictwo Demokratyczne, a left-wing breakaway from Sanacja) and the small Communist Party (about which more below) did not advocate mass Jewish emigration. In the atmosphere that prevailed in Poland in the last years before the war, denouncing anti-Semitism was tantamount to declaring oneself "for the Jews," and took considerable political and personal courage.

After Marshal Piłsudski's death in 1935, his heirs drew politically closer to both the Church and the Endecja, and diplomatically to Nazi Germany. This was a Polish government increasingly preoccupied, indeed obsessed by, the "Jewish question."[36] In December 1938, after Poland had participated in the dismemberment of Czechoslovakia, a government spokesman declared that "the more normal division of the Jews among the countries of the world" was "the pressing matter of the international political scene," and that the "Jewish question" was one of "the chief and most difficult problems facing the Polish nation."[37] The solution to this problem was sought in mass Jewish emigration. Most controversial of numerous schemes was the government's negotiations with Vladimir Jabotinsky of the Zionist Revisionists for the "evacuation" of hundreds of thousands of Polish Jews to Palestine, an episode that led to enormous publicity but no results. It is doubtful whether the government seriously expected any of these plans (none of which, it should be noted, involved forced emigration) to succeed. Such schemes emerged out of the same political atmosphere that turned the prohibition of Jewish ritual slaughter [shekhita] into a cause célèbre voluminously debated in the Polish parliament and press on the eve of World War II.[38] The Polish pluralist tradition was moribund; instead, the "Jewish question" hung over public life and imbued it with a peculiar aura of unreality. Rooted in the most fundamental problems of Polish national development, the "Jewish question" made it difficult to see those problems, as well as the truly menacing developments just beyond Poland's borders, with any clarity.

2

Poles and Jews During the Holocaust
1939–1944

O n September 1, 1939, German troops invaded Poland. Polish
    defenses quickly crumbled before an overwhelming German
assault that included intensive aerial bombardment of civilian areas.
After two weeks Germany controlled the western half of the country except for Warsaw, which, besieged and burning, abandoned
by the government and the general staff, held out for two more
weeks. Meanwhile, on September 17, the Soviet Union invaded
Poland from the east. For almost two years, according to the treaty
signed with Germany just before the war, the Soviets ruled half
the territory of prewar Poland, the area east of the Bug River, essentially the eastern borderlands. In June 1941, the Germans turned
on the Soviets and forced the Red Army out of Poland and eastward into the Russian heartland. For three years, all of prewar
Poland was occupied by the Germans. In January 1944, the Red
Army reentered prewar Polish territory, and by the beginning of
1945, swept the last of the German forces out of Poland.

The German occupation of Poland was the cornerstone of Nazi
plans for a Eurasian empire stratified by race, in which German
masters would rule over "racially inferior," primarily Slavic, peoples.[1] The war offered the Nazis the opportunity to begin building this "New Order," but not to complete it—that would have to
await final victory. Immediately after their conquest of the west-

ern half of Poland, the Nazis divided it in two. The northwestern regions, including important industrial and mining centers, were directly incorporated into the Reich, and much of their non-German population, primarily Poles and Jews, was expelled into the remaining area, which the Nazis called the Generalgouvernement. Over the next five years, the Generalgouvernement, consisting of one-third of the territory of prewar Poland, including the major cities of Warsaw, Kraków, and Lublin, and nearly half the population, became the center of the Nazi occupation.[2] As a dumping ground for all the "racial garbage" in occupied Poland, the Generalgouvernement became the focus of Nazi "clean-up" attempts: the organization of slave labor and mass murder.[3] At the same time, it was also where some fifteen million Poles managed to eat, sleep, work, and occasionally sit in a café or theater for the duration of the war, under conditions that, however bad, would doubtless have worsened had the Germans won the war.

For the time being, what the Germans instituted was a regime of total exploitation. Their intention was to extract from the Poles the maximum possible labor to support the German war machine, while allowing them as little as possible in return. All Poles fourteen years of age and older were required to work; workers were often bound to their workplace, with work papers used as identification. As a result of frequent, unpredictable roundups, more than a million Poles were deported to work in Germany; such roundups, as well as sentences for a host of major and minor transgressions of Nazi laws, resulted in some two million more being condemned to work in the vast network of Nazi concentration camps, labor camps, and prisons established within Poland.[4] Meanwhile, prices skyrocketed, wages (for those who were paid them) fell, and from the official rationing system, it appeared that the Nazis were rather indifferent about the survival of their Polish labor force.

Nazi policies in Poland were intended not just to control a potentially rebellious population, but to begin to shape its future. Although the Nazis made use of hundreds of thousands of municipal employees, railroad workers, police, and other local officials, who continued their accustomed work under German orders, in Poland, unlike elsewhere in Europe, the Nazis did not seek political collaborators, nor were there many interested in collaborating. Poles were not to be bargained with or cajoled; they were to be broken, reduced to the common denominator of helots for their Nazi lords. To do this, the structures and values that bound Polish society together, its social glue, so to speak, had to be dissolved. The Nazis began with a campaign to wipe out Polish elites. In 1939 and 1940, thousands of teachers, military officers, landowners, priests, and professors were rounded up and murdered. Secondary schools and universities were closed and most cultural activities banned, education was limited to the fourth grade, entertainment to operettas, cabarets, and pornography, and drinking was strongly encouraged. Above all, and throughout the years of occupation, random, meaningless violence, unrelated or out of proportion to any crime, was the preferred means of enforcing obedience.[5] The death penalty was the mandated punishment for a slew of transgressions, great and small; collective punishment—the execution, for a single act of real or imagined resistance, of scores or hundreds of innocent people—was a common occurrence. Nazi terror created an atmosphere conducive to terror of other kinds: banditry and armed attacks by political and quasi-political groups, including the slaughter in eastern Poland of some one hundred thousand Poles by Ukrainian nationalists.[6]

The Nazi assault on Polish society evoked two different but not necessarily exclusive reactions. Faced with the apparent impossibility of reasoning with the occupier, Poles soon discovered that there was one language the Germans understood well, and that was corruption. Under a system in which Poles had no rights whatsoever, every aspect of life, sometimes life itself, became a privilege to be negotiated with particular officials in return for particular financial considerations. Money suddenly became the measure of all things, and in this respect corruption complemented the work of terror by further wrecking traditional values: extortion, blackmail, and informing poisoned human relations. German greed combined with the inadequacy of official rationing to stimulate an alternative economy; the black market provided for some 80 percent of the needs of the Polish population.[7] Here, in cheating the Germans and helping Poles survive the war, corruption simultaneously played a positive social role as well. In the memoirs of Poles, as in the memoirs of Jews in the ghettos, the smuggler is frequently portrayed as a heroic figure.

German oppression bred another response as well: the most effective resistance movement in occupied Europe. Amid widespread demoralization, hundreds of thousands of Poles chose the opposite: exaltation and self-sacrifice. The raison d'être of this underground was less military than social; it aimed less to hurt the Germans than to counteract the atomization of Polish society, restore the social glue that the Germans sought to dissolve.[8] The underground organized clandestine secondary and higher education; cultural events, especially theater; and an underground press, the most extensive in occupied Europe, which appeared in nearly two thousand separate publications and millions of copies. Most of all, participation itself bonded conspirators together and endowed them with an exalted sense of mission, a crucial antidote to the depravity fostered by the Nazis. Anti-Nazi resistance could be assimilated into the history of Polish freedom fighting, of martyrdom for the Polish cause. Joining the underground, in other words, meant resisting the Nazis in the most fundamental way: deciding to invest one's life, and probably one's death, with meaning.

Ultimate authority over the underground was wielded by the Polish government-in-exile, headed by Władysław Sikorski and after his death in 1943 by Stanisław Mikołajczyk, and headquartered in London. This government appointed a representative to organize in Poland what was known as the Delegate's Bureau [Delegatura], the underground's supreme political authority. The government-in-exile, in certain respects, represented a break with the immediate past: it repudiated the prewar Sanacja regime for its political and military blindness as well as its authoritarianism. Within occupied Poland, every prewar political party went underground and (except for the Communists) was overseen by the Delegate's Bureau. Each party produced its own publications, took part in underground social and cultural work, as well as in military matters. Similarly, the underground's military arm, the Home Army [Armia Krajowa, AK], was an umbrella organization of armed groups originally organized under the authority of individual political parties. Of the groups that remained outside the

Home Army's authority, the most important were the forces organized by the Communists: the People's Guard [Gwardia Ludowa, GL] and its successor, the People's Army [Armia Ludowa, AL], and most of those organized by right-wing nationalists: the National Armed Forces [Narodowe Siły Zbrojne, NSZ].[9]

The Home Army, estimated at 350,000 members in 1943,[10] directed an extensive campaign of sabotage against German factories and railroads, and coordinated the work of partisan groups particularly active in the eastern forests. For most of the war the Home Army undertook only limited direct attacks against German personnel. Vastly superior German firepower and the policy of collective punishment made armed resistance problematic and mass insurrection seem suicidal.[11] Nevertheless, in Warsaw large amounts of arms were hidden and plans developed for a general insurrection, which, it was hoped, would finish off the Germans in the final stages of the war. On August 1, 1944, with the Soviets approaching Warsaw, the Home Army launched the long-awaited Warsaw Uprising. On October 2, as the Red Army still dawdled across the Vistula River from Warsaw, with some 200,000 Warsaw residents dead and the underground destroyed, the Poles surrendered to the Germans. The Germans marched the surviving population out of the city, while demolition squads dynamited what remained of its monuments. On January 17, 1945, the Red Army occupied the ruins of Warsaw.

The ramified social, cultural, political, and military network that emerged to resist the German occupation of Poland has been dubbed by Polish historians, with considerable justification, an "underground state." Its development was facilitated by a number of factors, above all by the accessibility of the Polish collective memory of resistance against occupiers. In addition, although the underground emerged as a response to oppression, this oppression, for most of the war and for most Poles, damaged but did not destroy the fabric of everyday life.[12] Most important in this respect, although the German rationing system might have had terrible consequences for Poles, as a result of the black market hunger rarely led to starvation. Finally, the "underground state" had access to large financial resources that were channeled to it from London, beyond German reach.

With respect to all these factors as well as many others, the situation of Jews under the German occupation bore little resemblance to that of Poles. The fundamental difference was a function of German policy, a function, that is, of the German intention to murder every Jew. The difference is most simply illustrated in numbers: about two million Poles and three million Polish Jews died during the German occupation of Poland;[13] these figures represent nearly 10 percent of the ethnically Polish population but almost 90 percent of the Jewish population of prewar Poland. Nevertheless, nowhere else in Europe would such a comparison even begin to be necessary; nowhere else, that is, did the murder of Jews unfold amid such slaughter of the coterritorial people.

Within months of their conquest of Poland, the Germans launched the first phase of their "Jewish policy."[14] Throughout Poland, Jews were made to wear the yellow star, uprooted from their homes, and forced into "ghettos." These were portions of the prewar Jewish neighborhoods in some four hundred cities and towns primarily in the Generalgouvernement. Their Polish residents expelled, the ghettos were crammed full of additional Jews from smaller surrounding communities. By the end of 1941, Jews had been despoiled of all their means of livelihood and the ghettos nearly all sealed. Entrance and exit were strictly controlled, regulations enforced with characteristic savagery.

Behind the ghetto walls, a world that lived under a death sentence came into being. But this was a sentence that the Nazis did their best to conceal. Slave labor factories in many ghettos produced apparently important war matériel for the Germans; Jewish councils [Judenräte] and Jewish police [Ordnungsdienst], though established by German decree and operating under German control, played on the centuries-old tradition of Jewish autonomy: Judenrat and kehilla were intentionally confounded. Historical memory betrayed Jewish leaders into believing that the survival of at least a portion of the community was possible; entirely helpless, most consented to a degree of cooperation with the oppressor and called for Jewish endurance, a buying of time until the German defeat. Meanwhile, vast amounts of energy, both officially and clandestinely, were channeled into communal welfare: soup kitchens, clothing, housing, health, schools, and cultural ac-

tivities of every kind. Simultaneously, clandestine private enterprise, above all smuggling, that typically involved Polish partners,
huge profits, and deadly risks, maintained economic breaches in
the ghetto walls. Yet all this frenzied activity, both private and communal, was insufficient to offset the effects of a German rationing
system that in 1941 allowed the Jews of Warsaw 184 calories per
person per day, one-quarter of the meager Polish ration.[15] In that
year in the ghetto, starvation combined with disease and outright
murder to produce a death rate of more than 10 percent.[16]

With their invasion of the Soviet Union in June 1941, the Nazis
decided to augment this rate. For Hitler, war in the East heralded
the New Order, a world about which much was in doubt but one
thing certain: it would contain no Jews. As the Germans swept the
Red Army before them through eastern Poland and into Russia,
mobile "special operations" units [*Einsatzgruppen*] operating behind the front lines slaughtered more than one million Jews. In
December 1941, at Chełmno in western Poland, the "experimental"
mass gassing of Jews in vans began. During 1942, camps equipped
with gas chambers and crematoriums began to operate throughout the Generalgouvernement. In ghetto after ghetto, similar sce-
narios unfolded: the Judenräte were told to furnish Jews for
"resettlement in the East." Some starving Jews reported voluntar-
ily when promised a loaf of bread and some marmalade, or after
receiving encouraging postcards from relatives; many attempted
to hide but were rounded up with extraordinary violence; all were
packed into freight cars and dispatched to their deaths. By the end
of 1942, nearly four million Jews, including most of the Jews of
Poland, were dead.

In the ghettos that remained, populated by handfuls of slave laborers and the "illegals" who had managed to avoid "deportation," awareness of Nazi intentions was now inescapable. A Jewish
underground had existed since the beginning of the German occupation. Composed primarily of youthful Zionist and socialist
activists who remained after the flight or murder of the prewar
Jewish political leadership, the underground had developed a pro-
lific clandestine press and struggled against divisions in its ranks
and among the masses of starving, isolated ghetto inmates. The
survivors of this ghetto underground now offered the surviving

Jews their leadership in a fight, not for survival, but for what they called "death with honor," meaning death with a weapon in hand. The most effective and symbolically important ghetto revolt occurred in Warsaw, after the removal and gassing at Treblinka, from July to September 1942, of over a quarter of a million Warsaw Jews. The Warsaw Ghetto Uprising, that began on April 19, 1943, pitted about 750 barely armed youngsters and some 40,000 unarmed Jews dug into underground bunkers against 2,000 superbly armed German troops. It was a contest, remarked Emmanuel Ringelblum, between a fly and an elephant.[17] The uprising, nevertheless, lasted more than a month; its defeat required the incineration of nearly every building in the ghetto—the old Jewish quarter of Warsaw was transformed into a lunar landscape. Individuals and groups also organized escapes from this and other ghettos; handfuls managed to flee from the death trains and camps. Some of the escapees formed Jewish partisan units or joined existing Russian and Polish groups who fought in the Polish forests. Others attempted to hide among non-Jews, both in cities and in the countryside. During the last two years of the war, the Germans expended great effort in tracking down and killing these survivors.

How did Poles, themselves the object of murderous repression, respond to the mass slaughter of their Jewish neighbors?[18] Polish response, it should be emphasized, was immensely varied; it ran the gamut from acts of altruism that risked (and sometimes required) one's own and one's family's life, through indifference, all the way to active participation in the killing. The responses of individuals, moreover, were not the same as collective responses, most importantly, those of the government-in-exile and the Polish underground. Polish response to the Holocaust, furthermore, was conditioned by a tangle of political, social, and psychological factors; present and past, reality and fantasy interacted to create immense barriers not just to helping Jews but to wanting to help them.

For a brief period after the German invasion, particularly as Poles and Jews dug trenches side by side in embattled Warsaw, Polish-Jewish relations were transformed; Warsaw Jews, as Emmanuel Ringelblum reported, were seized with an enthusiasm reminiscent of the solidarity experienced during the insurrections of the nineteenth century.[19] But the imposition of German rule, specifically intended, among other things, to poison relations between Jews and Poles, marked an irreversible change for the worse. While Nazi-orchestrated pogroms by Polish hoodlums (the Germans then "protecting" the Jews against their neighbors' "wrath") were a feature of only the first months of the occupation, the awareness that street toughs could do what they pleased to Jews accompanied the entire occupation, as did the venomous anti-Semitism of films, posters, and the official Polish-language press. Hooliganism set the tone; the "squeamish" and the "sentimental" could do little else in public than look the other way. Moreover, as Poles observed German policy toward the Jews during the first two years of the war, it may not have seemed entirely clear that Jews had it worse. Although it was apparent that the Nazis lavished exceptional sadism on the Jews, the overall thrust of German repression before the mobilization of the death camps may have appeared separate but equal: political in nature, including the murder of elites, against the Poles; primarily economic against the Jews.[20] Ghettos, termed "Jewish residential quarters" by the Nazis to parallel Polish and German "quarters," removed Jews, many with Polish neighbors and friends, from the midst of Polish daily life and banished them to a realm of rumor and myth. Until the ghetto uprisings and especially during the deportations, the Polish underground press stereotyped Jewish response to the Nazis as passivity and contrasted it with Polish resistance. When someone managed to escape onto an "Aryan" street from behind ghetto walls plastered with Nazi posters proclaiming "Jews, Lice, Disease," it required an effort for Poles to remember how recently this Jew had been their neighbor.

Furthermore, for many Poles the fate of the Jews proved economically profitable. Beyond the money to be made smuggling to and from the ghettos, as well as blackmailing and informing on Jews hidden on the "Aryan side," activities that involved relatively few Poles, the German expropriation of 3.5 million Jews amounted to an economic revolution.[21] While the Germans, certainly, took the lion's share of factories, warehouses, luxury residences, fancy furniture, and clothing, the leftovers went to Poles. Throughout Poland, in cities as in the smallest towns, ownerless stores, merchandise, workshops, raw material, land, and houses quickly found new owners. All of this bore a striking resemblance to the popular prewar demand of Polish nationalists for the elimination of Jews from the Polish economy. Resentment over the alleged Jewish stranglehold on Polish economic life and the conviction that Jewish property rightfully belonged in Polish hands combined with the lure of opportunity to stifle the scruples of the "inheritors" of Jewish property. Indeed, contemporary accounts made it clear that many Poles regarded the new economic situation as a fait accompli and would react rather badly should Jews attempt to return after the war to reclaim their property. Thus, for example, an assessment of the "Jewish question" as it would appear in postwar Poland, sent to the government-in-exile by an official of the Polish underground in August 1943, included the following:

In the Homeland as a whole—independently of the general psychological situation at any given moment—the position is such that the return of the Jews to their jobs and workshops is completely out of the question, even if the number of Jews were greatly reduced. The non-Jewish population has filled the places of the Jews in the towns and cities; in a large part of Poland this is a fundamental change, final in character. The return of masses of Jews would be experienced by the population not as restitution but as an invasion against which they would defend themselves, even with physical means.[22]

Such reactions were reinforced by Polish political parties. Of the parties whose collaboration enabled the "underground state" to function, most continued to regard the presence of Jews in Poland as a burden. Although only the extreme Right condoned killing Jews, most of the underground (except for the PPS and several smaller parties) opposed equal rights for Jews in postwar Poland and favored emigration of the one or two million anticipated survivors as the only acceptable resolution of the "Jewish question."[23] The Poland that would arise after the agony of the war, it was felt, must be a new Poland, free of the debilitating influence of the Jews. In Western Europe, local anti-Semites had cordially received the Nazis and often collaborated politically with them. As a result, after the German defeat, anti-Semitism was associated not only with the fate of the Jews but also with treason, and was therefore discredited and banished to the margins of public life. But in Poland, where there was no political collaboration, the most blood-thirsty anti-Semite typically remained a Polish patriot, fought the occupier, and found a place for his views in the underground press. Indeed, part of the Endek heritage was a special antipathy to Germans. Anti-Semitism in Poland, therefore, both during the war and in the years after, remained embedded in society; in many circles, being a "good Pole" and detesting Jews easily coexisted. This Polish anti-Semitism, however, was not simply a carryover from the prewar period; beginning with the war, it received a powerful new impetus from the Poles' encounter with their eastern neighbor, an experience that was to have momentous implications for the future.

For twenty-one months, from September 1939 to June 1941, the Soviet Union ruled the *kresy*, an area that made up half of the prewar Polish state but in which Poles constituted only a minority of the population.[24] The goal of the Soviet occupation was the incorporation of this region into the Soviet system, a transformation of its political, economic, and social structure that, in its own way, paralleled the Nazi effort to make the rest of Poland part of its New Order. The Soviet method was, first of all, to portray themselves as the liberators of the region from both class and national oppression, which meant appealing to Ukrainian and Belorussian peasants and impoverished Jewish workers, while destroying the Polish political and social infrastructure. Thus, on the heels of the advancing Red Army, Belorussian and Ukrainian peasants were incited to take violent revenge against their Polish landlords. The Soviets also established new schools, courts, and other institutions, and mounted an assault on religion intended particularly to co-opt young people into the new world of "proletarian values." Finally, the Soviets institutionalized the system of terror that Stalin had perfected in the 1930s. This system was based both on NKVD [political police] identifications of "class enemies," as well as denunciations solicited from all corners of society, the victims chosen according to no logic that anyone could fathom. In eastern as in Nazi-occupied western and central Poland, Poles trembled at the sound of car brakes screeching to a halt in the night before their homes.[25] Arrest, imprisonment under barbaric conditions, torture, execution, or most commonly, deportation to the far reaches of the Soviet Union (especially, as the saying went, "to the polar bears") swept up immense numbers of people. In the course of four waves of deportation in 1940 and 1941, more than half a million Polish citizens were rounded up without warning, loaded into sealed and unheated freight cars, and transported thousands of miles to gulags, prisons, and penal exile in Siberia and Central Asia.[26] As in German-occupied Poland, Polish elites were particular targets of repression.

After the German invasion of the Soviet Union and the rapid retreat of Soviet forces from Polish territory, Stalin initiated relations with the Polish government-in-exile. This uneasy alliance lasted two years, during which the Soviets released most Poles from detention and permitted them to recruit a Polish army in the Soviet Union. But in April 1943, in the Katyń Forest near Smolensk, Germans discovered the bodies of four thousand Polish officers who had been arrested and then murdered by the Soviets at the beginning of the war. The Katyń massacre, which the Soviets denied and then used as a pretext for severing diplomatic relations with the London government, was to become Communist Poland's greatest historical taboo, a collective symbol of the many Soviet atrocities committed against the Poles, but which, unlike Nazi crimes, went unpunished and, indeed, risked being effaced from historical memory.

Having broken with the London government, Stalin proceeded to plan Poland's future independently of it. First he began to build within Poland an underground military and political base devoted exclusively to Moscow. A small group of Polish Communists who had fled to the Soviet Union at the start of the war had already been parachuted into the Generalgouvernement in January 1942 to establish a new Communist party. This was the Polish Workers' Party (Polska Partia Robotnicza, PPR), the previous Polish Communist party having been liquidated by Stalin just before the war. This cadre then helped set up the People's Guard and later the People's Army, whose membership made it a small fraction of the size of the Home Army, but which neverthless proclaimed itself the legitimate Polish underground. Simultaneously, throughout the

Nazi-occupied eastern borderlands, Soviet partisan units fought the Germans and prepared the region for reannexation by the Soviets. Meanwhile Stalin played his other hand, that of diplomacy. As a result of three international conferences, at Tehran, Yalta, and Potsdam, from 1943 to 1945, he obtained Allied approval for a postwar Poland shorn of the *kresy* and definitively within the Soviet orbit. From positions across the Vistula River in October 1944, Red Army units, apparently purposely uninvolved, observed the end of an era in Polish history: the defeat of the Warsaw Uprising and the destruction of the Home Army, the last major link to Poland's prewar past.

Even before the Soviet invasion of eastern Poland, the so-called *Żydokomuna* (pronounced "zhidokomuna"), or "Jew Commune," had occupied a prominent place in nationalist diatribes. Here, supposedly, was the modern means to the long-attempted Jewish political conquest of Poland; the *Żydokomuna* conspirators would finally succeed in establishing a "Judaeo-Polonia." Beginning with the accusation that they sided with the Bolsheviks during the Polish-Soviet war of 1919–20, Jews were accused of masterminding Polish communism. The interwar Polish Communist Party [Komunistyczna Partia Polski, KPP] was a small, sectarian organization that Stalin dissolved in 1938 for "Fascist and Trotskyite infiltration,"[27] while summoning its leaders to Moscow where most of them were murdered. Most Poles saw the KPP as little more than a tool of their hereditary eastern enemy; the vast majority of Polish Jews preferred to support Zionist, Socialist, or Orthodox parties. Yet while the number of Jews in the KPP represented an insignificant fraction of the Jewish population of Poland, the Jewish share in party membership was far higher than the Jewish share in the general population. During the 1930s, Jews made up about one-quarter of the membership of the party; in large cities and in the *kresy* the proportions were considerably higher. Above all, Jews made up more than half of the local party leadership and most of the members of the Central Committee were of Jewish origin.[28] Most of the Jews in the KPP, it should be stressed, certainly those in positions of leadership, strongly deemphasized their Jewish origins. It should not be surprising that an ideology, indeed a militant faith, that guaranteed the overcoming of all national antagonisms in an internationalist world of the future, would entice Polish Jews more easily than Poles. Soviet practice, moreover, seemed to support the theory; for much of the interwar period, anti-Semitism in the Soviet Union was taboo, combatted, although with diminishing commitment, by state institutions.[29]

The invasion of the eastern borderlands by the Soviet Union signified something quite different for the Jews of the region than it did for the Poles.[30] First of all, after years of news reports from Nazi Germany and the testimony of masses of refugees from Nazi-occupied Poland, Jews in eastern Poland were convinced that whatever awaited them under the Soviets would be preferable to Nazi rule. Furthermore, particularly in the hundreds of impoverished *shtetlekh* that filled this region, there was considerable resentment against Polish rule, as there was, indeed, in Belorussian and Ukrainian peasant villages. In many towns, Jews and other minorities participated in greeting the Red Army with flowers and cheers; Jews apparently were particularly conspicuous for kissing Soviet tanks.[31] The Jewish response to the Soviets was also class related. While the middle class, whether traditionally oriented or Polish assimilating, generally minimized its contact with the occupier, some of the working-class youth, suddenly offered unprecedented educational and vocational opportunities, enthusiastically embraced a system in which being born Jewish was declared irrelevant; some even joined the Soviet security apparatus.

All this was carefully noted by the beleaguered Poles. Conflicting Jewish interests in a situation of vital significance to Poles were filtered through anti-Semitic fantasies to create a myth of Jewish vengeance. In this case, especially after the Germans united all of prewar Poland under their rule in 1941, rumors about the Soviet occupation of the east inundated the Generalgouvernement. These rumors typically embellished upon the theme of "what *they* [the Jews] did to us on the other side of the Bug." Poles, moreover, it was said, had two enemies, the Germans and the Soviets, but the Jews had only one. The irony is that after several months of life under the Soviets, most Jews, regardless of their initial reactions, were not exactly Soviet devotees. A contemporary anecdote told of two trains going in opposite directions meeting at the new German-Soviet border. One is carrying Jews fleeing German-occupied Poland for the Soviet zone, the other Jews fleeing the Soviets for the Germans. On each train a Jew leans out and shouts at the Jews on the other train: "Where are you going? Are you crazy?"[32] The fate of some three hundred thousand Jews from western and central Poland who fled to the Soviet sector during the first months of the war is also instructive. In the spring of 1940, these refugees were registered by the NKVD and offered two choices: either accept Soviet citizenship or declare themselves willing to return to their homes in German-occupied Poland. Most of these refugees indicated their readiness to return to the Nazis, whereupon they were accorded the standard Soviet treatment for those suspected of disloyalty: they were deported to labor camps deep in the Soviet Union. The ultimate irony is that most of these Polish Jews, by far the largest group to do so, thereby survived the Holocaust.

Bearing in mind the resentments, hatreds, and misunderstandings that shaped Polish attitudes to Jews during the war, as well as the severity of Polish suffering, we can return to the question of Polish reactions, institutional and individual, to the slaughter of their Jewish neighbors. The Polish underground was involved in various political, social welfare, and military activities. But for all its exemplary democratic structure and its exalted national mission, or perhaps more accurately, because of them, the "underground state" was essentially for Poles only. In this respect it was a departure from the historical tradition it claimed to represent. Its powerful bond to the community it defended was based on culture and blood, not citizenship, and this intimacy implied its mirroring of popular attitudes, including those about the Jews. In contrast, the government-in-exile had to walk a tightrope. On one hand, contending with Stalin for influence in Washington and London, it was exposed to western scrutiny and especially to that of American and British Jews, who found denouncing Polish anti-Semitism easier than criticizing their own governments' inaction in saving Jews. On the other hand, the government-in-exile was sensitive to reports from Poland stressing the danger of being perceived by Poles as a "government of the Jews." While the government-in-exile had two Jewish representatives on its National Council in London, in Poland, Jews were not represented in the Delegate's Bureau.

Beginning in October 1941, the Polish underground relayed accounts of the mass murder of Jews, first in the eastern territories, then in the gas vans at Chełmno. Several days after the start of transports from the Warsaw Ghetto to Treblinka, the underground provided a detailed report.[33] Such information was dispatched to the government-in-exile and also published in numerous underground publications. What happened to this information once it arrived in London, how it was treated by the government-in-exile, as well as by the BBC, Jewish groups, and Allied governments, is a complex matter, but what is undeniable is that, despite occasional vacillation, the Polish government-in-exile was the key channel through which word of the Holocaust reached the West. Crucial in this respect was the work of the Home Army courier, Jan Karski, who in October 1942 was smuggled into the Warsaw Ghetto and into a concentration camp, then recounted what he had seen in London and Washington; his visit to Washington in July 1943 included a personal audience with President Roosevelt.[34]

Both the government-in-exile and the Polish underground accompanied their documentation of the slaughter with expressions of outrage.[35] In October 1942, Prime Minister Sikorski, the main speaker at a protest demonstration at the Albert Hall in London, denounced the Nazi murder of the Jews, warned the Germans that they would pay for their crimes, and promised Jews equal rights in postwar Poland.[36] But with rare exceptions, what was missing in these statements were appeals to Poles to help the Jews.[37] In the Polish underground press, calls for assistance to Jews were no more frequent than condemnations of anti-Semitism; a typical reaction was speculation about whether Poles would be next to be murdered. For the underground press, the fate of the Jews was a distant second to the fate of the Poles.[38]

Although sporadic contacts between Polish and Jewish underground groups, chiefly between the PPS and the Bund, existed since the beginning of the war, not until the end of 1942 did the leadership of the Polish underground make attempts to aid Jews. In October of that year, when the Germans paused after killing 250,000 Warsaw Jews, the Warsaw Jewish underground managed for the first time to establish contact with the Home Army. Not long before the start of the ghetto uprising in April 1943, the Jewish underground was given a small quantity of arms and some weapons training. During the uprising, several AK units mounted attacks on the Germans; after the uprising, a handful of surviving fighters were led by AK guides through the sewers and out of the burning ghetto. Detachments of the People's Guard also aided the Jewish fighters. The Warsaw Ghetto Uprising marked a high point in the attitude of most of the Polish underground to the Jews; at last, it was felt, Jews had responded to the Nazis in a "manly" way. Nevertheless, Polish and Jewish interests diverged even here; the Home Army leadership resisted being drawn into a premature insurrection, while the Jews did not have the luxury of choice. Throughout the war, there were also Jews (often passing as "Aryans") who fought in Home Army partisan units, as well as some Jewish units who cooperated with the Home Army. Overall, however, Jews found it easier and safer to work with Soviet and PPR groups, because many NSZ and right-wing Home Army units treated Jews (and Bolsheviks) no differently than they did Germans.

More significant than military aid was the founding, in September 1942, of a clandestine Polish organization devoted to helping Jews survive on the "Aryan side." This was Żegota, code name of the Council for Aid to Jews (Rada Pomocy Żydom), that was incorporated into the Polish underground and funded until the end of the war by the Polish government-in-exile and western Jews. Primarily active in Warsaw, the several dozen members of Żegota located housing, forged documents, secured regular financial support, and organized medical care for thousands of Jews. The organization developed a special section devoted to hiding children and functioned as an advocate for Jews within the Delegate's Bureau.

The initiative for Żegota's creation was a leaflet written and distributed in Warsaw in August 1942, while trains were being loaded for Treblinka. The author, Zofia Kossak-Szczucka, a Catholic nationalist, reminded Poles of what was taking place behind the ghetto walls, then condemned the world's silence, which she equated with complicity with the murderers, and insisted that the duty of Catholics and Poles was to protest. She then continued:

> That is why we, Polish Catholics, are speaking out. Our feelings about the Jews have not changed. We have not ceased to regard them as political, economic, and ideological enemies of Poland. Furthermore, we recognize that they hate us more than the Germans, that they hold us responsible for their misfortunes. Why, for what reason—that remains a secret of the Jewish soul, nonetheless it is a fact that is continually confirmed. Our awareness of these feelings, however, does not free us from *the responsibility of denouncing the crime.*[39]

Kossak's views were not those of Żegota as a whole, but they were hardly unique; there were cases of other anti-Semites who, revolted by the Nazi resolution of the "Jewish question," devoted themselves to saving Jews. The point, rather, is that if even a founder of Żegota was an anti-Semite, what could one have expected of the average Pole, lacking, let us assume, Kossak's extraordinary ethical sensibility? It has been suggested, in Kossak's defense, that she was not herself an anti-Semite, but may have felt that referring to Jews as enemies of Poland would "make her appeal more effective," a suggestion even more revealing of the attitudes of her contemporaries.[40] In the words of the literary critic Jan Błoński, an astute recent commentator on these issues: "Kossak-Szczucka's leaflet—better than many direct testimonies—takes us into the thinking and feeling of a significant (majority?) portion of contemporary Polish society."[41]

Given the demoralization of much of Polish (and Jewish) society under Nazi rule, the fierce anti-Semitism, and the profits to be made from Jews, the prevalence of informing, blackmail, plunder of various kinds, as well as the outright murder of Jews should not surprise us. City streets in the "Aryan quarter" were the terrain of specialized gangs of blackmailers (the so-called *szmalcownicy,* from *shmalts,* Yiddish for grease), who scanned the physiognomy and posture of passersby seeking potential prey; in the forests, peasants, with or without German escort, hunted for Jews, whom they killed on the spot or turned over to the Germans. Certainly, not only Jews were betrayed; the first commander of the Home Army, Gen. Stefan Grot-Rowecki, was denounced to the Nazis by a fellow officer. Hunting Jews, however, was easier; all one needed was a knack for "sniffing them out." It was also less dangerous;

despite Żegota's efforts, the number of Poles whom the underground sentenced to death for crimes against Jews was only 1 percent of all the Poles executed by the underground.[42] As Emmanuel Ringelblum noted, in "Aryan" Warsaw the cry "Catch that Jew!" was used by the Nazis to enlist the help of passersby in capturing fleeing members of the Polish underground.[43]

On a popular level, the murder of the Jews evoked a range of responses, from compassion, to the opinion that their fate was "not our business," to the judgment that the Germans had provided an unpleasant but necessary solution to an intractable problem. For most Poles, however, none of these feelings inspired any action. No different, in this respect, from other non-Jews under Nazi occupation, most Poles were passive witnesses to the fate of the Jews. Yet for Poles this passivity was reinforced by three factors: the difficulty of daily life under German occupation, especially the extreme terror; the imposition of the death sentence against those accused of aiding Jews; and the widespread perception that Jews were beyond the Polish universe of obligation, that they were not, in other words, "ours."[44]

Nevertheless, throughout Poland, Jews were helped by thousands of individual Poles, most unaffiliated with Żegota. This assistance ranged from the most unpremeditated of gestures, such as offering someone on a death transport a drink of water, all the way to building and maintaining elaborate hideouts where scores of people survived for months and sometimes years. There were Jews hidden for the entire war by the Polish families into which they had married and those taken off the street, housed and fed for years by total strangers. Some of these Poles were paid for their assistance, others were not, but payment could not compensate for the risks involved. Hiding Jews was punishable by death, and there are records of hundreds of Poles who paid that price, sometimes along with their families.[45]

Yet what limited Polish aid to Jews was not just fear of the death penalty. In occupied Poland, death was mandated for a host of transgressions great and small, and was sometimes merely a result of being on the street at the wrong time. Nor did the fear of death keep hundreds of thousands of Poles from joining the underground. It is true that hiding Jews was more dangerous than distributing underground literature. But the reason for this dif-ference lay above all in popular attitudes about Jews, as a result of which someone hiding a Jew could be much less certain of his or her neighbor than someone distributing an underground paper. Hiding Jews required, within the individual, more than courage and as much as compassion, a powerful system of personal val-ues independent of social norms. Those who saved Jews came from all classes of society; what many of them had in common was a trait that the sociologist Nehama Tec has called "marginality," or more positively, "individuality."[46] This rare quality permitted such people to face not only Nazi terror but also the indifference and hostility of much of their society. It permitted them to see Jews, despite the weight of history, as human beings in need of help. Not the informing or the indifference, but the existence of such in-dividuals is one of the most remarkable features of Polish-Jewish relations during the Holocaust.

3

Memory's Wounds
1944–1948

The Polish state that emerged from the devastation of the Second World War was strikingly different from the Second Polish Commonwealth of the interwar years. First of all, according to agreements worked out by the Allies at Tehran, Yalta, and Potsdam, the boundaries of the new state were shifted greatly to the west. Some seventy thousand square miles, the multiethnic *kresy,* were ceded to the Soviet Union; in exchange, forty thousand square miles of what had been the German Reich, including East Prussia, Pomerania, and Lower Silesia, became Polish. This geographic transformation, accompanied by the forced expulsion of millions of Germans and Ukrainians out of the western and eastern regions, respectively, of the new state, created a demographic revolution. For the first time in history, a Polish state would be populated almost exclusively by ethnic, Roman Catholic Poles. Ironically, this goal of several generations of Polish nationalists, first realized in the experience of the Home Army's "underground state," whose strength had rested precisely in its "Polishness," was attained under Communist rule. For no longer as the Commonwealth, but as the People's Republic of Poland, the new state, like its neighbors to the east, west, and south, would be incorporated for more than four decades into the Soviet bloc and governed, in practice, by one political party "in the interests of" its citizens. The imposition of totalitarian rule transformed everything in Poland, from the structure of its economic development to the consciousness of its intelligentsia to the minutiae of everyday life. Politics—the rise, victory, decline and fall of Polish communism—is the baseline of postwar Polish history, the ground against which all other aspects of that history acquire definition.

The key role of politics is apparent in the immediate postwar period. As Norman Davies points out, it is rather out of place to speak of a Communist "seizure of power" during the years 1944 to 1948.[1] According to Allied understanding, Poland was to belong to the Soviet sphere of influence; the presence in Poland of the Red Army, accompanied by the inevitable political commissars and secret police, guaranteed this outcome. With the destruction of the Home Army during the Warsaw Uprising of August–October 1944, and the withdrawal of United States and British support for the government-in-exile, there remained little significant political opposition to the installation of a Polish government subservient to Moscow. Subsequent events were less a seizure than simply a consolidation of power by the Communists: the succession of provisional governments (beginning with the so-called Lublin Committee organized as early as July 1944) consisting of what was termed "all democratic and anti-Nazi elements" that ruled Poland until February 1947; the rigged national referendum of 1946 supporting the government; the elections of 1947 that brought Bolesław Bierut, a Communist who had spent the war years in Moscow, into power as president of the republic; the flight from Poland in late 1947 of Stanisław Mikołajczyk, the last major independent political figure (upon his appearance in London, Churchill expressed surprise that he was still alive); the founding the following year (out of the PPR, part of the PPS, and several smaller parties) of the Polish United Workers' Party [Polska Zjednoczona Partia Robotnicza, PZPR] that was to rule Poland for four decades, with Bierut also as its general secretary.

In the immediate postwar years, there was a degree of sympathy in Polish society, particularly among workers, peasants, and the intelligentsia, for the program of reconstruction and reform promised by Communist leaders. It was argued by some intellectuals, for example, that communism would end the "impracticality" of the Polish intelligentsia, historically alienated from the rest of society because of its *szlachta* origins.[2] Nevertheless, as Stalin is said to have remarked, imposing Soviet-style communism on Poland was ultimately like trying to saddle a cow. Communism in Poland had had only a limited following, unlike in interwar Czechoslovakia, or in Yugoslavia, where the Communists' role in the anti-Nazi resistance legitimated their claim to national leadership after the war. Indeed, in Poland just the opposite was the case; the Home Army and its "underground state" had been betrayed by the Communists. Furthermore, communism had no links to either of the national orientations that had developed at the end of the nineteenth century; it traced its origins, in fact, to a tiny clandestine party that had explicitly renounced the need for Polish independence.[3] In postwar Poland, communism largely remained an alien system, imposed by the "eastern enemy" for "reasons of state." The sense of victory at the conclusion of the war was fleeting at best, and quickly gave way to the perception that one occupier had simply replaced another, and that Poland had been betrayed and abandoned by the West. Such feelings, compounded by the increasing mockery that Communist ideology made of pluralist and universalist discourse, all tended to reinforce the exclusivist, indeed the paranoid, tendencies in Polish popular consciousness. For many Poles, the aftermath of the war confirmed a bitter vision of a world awash with enemies and false friends, a world in which the cardinal error was trusting anyone other than oneself.

The consciousness of political defeat played itself out in a wider atmosphere of demoralization. As in the years after World War I, but to a much greater extent, the aftermath of war was widespread lawlessness and violence that approached civil war; human life continued to mean very little. Alongside private vendettas and often indistinguishable from them, paramilitary units linked to three political groups launched attacks claiming thousands of victims against the government and whomever they identified as its sympathizers. There were the National Armed Forces (NSZ), right-wing nationalists who had remained outside the Home Army during the war; Freedom and Independence [Wolność i Niezawisłość,

WiN], made up of remnants of the disbanded Home Army; and the Ukrainian Insurgent Army [Ukrajinska Powstanska Armija, UPA], who fought for a Ukrainian state in eastern Poland. At the same time, both responding to the right-wing violence and provoking it, the Soviet terror apparatus well known to Poles from the occupation of eastern Poland in 1939–41 swung into action; indiscriminate murders, arrests, and deportations swept the country. Not only former Home Army officers and sympathizers of opposition parties learned to dread the midnight knock on the door.

This was the atmosphere in which survivors of the Holocaust began to emerge from concentration camps and places of refuge. Determining their number is difficult. There was continuous traffic across the Polish borders, recordkeeping was unreliable, and above all, existing statistics reflect only the Jews who chose to identify themselves as such to local Jewish committees. Thus statistics from January 1946 show 86,000 Jews in Poland, most of whom, we may assume, had hidden on the "Aryan side" or survived concentration camps, with smaller numbers surviving as combatants in partisan units and in the Polish army, and in hiding in forests and bunkers. From February to August 1946, according to the terms of a Polish-Soviet repatriation agreement, more than 100,000 Jews, prewar Polish citizens who had escaped the war deep in the Soviet Union, returned to Poland, swelling the officially registered Jewish population to a postwar peak of 244,000.[4] There is no way even to estimate the additional number of Jews who, having passed as Poles on the "Aryan side," chose to remain that way.

During these years, it briefly seemed as if organized Jewish life in Poland might regain its prewar shape if not its magnitude. Headed by leaders who had returned from the Soviet Union, all the prewar Jewish political parties began to rebuild their activist networks. Alongside them, and involving many of the same leaders, the Central Committee of Polish Jews [Centralny Komitet Żydów Polskich, CKŻP], established in late 1944 with the cooperation of the pro-Soviet authorities, pursued a program aiming at the economic, social, and cultural revival of the Jewish community in Poland.[5] For understandable psychological reasons, as well as reasons of security, few Jews attempted to resume their lives in the places they had lived before the war. With the encouragement of the Polish government and financial support from American Jews, the CKŻP helped settle Jews in the new western areas of Poland, particularly Lower Silesia, where there were industrial jobs. Jewish farming and artisanry were also developed, along with a network of producers' cooperatives. The CKŻP set up Jewish schools providing primary, secondary, and vocational instruction in Yiddish and Polish, as well as clinics and orphanages (the latter attempting to cope with the unique needs of child survivors). Numerous Jewish periodicals were published, two Yiddish theaters and various cultural organizations were established. Religious life was organized by local associations modeled on the prewar *kehilla;* a national union of these congregations was recognized by the government alongside the CKŻP.

Contemporaneously with the founding of the CKŻP, under its aegis and with the government's support, a handful of surviving Jewish historians founded the Central Jewish Historical Commission [Centralna Żydowska Komisja Historyczna, CŻKH]. The commission opened branches in several Polish cities and dedicated itself to gathering documentation of the Holocaust. Its activity paralleled that of Polish historians working in the High Commission to Investigate Nazi Crimes in Poland [Główna Komisja Badania Zbrodni Hitlerowskich w Polsce], established by the Polish government in 1945.[6] The primary task of the High Commission, under the auspices of the Ministry of Justice, was to gather material for the prosecution of war criminals before the International Military Tribunal at Nuremberg and the Supreme National Tribunal in Poland. The best-known of the Polish trials was that of Rudolf Hoess, the commandant of Auschwitz, who was executed at the site of the camp in 1947. Both the High Commission to Investigate Nazi War Crimes and the Central Jewish Historical Commission published considerable material. In the case of the latter, during 1945 to 1948 this material amounted to more than twenty volumes of documents, histories, memoirs, and literary works.[7] In 1947, the Jewish Historical Commission moved permanently to Warsaw, and as the Jewish Historical Institute [Żydowski Instytut Historyczny, ŻIH], became the repository of archives relating to Jewish life before and during the Holocaust, above all, the Ringelblum Archives, which were dug out of the rubble of the

Warsaw Ghetto in 1946 and 1950. Although most of its founders soon left Poland, the institute nevertheless continued with research and publishing, its quantity and quality depending on the political climate, through all the subsequent years of Communist rule, the only Jewish research institution in the Soviet bloc that managed to do so.[8]

That the upsurge of Jewish activity in the immediate postwar years was supported by the new Polish government should not be surprising. Certainly, until the late 1940s, the goodwill of the West and of western Jews was important both to the Soviet Union and the new Polish state, especially when such goodwill was accompanied by financial aid. Support for Holocaust survivors in Poland coincided with Soviet politics internationally; in 1947, the Soviet Union voted in the United Nations for the creation of a Jewish state. Nor did the Polish government in the immediate postwar period hinder Jewish emigration to Palestine. Throughout the world these years seemed to mark the victory of good over evil. The notion that "peace and progress" had triumphed over "fascist barbarism" was much more than a Communist slogan. Based on these beliefs, official commemorative activity was quickly undertaken. Even before the end of the war, the remains of the concentration camps at Majdanek, Stutthof [Sztutowo], and Auschwitz-Birkenau [Oświęcim-Brzezinka] were declared memorial sites by the provisional government,[9] and in 1947, the Polish parliament made these and similar locations the responsibility of a Council for the Protection of Memorials to Struggle and Martyrdom [Rada Ochrony Pomników Walki i Męczeństwa].

The new Polish government legitimized itself by claiming to represent a complete break with everything "reactionary" in the Polish past, in particular, with the heritage of anti-Semitism. This was, it turned out, only a step along the path to triumphant Stalinism, which would shortly disown the entire Polish past as "prehistory," the product of class oppression, Year One of real history beginning with the establishment of the People's Republic. For the time being, however, the government and its supporters contented themselves with constructing a rhetorical image of the enemy out of the attributes "reactionary," "nationalist," "anti-Semitic" and "criminal."[10] Little distinction was made between the NSZ and the AK; both were attacked as Nazi collaborators who equally murdered Jews and partisans. Jewish resistance, and above all the Warsaw Ghetto Uprising, was easily absorbed into this narrative. An extreme but instructive example: the writer Jerzy Andrzejewski reports seeing two posters affixed to walls amid the ruins of Warsaw in April 1945; one read "Glory to the Heroic Defenders of the Ghetto," while another alongside it declared "Shame to the Fascist Flunkeys of the Home Army."[11] Three years later, on the fifth anniversary of the Warsaw Ghetto Uprising, this distinction was literally graven in stone with the unveiling of Nathan Rapoport's memorial. This celebrated monument and the large public square in front of it quickly became the preeminent site for all Polish commemorations of the Holocaust.[12] Although official attitudes to the Home Army and the Warsaw Uprising softened considerably over subsequent decades, it nevertheless required forty years until a comparable monument was erected to commemorate the Polish uprising. Indeed, at the time the ghetto monument was raised, the only other war memorial that had been erected in Warsaw commemorated fallen Soviet soldiers. Rapoport's creation stood alone in a vast field of rubble, easily read by Poles as a symbol of the new government's decision to honor the Jews, while consigning the Polish national struggle to the dustbin of history.[13] Similarly, Polish secondary school textbooks of the early 1950s devote more attention to the history of anti-Semitism and the Holocaust than any subsequent versions, but the context for this information is a narrative in which the AK is described as collaborating with the Germans.[14]

Such "proofs" by the government only reaffirmed what many Poles already felt they knew: Jews were the government and the government was Jewish. In the propaganda of the nationalist underground and in a considerable portion of popular consciousness, a likeness of the enemy, the mirror image of government propaganda, was assembled out of the attributes "alien," "Communist," "Jewish," and "traitorous." It was an image that was to long outlive its competitor. The product of labyrinthine interaction between systems of myth and stereotype on one hand and historical experience on the other, the image weaves fantasy and reality into an apparently seamless whole. The image reaches back to the oldest strata of European Jew hatred, the Jew as Judas Iscariot, medieval sorcerer and well-poisoner. It receives further sustenance from late-nineteenth-century anti-Semitic stereotypes, above all that of the Jewish plot, be it through capitalism, Zionism, revolution, or some combination thereof, to rule the world. The image of the Jew as Bolshevik conspirator assumed a specifically Polish form already before the war in the notion of the *Żydokomuna*. During the Soviet occupation of eastern Poland, the interaction between this stereotype and aspects of Jewish behavior led to a specific belief in Jewish vengeance on Poles. Now, in the years immediately after the war, a similar process led to the conviction that the *Żydokomuna* had finally conquered Poland. Characteristic is a report written in London in October 1945 by a military courier who had just returned from Poland. Upon the appearance of the new political authorities, Jews, he claims, "immediately began to falsely accuse those who had concealed them of blackmail and extortion, denounced members of the AK, and permitted themselves to beat and torture Poles in the camps the Jews administered for the Soviets. . . . It is a fact that Jews along with the Bolsheviks rule Poland. The ridiculed prewar slogan '*Żydokomuna*' has currently been realized. Polish Communists have no power, even in the PPR."[15] The Jews are held responsible, in a word, for the enslavement of Poland.

The kernel of truth in such accusations was related to the vast difference between the situation of Poles and Jews in the new Poland. Because so many Jews owed their survival to having spent the war years in the Soviet Union and because the postwar Polish government seemed the only force capable of defending Jewish rights and safeguarding Jewish life and property after the war, most Jews in Poland and throughout the world, although not without many reservations, supported the new government. In the fictionalized memoirs of Hanna Krall, a Jew who survives the Holocaust in the Soviet Union and subsequently returns to Poland as a political commissar defines his tragicomic fate as follows: "He couldn't even hate Stalin like the others [Poles], but had to love him a little after all."[16] Yet only a minority of Jews served in the government. The answer to the question how many depends, first of all, on how one defines who is a Jew. Except for a handful of Yiddish-speaking Communists who would oversee the officially organized Jewish community in Poland from 1948 to 1968, most of the Jews who served in the Polish government had assimilated linguistically and culturally to Polish norms or were attempting to do so. For most of these officials, their connection to anything Jewish amounted to an accident of birth. Even as we examine the presence of such individuals in the Polish government, we should be aware that such an investigation accepts a racial definition of what constitutes a Jew.[17]

The prevalence of such Jews in the postwar Polish government, then, is reminiscent of their prevalence in the KPP, the prewar Polish Communist Party; only a tiny proportion of all Jews, their representation in the party was considerably higher than their share in the general population.[18] Indeed, the group of Communists who took power in postwar Poland were primarily former KPP members who had spent the war in Moscow, and therefore included a particularly high proportion of individuals of Jewish origin who had thereby survived the Holocaust. For most such lifelong activists, the postwar years provided the opportunity to create the kind of Poland of which they had dreamed. Nor should it surprise us that even Jews who were not Communists might be attracted by the opportunity to serve in the government, from which Jews had been excluded before the war. Many Jews in the party and the government, moreover, partly at the urging of their superiors or the NKVD, adopted more Polish-sounding names to arouse less hostility. This practice often backfired, and fed the stereotype of "hidden Jews," speculation about whom became a popular pastime for decades to come. But the deadliest part of the stereotype as it developed in the postwar years was the widespread belief that the security apparatus, the dreaded UB (Urząd Bezpieczeństwa), was in Jewish hands and that Jews were thereby responsible for the torture and murder of Polish patriots. The reality was that Jewish representation was somewhat greater than the Jewish share of the population, but nowhere near the claims of the stereotype.[19]

Accompanying the development of the stereotype and its fixation in popular consciousness in the postwar years was the worst anti-Jewish violence in the history of Polish-Jewish relations. In Poland from 1944 to 1947, between fifteen hundred and two thousand Jews were murdered, most of them specifically because they were Jews.[20] Most were killed individually or in small groups when they returned to scores of localities throughout Poland to discover the fate of their families or reclaim homes and businesses. Jews were also pulled from trains to be beaten and murdered, and several Jewish institutions were bombed. Finally, in about a dozen cities and towns, Jews lost their lives in pogroms. The worst and the last of these attacks occurred in Kielce in July 1946; forty-two Jews were killed and more than one hundred were wounded when a mob attacked a communal residence for Holocaust survivors.[21] The violence as a whole, and above all the Kielce pogrom, that brought international notoriety to postwar Poland, strengthened the government's claim to being the only force that could oppose "reaction" and protect the Jews. The pogrom was also a turning point in the attempt to rebuild a Jewish community in Poland. Kielce convinced most survivors that Poland held no future for them; by 1951, when the government prohibited emigration to Israel, the Jewish population of Poland had shrunk to less than eighty thousand.[22] Many of those who stayed had political reasons for doing so; their group profile ever more closely resembled the mythic *Żydokomuna*.

What caused the waves of anti-Jewish violence that swept Poland after liberation? Certainly political factors were of great importance. Some of the perpetrators, often still in uniform, were indeed the "fascist bandits" of government propaganda, the "boys from the woods" of the NSZ. Wiping out Jews was as much a part of their political credo as eliminating Bolsheviks; their leaflets ended with the slogan "Kill the Jews and save Poland."[23] The Kielce pogrom has also inspired a good deal of speculation that it was a provocation orchestrated by the NKVD, intended to turn world sympathy against the opposition just as it began to protest the rigged results of the 1946 referendum.[24] More generally, the Jews, it can be said, found themselves victims of the most explosive conflicts in postwar Poland, and these conflicts were essentially political. As the historian Krystyna Kersten has recently put it, the core of the problem was "the result of linking the Jewish question to the system of rule imposed on Poland. Mixed together in this syndrome in a truly surrealistic manner were the real world and the mythologized world, reason and phobia, political morality and political pragmatism, manipulation and spontaneity, the past and the present, nationalism and communism."[25] Compared to the prewar period, when hostility to Jews was entangled in economic factors, the postwar situation was new. At the same time, there was an abiding continuity in the negative stereotype of the Jew: whether before, during, or after the war, his image was available as that of the spoiler, the avenger, the foe of everything Polish.

But this apparent continuity inspires an obvious question: how could it have survived the Holocaust? How could the experience of being the prime witnesses of the Holocaust have left conventional attitudes to Jews unchanged? The characteristic Polish stance in relation to the Holocaust was passive witnessing. Having examined the reasons for the passivity, we must now consider a more difficult problem: the subjective nature of the witnessing. It is Poles, after all, who saw the ghetto walls go up and watched their neighbors imprisoned behind them. Poles watched the ghettos burn, saw their neighbors herded into sealed trains, watched the "transports" arrive at their destination, smelled the smoke of the crematoriums, witnessed the hunting of escapees. Individual impressions were confirmed by the accounts of family and friends and by the underground press. It should not have been difficult for Poles to conclude that they were witnessing the attempt to murder every Jew in Poland, perhaps every Jew in Europe.

Yet is it possible that the Holocaust was not truly or fully witnessed by Poles, that its events were seen but not comprehended? There is testimony that something like this was indeed the case. A student of attitudes to Jews in recent Polish literature cites the following passage as typical of the Polish reaction to the fate of the Jews: "Collective life and my own life went on beside the life of the ghetto. It occupied me little then; I treated its misery as one of the many astonishing aspects of the war, unnamed in their ghastliness, to which we somehow became accustomed."[26] Krystyna Kersten, analyzing references to Jews in memoranda written from wartime Poland to the government-in-exile, points out "the nearly total separation of the martyrdom of the Jews from the so-called Jewish question. The annihilation of the Jewish people occurring before the eyes of Poles seemed not to have changed in any way the stereotype, encoded in the collective imagination, of the Jew as threat. . . . Between the effect—Poland without Jews, and the cause—a crime without precedent, on a scale that does not permit it to be grasped by the imagination of those who were not its witnesses—the link was broken." It is this, according to Kersten, that allowed the Catholic activist Zofia Kossak to demand Polish aid for Jews during the war even as she termed them enemies of Poland.[27]

The inability to accept, to assimilate, to grasp, that is, truly to witness the events of the Holocaust as they were occurring was not unique to Poles. It was inherent in the incredulous response of Americans who read the news of death camps printed in the corners of their newspapers because the editors, in turn, had found the information too "unbelievable" to put on page one. It was true of most of the perpetrators, the bureaucrats who did not want to know and were systematically kept from knowing the truth, carefully cloaked in euphemisms. It applied to Jews in the ghettos, who assumed that making themselves useful to the Germans would guarantee survival, and later, when they entered gas chambers believing they were showers; and it was true of the survivors, who typically questioned whether they could bear witness to themselves, much less to the world, about what they had experienced.[28] In this context, the Holocaust has been termed *"an event without a witness,* an event which historically consists in the scheme of the literal *erasure of its witnesses* but which, moreover, philosophically consists in an accidenting of perception, in a *splitting of eyewitnessing* as such; an event, thus, not empirically, but cognitively and perceptually without a witness both because it precludes seeing and because it precludes the possibility of a *community of seeing."*[29]

If the failure to witness the Holocaust was common to all its contemporaries, then its surviving victims, perpetrators, and bystanders have all, in the years since the Holocaust, had to cope with the consequences of this failure. As we are only now beginning to understand, the unwitnessed event haunts us all; long after its historical terminus, its imprint remains in our consciousness and behavior, affects the shape of our politics and culture. Postwar Poland is no exception.

There is, first of all, the common Polish reaction to the resurfacing of Jews in Poland. Beyond the violence, Jewish sources uniformly attest to the pervasive mixture of surprise, derision, and animosity punctuated by the inevitable refrain "What? They're still alive?" with which survivors were greeted as they appeared on roads, in train stations and town squares.[30] There is also the reappearance in postwar Poland of the blood libel, the belief, dating back to the Middle Ages, that Jews used the blood of Christian children for their religious rituals. Tales of Jewish ritual murder swept the country; most pogroms, including the one in Kielce, began with rumors about the disappearance of Polish children.[31] Finally, and perhaps most troubling, is the widespread hostility directed not just at Jews but at Poles who had saved Jews. Michał Borwicz, one of the founders of the Jewish Historical Commission, who, like most of his colleagues, subsequently emigrated from Poland, found it necessary to respond in 1958 to charges that Jews had kept silent about the Poles who saved their lives during the war, by recounting what happened when he began to publish such accounts in Poland just after the war.

> I began to receive paradoxical visits. People cited by name (and this as saviors!) arrived dispirited, complaining that in publishing their "crime," which consisted in aid rendered at the risk of their life, we exposed them as prey for their neighbors' vengeance. In turn, with similar complaints, certain Jews who had been saved began to appear, sent to us by those who saved them. Still others (the authors of written but as yet unpublished testimonies) came "preventively," to prohibit the future publication of their names. There were cases in which—at the demand of those who saved them—certain individuals refused permission to publish their testimonies at all, even without citing the relevant names, since "from other details (the name of the locality, etc.) their neighbors might guess who was meant."[32]

Borwicz then cites from the introduction to a contemporary collection of testimonies of child survivors.

> In this book, in many testimonies those who saved Jewish children are mentioned by name, but in others only initials are used. Why—

if the names are known? I don't know if anyone beyond the borders of Poland will absorb and comprehend the fact that saving the life of a defenseless child hunted by a murderer can cover someone with shame and disgrace, or make trouble for him.[33]

A confidential memorandum written in February 1946 to a U.S. Embassy counselor in Poland recounts the plight of Jewish children who had been saved by Poles in Kraków: "Until this very day those children are kept in the garret of the house, hidden away from the neighbors for fear that the neighbors discover that the Christian family saved the Jewish children and vent their vengeance on the whole family, and this one year after liberation."[34]

What is the source of such bizarre hatreds, of behavior that seems to undermine our most elementary assumptions about humanity, behavior apparently triggered by little more than the appearance of a handful of survivors of the worst slaughter in history? Our political paradigm alone is insufficient to make sense of such testimony. The need for a psychological perspective on such responses has been noted parenthetically by occasional observers, but such an approach has never been systematically pursued. As early as 1957, the editors of the émigré Polish journal *Kultura*, attempting to understand the overwhelming lack of response combined with outright denials and occasional breast-beating occasioned by their attempt to poll their readers about anti-Semitism, suggested that Polish anti-Semitism was perhaps a "collective psychosis."[35] More recently, the sociologist Zygmunt Bauman has mentioned that Polish reactions to "the crime committed on their soil, before their eyes . . . were as if drawn from a psychology textbook."[36] But what sort of psychology? As Eric Santner has argued, albeit in a different context, "Nazism and the 'Final Solution' need to be theorized under the sign of massive trauma, meaning that these events must be confronted and analyzed in their capacity to endanger and overwhelm the composition and coherence of individual and collective identities that enter into their deadly field of force."[37] The development of such an analysis has long been the work of the psychiatrist and historian Robert Jay Lifton, who has devoted decades to studying the effects of

massive, traumatic exposure to death in various situations including the Holocaust.

In his work of synthesis, *The Broken Connection*, Lifton summarizes several "characteristic themes" or "struggles" within the
survivors of massive death trauma.[38] The first of these is what
Lifton calls the "death imprint" and defines as "the radical intrusion of an image-feeling of threat or end to life." The more extreme, protracted, grotesque, absurd, or otherwise unacceptable is
the image of death, the more unassimilable is the death imprint,
and the more anxiety it evokes. Beside the experience of death is
that of guilt, what Lifton terms "death guilt." It arises from the encounter with a situation in which the possibilities for physical and
even psychic response are nonexistent. "One feels responsible for
what one has not done, for what one has not felt, and above all for
the gap between that physical and psychic inactivation and what
one felt called upon . . . to do and feel." What Lifton calls "the
heart of the traumatic syndrome" is "psychic numbing." These are
strategies, often involuntary and unconscious, that diminish the
capacity to feel, that is, to witness. They include images of denial
as well as, for example, the strategy of "interruption of identification ('I see you dying, but I am not related to you or to your death')."
Psychic numbing severs the self "from its own history, from its
grounding in such psychic forms as compassion for others, communal involvement, and other ultimate values . . . [since it] under-
mines the most fundamental psychic processes . . . we can speak
of it as the essential mechanism of mental disorder." Psychic numbing is characteristically accompanied by anger, rage, and violence
through which the survivor attempts to regain some sense of vitality. It is also accompanied by a symptom that Freud first noted
and termed the "repetition compulsion." Unable fully to witness
the traumatic experience, the survivor obsessively repeats images
and even behavior associated with it. Utimately the survivor
struggles toward what Lifton calls "formulation," a restructuring
of the psyche, its values and symbols, that includes the traumatic
image. This process ideally ends in psychic and moral renewal; its
goal is "emancipation from bondage to the deceased."[39]

But what happens if this healing is blocked? History, particu-

larly in the twentieth century, furnishes examples of entire societies that have experienced massive death trauma without the
opportunity for renewal. The consequences have been the rein-
forcement of guilt, denial, anger, and psychic numbing, "a vicious
circle of unmastered history," as Lifton puts it, referring in this
case to postwar Germany. Particularly during periods that Lifton
calls "protean historical situation[s]," moments at which "in
terms of imagery and sometimes behavior, everything becomes
possible," traumatized societies are often attracted to new "total-
istic programs" rooted in violence and death. Such "totalisms,"
the model for which are modern fascist movements, seek "to master the death immersion—the 'traumatic situation'—by having it
in some way reenacted (on the order of the 'repetition compulsion'), changing or rearranging the participants, but always with
an onrush of survival on the part of oneself or one's group." In-
separable from this strategy is victimization, the creation of "a
death-tainted group," a group of scapegoats that allows the survivors to turn themselves from passive victimized to active victimizers, while nevertheless retaining the image of themselves as
victims. The result is "a perpetual victim-victimizer ethos [such
that] every act of aggression against the target group is understood as anticipatory 'defense,' appropriate revenge, or a combination of both."[40]

To apply this paradigm to postwar Polish history, we must
modify it in several ways that, if anything, reinforce its thrust.
The first concerns the role of guilt. For Poles, the sense of guilt in
witnessing the destruction of the Jews not only resulted from
helplessness before the machinery of murder, what Lifton calls
"death guilt," but also was evoked by two factors rooted in the
specific history of Polish-Jewish relations. First, by the 1930s and
continuing throughout the war, most Poles, to put it most simply,
did not like Jews. Whether this dislike was a result of prewar Jewish economic power or Jewish sympathy for Bolshevism, whether
it emerged out of Church doctrine or the ideology of exclusivist
nationalism or Nazi propaganda, whether or not, in short, it depended on anything the Jews did, does not matter in this respect.
What *does* matter is that this dislike did *not* as a rule mean that
Poles wished to see the Jews murdered. In this context we should

probably even avoid the term "anti-Semitism"; it is feelings, not ideology, that we are after, and moreover, there were doubtless more Poles who disliked Jews than there were "anti-Semites." On the other hand, this dislike *did* mean that many Poles wished that Jews would simply disappear. This wish is borne out by the widespread popularity in Polish society, both before the war and during it, of mass emigration as a solution to the "Jewish question." Jan Błoński describes Zofia Kossak as follows: "She was prepared to give her life for Jews; if nevertheless—through some miracle— they vanished without any particular harm being done to them, she would have been relieved, since she saw neither the need nor the possibility for co-existence."[41]

Second, even during the war, the fate of the Jews had proved economically profitable for Poles. Now, with the defeat of the Germans, what had once belonged to the Jews and still remained in Poland passed into Polish hands. Indeed, an important aspect of the Polish postwar demographic transformation was the movement of peasants from villages on the outskirts of *shtetlekh* into their center, to occupy the traditional Jewish quarters surrounding the marketplace. One of the rare contemporary reflections on the psychic and moral effects of this phenomenon was penned by the literary critic Kazimierz Wyka, writing just as the war was ending.

> From under the sword of the German butcher perpetrating a crime unprecedented in history, the little Polish shopkeeper sneaked the keys to his Jewish competitor's cashbox, and believed that he had acted morally. To the Germans went the guilt and the crime; to us the keys and the cashbox. The storekeeper forgot that the "legal" annihilation of an entire people is part of an undertaking so unparalleled that it was doubtless not staged by history for the purpose of changing the sign on someone's shop. The methods by which Germans liquidated the Jews rest on the Germans' conscience. *The reaction to these methods rests nevertheless on our conscience.* The gold filling torn out of a corpse's mouth will always bleed, even if no one remembers its national origin.[42]

Neither for the Polish shopkeeper occupying his competitor's premises (shortly to be dispossessed in turn by Communist bureaucrats), nor for the millions of Poles moving into what had been Jewish homes, offices, synagogues, and communal institutions, making use of land, factories, warehouses, money, jewelry, furniture, clothing, dishes, and linen that had belonged to Jews, would it be simple morally or psychologically to accept this new order of things. To dislike one's neighbor, to wish him gone; then to observe his unprecedented total annihilation; finally to inherit what had once been his: such a sequence of events can only add immeasurably to the guilt occasioned by the trauma itself. The resulting self-accusation is all the more powerful for being unrelated to any actual transgression. In this respect the postwar German situation was less complicated; a small portion of the guilty could be punished, the crime could thereby be symbolically expiated, and the society, for better or for worse, attempt to move on. But as witnesses Poles had committed no crime, there was nothing to expiate—yet Polish history had loaded the act of witnessing the Holocaust to spring a psychological and moral trap from which there was no apparent exit. The unacceptable, unmasterable guilt could only be denied and repressed, thereafter to erupt into history in particularly distorted forms.

Furthermore, unlike other traumatized societies, Poles in the postwar period had no need either to invent new "totalisms" or new notions of victimization. Abandoned by their erstwhile western allies to Stalin's mercies, in their isolation Poles found ready to hand a familiar explanatory system: a reading of history as their ongoing victimization by traditional enemies and above all by the Jew, the eternal enemy within. The postwar period, and especially its first several decades, thereby functioned not as a "protean historical situation [in which] everything becomes possible," but just the opposite. The imposition of Communist rule evoked an old mode of symbolic response and then congealed it into immobility: the exclusivist vision of turn-of-the-century Polish nationalists became a conspiratorial and paranoid worldview, a frozen psychosocial grimace. The image of the Jew in postwar Poland was thereby weighted with an extraordinary psychic load. Transformed into Bolshevik minister and security policeman, the "Jew" attracted hostility that conveniently substituted for other, politically inadvisable, aggression. But this hostility was also rooted in the Polish experience of the Holocaust, in the new accusatory death-tainted image of the Jew that infused the traditional stereotype. With no hope of healing within the growing frost, Poles could only move, according to Lifton's formulation, from passive victimized to active victimizers, while nevertheless retaining the image of themselves as victims. Thus the stage was set for a future "victimization competition" expressed in the ritualized Polish insistence that they had suffered during the war as much as Jews, as well as the "anti-Semitism without Jews" that would so puzzle and fascinate western observers. For Poles, in a world comprehended through the myth of their own eternal victimization, the Holocaust would begin to feel like their ultimate victimization by Jews.

The guilt-driven hostility and violence that greeted Jews in postwar Poland resulted, in the deadliest of cycles, in the creation of even more guilt. The repression of the new guilt required rationalization of the new aggression through further recourse to the notion of victimization by the *Żydokomuna*. Thus, for example, in the aftermath of the Kielce pogrom, beside government propaganda and the outcry of a few independant intellectuals,[43] Cardinal Hlond, who had decried anti-Semitism several months previously, now issued a statement blaming deteriorating Polish-Jewish relations on "Jews today occupying leading positions in the Polish government and attempting to introduce a governmental structure which the majority of the nation does not desire." Typically, the statement also included a reminder about Polish aid to Jews during the war.[44] After the trial, conviction, and sentencing to death of nine of the Kielce rioters, sit-down strikes by workers protesting the sentences spread to a number of cities, as did rumors that this and other pogroms had been instigated by Zionists to stimulate Jewish emigration. Among the sources of this rumor was a nun who had saved Jewish girls during the Holocaust.[45]

4

Memory Repressed
1948–1968

In attempting to trace Polish reactions to the Holocaust in the period after 1948, most of the evidence at our disposal, above all during the first several decades, concerns the actions and attitudes of party and state. With the totalitarian system in place, popular violence, indeed popular expression of any kind, was rare; even when some unplanned outburst occurred, its traces were quickly and generally successfully erased from public record. Certainly on most issues there was a vast gulf between official pronouncements and the private opinions of "average" Poles. Indeed, this was one of the defining characteristics of the ruling system. Yet it would be an oversimplification to distinguish absolutely between rulers and ruled, to suggest, that is, that "popular" and "official" realms were always incommensurable. The "official" world included, after all, several million bureaucrats who had been raised, not in some Soviet incubator, but in Poland, before, during, and after the war. Poland under communism was not simply a creature of Soviet manipulation, but a product of the interplay between this manipulation and the particular constraints of Polish history. Rulers and ruled in postwar Poland were indeed distinct, but they were also all Poles. Nowhere was this more true, as we shall see, than in relation to the "Jewish question" and the memory of the Holocaust.

As elsewhere in Eastern Europe, Soviet domination was strongest at the start of this period. From 1948 until 1956, Poland was governed by a group of ideologues intimately linked to the Soviet Union who attempted to impose on the country a system of economic, political, and cultural life that has been called "Stalinism."[1] But Polish Stalinism, the first and crudest attempt to saddle the Polish cow, never attained the extremes of its counterparts in neighboring Communist countries, and this made a fateful difference in Poland's postwar history as a whole. Thus, fulfilling the Stalinist dogma of claiming to rule in the exclusive interests of workers and peasants, Bierut and his circle devoted great energy to developing heavy industry and collectivizing agriculture. Yet simultaneously vast funds were spent on the meticulous reconstruction of Warsaw's devastated Old City, while already in 1953, with the death of Stalin, collectivization was curtailed, and was stopped altogether in 1956. Poland became the only Soviet bloc country whose agriculture remained overwhelmingly in private hands, partitioned into innumerable small holdings typically worked with horse and plow.

Like its neighbors, the country was transformed into a police state radiating paranoia. Links to the West were associated with espionage; informers and the fear of informers were ever present. Yet although arrests and prison sentences were common, there were comparatively few executions. Newspapers and books were strongly censored; artists and writers who continued to create were required to adhere to the banal norms of Socialist realism. The Church too found itself under attack. Priests were arrested; even Cardinal Stefan Wyszyński, the Home Army chaplain who had succeeded Cardinal Hlond as primate of Poland, was placed under house arrest; and government-sponsored Catholic organizations were created to co-opt the faithful. Yet the Church was far from crushed; in 1956, Cardinal Wyszyński was freed, and for the next quarter of a century his immense moral authority oversaw the development of the most powerful church in the Communist bloc.[2] By the 1980s, Communist Poland would experience the highest rate of church construction in the world, a phenomenon that swept up even such places as Nowa Huta, the model workers' suburb outside Kraków that had been ostentatiously built after the war without churches. With great fanfare, its first church was dedicated in 1977 by Karol Wojtyła, archbishop of Kraków, who would shortly become John Paul II. Under a political system in which the state controlled all education and media, the Church also managed to retain the only exceptions: legalized religious instruction for the young and its own press.

The new regime attempted to accustom Poles to austerity through a rhetoric of present sacrifice for future generations. But for daily life, the reality was not just scarcity, but interminable delays and inefficiency in the expanding state bureaucracy along with growing corruption. The labyrinthine difficulties of obtaining anything from consumer goods to medicines to apartments were one of the most oppressive aspects of the system. In response, informal social and economic networks continued the tradition of *załatwienie*, or "taking care of business," that had developed under the Nazi occupation. Gradually, a full-blown alternative economy expanded into the abyss between official pronouncements and daily life.[3] This abyss was intellectual and moral no less than economic; what was proclaimed publicly bore less and less relation to what was believed privately. Out of this abyss wafted the "Communist stink" to which contemporaries referred privately; it was ongoing evidence of the ultimate illegitimacy of the prevailing political order, of a system founded on duplicity.

The overthrow of Polish Stalinism in 1956 and its replacement by a new group of leaders—the events of the so-called Polish October—were the most significant attempt during the postwar years to reestablish the legitimacy of the ruling system through reform. The crisis began amid the crisis of communism as a whole, in February 1956, with Krushchev's celebrated "secret" speech to the Twentieth Party Congress chronicling Stalin's crimes. It was followed by news from Moscow of the sudden death of Bolesław Bierut, who had been attending the proceedings. As factions in the PZPR's Central Committee jockeyed for power in Warsaw, workers in Poznań in June demonstrated under banners demanding "Bread and Freedom" and "Russians Go Home," and then fought police in the streets. In October, as the Red Army prepared to intervene in Poland (as it did in fact two weeks later in Hungary), the Central Committee selected Władysław Gomułka as general secretary. The choice of Gomułka, who had been expelled from the party and jailed during the Stalinist period for "nationalist deviationism," led Krushchev in person to arrive in Warsaw breathing fire, but Gomułka managed to defuse the crisis by convincing him of his loyalty to Moscow and ultimate political orthodoxy.

Gomułka's assumption of power climaxed a fateful factional struggle within Polish communism that dated to the war years. This was, first of all, a contest between groups who had had two different experiences of the war years: those, like Bierut, who had spent the war in Moscow, and those, like Gomułka, who had spent it in Poland. It was a confrontation, therefore, with both ideological and psychological overtones. The reputation of the former was that of hard-line ideologues totally identified with the Soviet Union, who had, however, risked little personally during the war; the latter, identified as "fighters" and "patriots," were reputed to be less dogmatic, more practical-minded, more willing to discover a "Polish road to socialism." This highly touted slogan, which at the time was filled with promise, was also taken up by a generation of Polish intelligentsia, who, it turned out, would be the last generation to believe that the Polish cow could still be saddled in a way that was good for the cow.

The "Polish road to socialism" of Gomułka and his circle, a version of the notion of "national communism" that made headway for several decades in the Soviet bloc, was a grab bag of contradictory tendencies advanced by competing factions. There were "revisionists" who sought to make the ruling system less repressive politically and culturally and less imitative of Soviet economic models. The first years of Gomułka's rule were indeed marked by a new sense of intellectual freedom, a considerable easing of censorship, and the disappearance of many Stalinist taboos. There was even a bit of room for the development of new theoretical perspectives, especially the notion of a humanistic socialism advanced by Leszek Kołakowski and his colleagues. Even when the pendulum swung toward greater censorship in the 1960s, the Polish cultural and intellectual atmosphere remained the freest in the Socialist bloc. But there were also those around the new regime much less enamored of attacking authoritarianism, concerned, rather, to rehabilitate the system by infusing it with "national" overtones. This

direction was particularly dear to a new generation of party functionaries, the so-called new class, primarily of peasant background,
who had joined the party after the war. Ideologically it entailed
the reemergence of ideas and slogans with a direct lineage to the
prewar Endecja, and their assimilation into "proletarian" rhetoric.
Here were the beginnings of a peculiar marriage of authoritarian
Communist and chauvinist nationalist tendencies that would later
be termed "Endo-Communism."[4]

With the end of the Stalinist period, in other words, in attempting to develop a greater measure of national legitimacy, Polish
communism began to manifest divisions resembling those characteristic of Polish politics ever since the end of the nineteenth
century.[5] What had once been discourse reemerged in the new
political context as intrigue, yet one of its key elements remained
unchanged, and that was the "Jewish question." It is true that anti-
Semitism within the party had something of a precedent even before Gomułka. During the Stalinist period, under pressure from
the Soviets, who, by the end of the 1940s, had begun to persecute
Jews and Jewish culture, and doubtless also with the hope of gaining greater popular acceptance, the PZPR had purged Jews from
positions in the military and the security apparatus.[6] Yet, at a time
when in the Soviet Union Yiddish writers were murdered and Jewish doctors accused of poisoning Stalin, while elsewhere in the Soviet bloc anti-Semitic show trials were the order of the day (best
known was the Slánský affair in Czechoslovakia), the Polish purges
were limited and above all unpublicized.

But with Gomułka's rise to power, the "Jewish question" began
to play an increasingly prominent role in intraparty intrigue. The
fall of the Polish Stalinists was hailed by the budding Endo-Com-
munists as the defeat of the Jews who had sat out the war in
Moscow and then returned to exploit Polish workers. Simultaneously the revisionists too began to find themselves labeled "cos-
mopolitans" and "Jews" out of touch with the needs of the Polish
masses; they were baited, moreover, as former Stalinists. Indeed,
among the popular designations for the two factions that rose to
power with Gomułka were "Żydzi" (Jews) and "Chamy" (boors,
suggesting dull, slow-witted peasants).[7] These epithets drew on
stereotypes that were centuries old. As in postwar Polish popular

consciousness as a whole, the emergence of the label "Jew" in intraparty intrigues doubtless bore some relation to the relative prominence of individuals of Jewish descent among the various factions, but its symbolic weight far transcended its relation to reality.

The introduction of the "Jewish question" into party intrigue and a portion of party propaganda was paralleled by an upsurge of popular anti-Semitism. Nowhere comparable in extent or intensity to that of the immediate postwar years, it included some physical attacks, with abuse particularly directed at Jewish schoolchildren, as well as the expropriation of apartments belonging to Jews.[8] A rare window on Polish attitudes during this period is the apparent prevalence of a comment attributed, in one of its versions, to a Łódź Jew: "Many of us died, it's true, but there are enough of us remaining to rule over you."[9] In excerpts from the diary of a young Jewish Communist newly arrived from France, published during a lull in censorship in 1956, there is shock at the extent of popular anti-Semitic feeling as well as the official silence surrounding it.[10] While the precise relation between public manifestations of anti-Semitism and party agitation is unclear, both were short-lived because, for the time being, the highest party authorities insisted on adhering to ideological orthodoxy and repressing them. In April 1957, the Central Committee of the PZPR issued a memorandum to party committees throughout the country denouncing "occurrences of chauvinism, antisemitism and racism" as well as "nationalistic, chauvinistic and racist views [propagated by] comrades holding responsible party or state positions."[11] Several years later, such concerns prevented *The Merchant of Venice* from opening at the state theater.[12] For another decade, the passions surrounding the "Jewish question" would be more or less successfully excluded from the public domain.

The events of the Polish October, combined with the lifting of the ban on Jewish emigration, were enough, nevertheless, to provoke a new wave of Jewish emigration. From 1956 to 1960, more than forty thousand Jews left Poland for Israel. These departures were only partially offset by the repatriation of eighteen thousand Polish Jews from the Soviet Union, some of whom remained in Poland. By the mid-1960s, the Jewish community in Poland numbered no more than thirty thousand.[13] This was an aging, fear-

ridden group that was supposed to conform to the profile of a Soviet-style "national minority." With no qualified rabbi, nearly no
shokhtim (ritual slaughterers), and only a handful of functioning
synagogues, the community was controlled by a small group of
Yiddish-speaking Communists who, with government approval
and American Jewish financial assistance, ostentatiously maintained certain vestiges of a secular Yiddish culture: a newspaper
(*Folksshtimme* [The people's voice]), a publishing house (Yidish
Bukh), and above all, a theater, directed until 1969 by the celebrated
Yiddish actress Ida Kaminska.

As the Gomułka regime, and indeed, all of Poland's Communist governments realized, successfully saddling the Polish cow
depended on working not just with the present but with the past.
The development of modern Polish national identity had been
rooted in claims to the past in the name of the present; no government professing to represent the Polish people could avoid this
task, and especially in relation to the war years. To discover meaning in the unprecedented suffering of that period would have
weighed on the imagination of any nation, all the more so one that
had chosen to define itself through a narrative of exemplary self-
sacrifice. The many-sided development, in a host of contexts and
mediums, of an acceptable narrative of the war years, was a process
crucial to the efforts of postwar Polish governments to legitimate
themselves to their subjects.[14]

The use of such a narrative as a form of legitimation, moreover,
was of importance externally as well as internally. Postwar Polish
governments, especially until the ratification of a treaty with West
Germany in 1972, were extremely nervous about Poland's new
western borders, which included land that, by any stretch of the
historical imagination, one would have been hard pressed to call
Polish. Fear of "German revanchism," that is, German territorial
claims on Poland, reinforced by the long memories of the millions
of Germans expelled from the "liberated lands," was an abiding
and sometimes overriding determinant of Polish foreign policy.
Here too, cultivating the memory of "Nazi crimes against the Polish people" played a central role. To memorialize the martyrdom
of Poles at the hands of the Germans was to demonstrate the historical justice of the new political geography.

For Communists, finally, the matter was loaded with even more significance. From Marx to Stalin, history had been the foundation of the Communist worldview, the final judge of human actions, the basis of all morality; everything was done and justified in its name. Accordingly, in the essential Communist narrative that developed in the postwar years, the war was invested with messianic significance. It was seen as the product of suicidal class and national hatreds that had climaxed in the destruction of the class system and the establishment of the rule of peace and justice in Poland and throughout the Soviet bloc. The war years were assimilated to an appropriately dialectical perspective of martyrdom and resistance, torment and heroism, the destruction of the old and the birth of the new. Both the heroism and the torment, furthermore, were "national in form, socialist in content," that is, while the "fighters and martyrs" represented many nations, their "resistance and martyrdom" were all in the interest of a single, historically inevitable, cause.

The fate of the Auschwitz-Birkenau camp is instructive. Here had stood the Nazis' largest and most dreaded slave labor factory, where from 1940 to 1942, tens of thousands of Poles, among them the Polish political and cultural elite, were shipped to be worked to death. From 1942 until the end of 1944, expanded by the addition at Birkenau of four sets of crematoriums and gas chambers, the camp, while never ceasing to be a slave labor center, also became the final destination for thousands of trainloads of Jews from Poland and every corner of Europe. According to a recent study, 960,000 Jews, as well as 73,000 Poles, 21,000 Gypsies, 15,000 Soviet POWs, and 10–15,000 citizens of other nations were murdered at this site.[15] Yet according to the mandate of the Council for the Protection of Memorials to Struggle and Martyrdom, ratified by the Polish parliament in 1947, Auschwitz was one of the sites at which "Poles and citizens of other nationalities fought and died a martyr's death."[16]

The Polish Communist narrative, which monopolized the symbolism of Auschwitz until the 1980s, turned this site into a monument to internationalism that commemorated the "resistance and martyrdom" of "Poles and citizens of other nationalities." With the consultation of the International Auschwitz Committee, a group of survivors and relatives of victims dominated by veterans of the largely Communist Auschwitz underground, barracks in the original work camp area, near the infamous gate marked "Arbeit macht frei," were turned over to twenty countries for use as "national pavilions." One of these structures became a "Jewish pavilion" that was usually locked and opened only on special occasions. Several kilometers from the original camp area, the vast grounds of Birkenau, where the tracks ended, Jews "disembarked," and Dr. Mengele made his "selections," and where the ruins of the crematoriums the fleeing Nazis had dynamited now lay, remained inaccessible and desolate, rarely viewed by visitors.

In 1967, as a result of efforts initiated by the International Auschwitz Committee soon after Gomułka's accession to power, an International Memorial to the Victims of Fascism was completed at Birkenau near the crematoriums. One week before its unveiling, the element surmounting the monument was changed; a group of three abstract figures of varying sizes suggesting a family was replaced by a polished marble square with a triangle at its center.[17] That is, a shape suggesting Jewish victims (almost all the families murdered were Jewish) was replaced by one recalling the insignia worn by slave laborers, those who had not been immediately gassed and who indeed represented a cross-section of nationalities. At the base of the monument were nineteen plaques in as many languages (including Yiddish), bearing the inscription: "Four million people suffered and died here at the hands of the Nazi murderers between the years 1940 and 1945." This inflated figure, widely accepted in the Soviet bloc, was based on the unexamined postwar testimony of both Auschwitz survivors and Nazi officials, and made it possible to inflate the numbers of Poles, Russian prisoners of war, and other non-Jews murdered at Auschwitz, thus providing further basis both for its "polonization" and its "internationalization." Auschwitz-Birkenau, or Oświęcim-Brzezinka, as it continued to be known in Poland, could thereby emerge as the central symbol of Polish martyrdom, but within an "inclusive" internationalist framework. Jews could be relegated to the formulaic "other nationalities" murdered at Auschwitz, a list in which, alphabetically and therefore "democratically," "Żydzi" came last.

Nevertheless, until the mid-1960s, in contexts where reference to Jews was unavoidable, their fate continued to be seen as something exceptional. "Genocide," the term used to designate the fate of the Jews, was, however, incorporated into a suitably ideological narrative. Seen as a result of passivity in the face of fascism, it was counterposed to redeeming acts of resistance. The Warsaw Ghetto Uprising became central to this narrative. It was seen, first of all, not only as the supreme but as the only act of Jewish armed resistance. Other cases of resistance, in other ghettos, partisan groups, and concentration camps, were forgotten. Moreover, anniversaries of the Warsaw Ghetto Uprising became the context for commemorating the Holocaust as a whole. Rapoport's Warsaw Ghetto monument, the focus of all Holocaust commemorations in Poland since the Stalinist period, was designed to express the requisite moral architectonically. At the front of the monument, framed by two large menorahs (lit once a year on the anniversary of the uprising) and dominating the surrounding square, a group of armed ghetto fighters seems to burst out of the stone. Below them, engraved into the pedestal, is an inscription in Yiddish, Hebrew, and Polish: "From the Jewish people to its fighters and martyrs." At the rear of the monument are the martyrs: a shallow bas-relief depicts a downcast procession of Jews that includes the monument's only religious figure, a traditionally dressed Jew gazing heavenward and bearing a Torah scroll, guarded by German soldiers. This image overlooks a side street.

Narrative accounts of the Warsaw Ghetto Uprising published during the Gomułka years are constructed around this duality. Typically, they also stress Polish solidarity with Jewish resistance and parallel Polish and Jewish suffering, thereby tending to blur, though not yet abolish, the distinction between the fate of Poles and Jews. The introduction to a popular volume of photographs of the uprising, for example, mentions both the "inconceivable crime [of] genocide" and "the invader's plans ... to be rid of everything that was not Germanic."[18] In a pamphlet designed for popular consumption published by the veterans' association Związek Bojowników o Wolność i Demokrację (ZBoWiD, Association of Fighters for Freedom and Democracy) on the twentieth anniversary of the uprising, the author, Wacław Poterański, begins with the sounds of battle and ends on a note of internationalism, linking the Ghetto Uprising both with the Polish Uprising and the anti-Fascist struggles of "all the freedom and peace-loving peoples."[19] Poles and Jews are also linked through the intentions of their persecutor. The Nazis, according to Poterański, slated both for extermination, but did not have time to complete the job on the Poles. Furthermore: "The overwhelming majority of the Polish nation condemned the crimes committed against the Jews, and stigmatized those who expressed satisfaction with 'Hitler's solution to the Jewish question' or manifested passivity."[20] Poterański also draws a parallel between the internal struggles of Poles and Jews around the issue of armed resistance. In both cases, we are told, "bourgeois and right-wing groups" preached passivity; among Poles, they waited for the Nazis and the Soviets to finish each other off on the eastern front; among Jews, they attended help from the West. Among both Poles and Jews, only the Left, and above all the PPR, consistently organized armed resistance from the beginning. The extremity of postwar attacks on non-Communists is considerably moderated, however; only the NSZ is accused of fascism, anti-Semitism, and collaboration. The AK, the government-in-exile, and even the Church are assigned roles that are honorable though secondary. The impact of the "Polish road to socialism" on the narrative of the war years is apparent in Poterański's list of who it was that helped save Jews: "communists, socialists, populists, democrats, scouts, officers and soldiers of the People's Guard and the AK, Catholics, priests and nuns, professors, doctors, workers and students."[21]

In the great variety of Polish commemorative activity during the Gomułka period, it is possible, especially in the earlier years, to discover other approaches as well. There is, for example, a large-format volume of photographs entitled *Miasto nieujarzmione* (Unvanquished city), dedicated to occupied Warsaw. Published in the liberal political atmosphere after Gomułka's accession to power, its emphasis is on the Home Army and the Polish Uprising, its tone is unabashedly nationalist. The afterword, printed in the national colors, white letters on a red page, refers to the uprising as "yet another insurrectionary impulse," and alludes to the ongoing need for Poles to "uncover the truth about the uprising—raw and grim, yet full of faith in man, his nobility and courage," and to incorporate it into national memory. Yet in this decidedly unofficial narrative of occupied Warsaw, out of 270 pages of photographs there are 2 pages on the ghetto and 4 on the Ghetto Uprising.[22] Relatively unmarked by official ideology was also much of the Holocaust scholarship produced by the Jewish Historical Institute from the late 1950s to the early 1960s, as well as a short history of wartime Poland, whose authors, one of them the director of the High Commission to Investigate Nazi Crimes in Poland, state that the Nazis intended to deport, but not murder, all the Poles.[23] There is also the powerful memorial at Treblinka, a site at which only Jews were killed. Designed by Adam Haupt and Franciszek Duszenko and completed in 1964, it consists of many thousands of broken stones, some bearing the names of destroyed Jewish communities, fixed in a huge field of concrete set amid a meadow. Overlooking the field is a monument that includes a carved menorah; text panels at the entrance also refer to Jews. At the unveiling of this memorial, nevertheless, the press spoke of Treblinka's victims as "800,000 citizens of European nations."[24]

How was all this commemorative activity received by its intended audience? We lack the evidence to answer this question definitively, yet it is reasonable to assume that most of it was widely mistrusted, if not dismissed. This doubtless applied to the invocations to internationalism, taken as a cynical reminder of precisely the opposite: the history of Soviet oppression, beginning during the war and continuing even under "national communism." More generally, by the 1960s, as political repression intensified, and above all, as the economic situation worsened, Gomułka's vaunted "Polish road to socialism" increasingly seemed yet another variety of opportunism. Daily life in Gomułka's Poland undermined all the affirmations of public discourse, and the abyss between the latter and private belief continued to widen. The following passage from the émigré writer Henryk Grynberg's autobiographical novel, set in Poland in the late 1950s and early 1960s, presents this disjunction, inaccessible through opinion polls, in its extremity:

> Speakers have to pretend that they believe what they say, and listeners that they believe what they hear, and it doesn't bother anyone that everyone knows that no one believes a single word. . . . Every speaker knows that no one believes him, and everyone

knows that he knows that everyone knows. . . . No speaker among us was embarrassed to give an official (as opposed to personal) talk, because he knew that anyone in his place would do the same, and the listeners, who also knew this well, were not in the least embarrassed to applaud or launch anemic hurrahs from strategic corners of the hall. . . . Was anyone among us embarrassed before anyone anymore? The press did not believe what it wrote, for it was not so stupid, nor was it embarrassed knowing that its readers could not believe it and perfectly well knew that it knew, and none of this surprised anyone. . . . It was the same with radio and television, exhibitions, films, books, students and teachers, and pretending no longer tired anyone, for everyone was accustomed to it. . . . One didn't even have to pretend so carefully, knowing that in any case everyone knew. Very little was demanded, just enough for the show to go on.[25]

Although those who continued to live in Poland may not have perceived the disjunction between public and private discourse in terms that were quite so absolute,[26] what was believed about the war years was doubtless above all what was received behind closed doors: the personal accounts of family and friends. While the prioritizing of private narrative was everywhere a cornerstone of popular resistance to communism, Polish private narratives of the war, punctuated by the rumors, resentments, and silences inherited from the war years and the years immediately following, were a legacy particularly subject to distortion.[27] Unlike during the immediate postwar years, however, these beliefs scarcely marked the surface of history. Elsewhere in the novel just cited, its author, who toured Poland for several years with Ida Kaminska's Yiddish theater troupe, recounts how in one city, as the actors left the theater, a group of local residents confronted them: "They didn't make any real disturbance, and didn't even throw stones as we departed, but only repeated, over and over, 'Leave us alone!'"[28] In consigning the memory of the Jews to that of the "other nations" martyred by the Nazis, or to an official narrative woven around a small number of explicitly "Jewish" sites and symbols, a narrative whose effect was to marginalize, "ghettoize," its subject, official Polish attempts to deal with the memory of the Holocaust doubtless reflected, after all, a popular need.

1. *Jews through Polish eyes:* Contemporary Polish folk sculptures. The figure on the right, with realistically rendered earlocks [*peyes*], coat [*kapote*], and hat [*shtrayml*] made of real fur, strikes a "Jewish" pose (transmitted into American culture via Jack Benny). In the more ambiguous figure on the left, note the large "Jewish" ear and the bag. Is he the Wandering Jew? What does he have in the bag? Naughty Polish children were traditionally warned that they would be sold to the Gypsy or the Jew. Courtesy of the author.

2. *Jews through Polish eyes:* Warsaw cymbalist Mordko Fajerman. This was the instrument on which Jankiel the tavernkeeper in Adam Mickiewicz's *Pan Tadeusz* performed a patriotic polonaise for his Polish audience (see p. 10). Woodcut by an unknown artist (1867) after a photograph by Karol Beyer.

3. *Jews through Polish eyes:* A Jew at prayer. Woodcut by Michał Elwiro Andriolli (1876).

4. *Jews through Polish eyes:* "Serving" the gentry. The young gentleman, still in morning clothes, listens attentively as his agent attests to the honesty of the money lender he has brought him, and encourages him to sign the promissory note. Lithograph by Jan Feliks Piwarski (1859).

5. *Jews through Polish eyes:* In front of the bank in Warsaw. In the center, the bankers, showing signs of assimilation, wear top hats; one wears a shortened coat and carries an umbrella. On the left, their poorer cousins, hoping for a piece of some action, are dressed more traditionally with caps, canes, longer coats, and beards. Woodcut by Franciszek Kostrzewski (1871).

6. *Jews through Polish eyes:* Warsaw street vendor. Woodcut by J. Konopacki (1884).

7. *Jews through Polish eyes:* Warsaw porter. Hauling loads on one's back was most often a Jewish occupation. Zincotype by Józef Pankiewicz (1887).

8. Marketplace, shtetl of Kazimierz Dolny, interwar period. Courtesy of YIVO Institute for Jewish Research.

9. Gęsia (Goose) Street, heart of Jewish Warsaw, interwar period. Courtesy of Roman Vishniac and YIVO Institute for Jewish Research.

10. Great Synagogue, Tłomackie Street, Warsaw, interwar period. Completed in 1878, the synagogue could hold 2,400 worshipers; it was the pride of Warsaw's Jewish plutocracy. Upon the defeat of the Warsaw Ghetto Uprising in May 1943, the Great Synagogue was dynamited by the Nazis. The building to the left survived the war and today houses the Jewish Historical Institute. Courtesy of YIVO Institute for Jewish Research.

11. Uncompleted office tower, Warsaw, 1980s. For many years, this abandoned and decaying construction project marked the site of the Great Synagogue. "What did they expect?" a cab driver once exclaimed to the author. "Of course they couldn't complete it, this is where the synagogue stood." Currently a new office building rises at the site. Courtesy of the author.

12. Memorial to the Jews of Zamość. This monument, constructed of broken Jewish tombstones [*matsevot*], stands amidst a housing project. Courtesy of the author.

13. Detail, rear wall, old Jewish cemetery, Kraków. The wall was constructed after 1957, when several Kraków synagogues were restored as well. Courtesy of the author.

14. Detail, rear wall, old Jewish cemetery, Kraków. Courtesy of the author.

15. Synagogue in Lesko, 16th–17th century. Reconstructed in 1980, now a regional museum. Courtesy of the author.

16. Synagogue in Zamość, 1610–20. Reconstructed in the 1950s, now the town library. Courtesy of the author.

17. Synagogue in Dębica, 18th century. Interior reconstructed for use as a department store. Courtesy of the author.

18. Ruined seventeenth century synagogue in Rymanów. The image, captioned "light as an eagle," is one of four polichromes illustrating a passage from *The Ethics of the Fathers:* "Be bold as a leopard, light as an eagle, swift as a deer, and strong as a lion, to do the will of your Father who is in heaven." Courtesy of the author.

19. Synagogue in Tykocin, 1642. Carefully restored, including interior polichromes; maintained as an historic site. Courtesy of the author.

20. Nożyk synagogue, Warsaw, end of nineteenth century. Restored in 1983, now used as a synagogue. The State Yiddish Theater and other Jewish institutions have offices next door. Courtesy of the author.

21. Warsaw Ghetto monument, front. Designed by Nathan Rapoport, built in 1948 (see p. 71). Courtesy of the author.

22. Warsaw Ghetto monument, rear. Courtesy of the author.

23. Solidarity demonstration, 1983. The occasion was the funeral of a young activist beaten to death by police during the period of martial law. Courtesy of the author.

24. Flower cross, 1983. This cross was next to the church of St. Anne in Warsaw (see p. 102). Courtesy of the author.

25. Unoffical demonstration at Warsaw Ghetto monument, April 1983 (see p. 108). Courtesy of the author.

26. Flower cross laid at Warsaw Ghetto monument, April 1983. Courtesy of the author.

27. Solidarity "stamps" with Jewish themes. The bottom stamp
commemorates Viktor Alter and Henryk Ehrlich, leaders of the
Jewish Bund murdered by Stalin during World War II. On the top
stamp, see p. 108. Collection of the author.

28. Wausau Ghetto monument. The inscription reads: "From the Jewish people to its fighters and martyrs." Courtesy of the author.

5

Memory Expelled
1968–1970

Beginning in the mid-1960s, efforts to appropriate the memory of the war years could less and less permit Poles to be left alone, could no longer avoid, that is, confronting the memory of the murdered Jew. The first of these confrontations climaxed in the years 1968–70 and was, appropriately enough, the most extreme, the most bizarre, and the most destructive. It was a confrontation, among other things, between two generations, one coming of age and the other coming to power. The first generation born after the war, with no direct memory of Jews, confronted a generation whose formative years had been spent watching them murdered.

This is hardly the way Poles have seen these events. In Polish popular awareness as in recent Polish historiography, the events of this period have been subsumed under the term "March 68," which organizes their significance around politics, specifically, the government's attack on striking Warsaw University students, which began that month.[1] The immediate cause of this attack was, typically, a conflict about the uses of the past: students had protested the banning of performances of Adam Mickiewicz's national epic *Dziady* (Forefathers' eve), which had supposedly inspired behavior hostile to Poland's "eastern ally." The government's heavy-handed response, probably planned in advance, quickly escalated events into a full-fledged confrontation between, on one side, students and intelligentsia, the proponents of political and cultural reform, and on the other side, the most repressive faction within the party, the so-called Partisans led by Gen. Mieczysław Moczar. The Partisans, whose name stressed their self-identification as "fighters" and "patriots" of the anti-Nazi resistance and who were strongly represented in the security apparatus, unleashed against the so-called *bananowcy* (a term implying the students' privileged consumption of delicacies such as bananas) the combined forces of the police, courts, and media, including a wave of carefully orchestrated "spontaneous demonstrations of popular outrage."

In the short run, the Partisans, unimpeded by Gomułka, won notable victories. The student movement and its allies were crushed, its leaders imprisoned or exiled; in Poland as throughout the Soviet bloc, most tragically in Czechoslovakia, revisionism was defeated. Moczar, however, did not succeed in replacing Gomułka, who weathered this storm only to fall to worker protests two years later. Although the succeeding government of Edward Gierek included many of Moczar's followers, Moczar himself was excluded from power. More important, the student rebels of 1968 learned crucial lessons from their defeat, above all that political change was not possible without the active participation of workers; in 1980, an alliance of workers and intelligentsia would produce the Solidarity movement. From this perspective, March 1968 can be seen as a turning point in postwar Polish history, the birth date of forces that would overthrow Polish communism.

But the years that set the stage for communism's last stand also witnessed a state-sponsored campaign of anti-Semitic agitation of hysterical intensity, unprecedented in Polish history, directed not only at the allegedly Zionist student rebels but also against Jews in general, both real and imaginary.[2] It was a campaign initiated by Gomułka in a speech after the Six-Day War in June 1967, in which he employed the term "fifth column" to refer to Jews in Poland.[3] It peaked between March and July 1968, after which Gomułka and the party central committee reined it in. It resulted, during the years 1968–70, in the ruin of thousands of careers, the emigration of some twenty thousand Jews, and in what was perceived as the definitive end of the millennial Jewish presence in Poland. From the perspective that organizes the meaning of these years around the term "March 68," these phenomena were the barbaric accompaniment of an essentially political struggle, an example of the ability of the authorities to "sink to anything" to defend their rule. The campaign against Jews, which was directed with particular ferocity at party functionaries of Jewish descent, has also been seen as an effort by the new generation of bureaucrats, who joined the party after the war, to advance their careers by making room for themselves in the party hierarchy. Yet these factors hardly exhaust the significance of the anti-Zionist campaign. Above all, the reemergence into public discourse of the "Jewish menace," in a particularly irrational form and at a turning point in postwar Polish history, was more than a coincidence.

The second half of the 1960s marked not only the emergence of a new kind of political opposition in Poland but also the beginnings of a transformation in the nature of public discourse, and this transformation applied to both sides in the struggle. Before this period, not only the government but also the intelligentsia operated within a more or less conventional Marxist worldview; at most the intelligentsia spoke of "socialism with a human face." March 68, as the sociologist Jerzy Szacki put it twenty years later, was "the funeral of communist ideology."[4] What replaced it? In the years after 1968, among both the authorities and the forces that gradually constituted the political opposition, in the words of the historian Marcin Król: "Slowly a patriotic-symbolic-religious language merged with the language permitted in public life. . . . Traditions that had been reviled and undermined by the authorities, but also by the intelligentsia, returned to public life with their entire ambiguous heritage."[5] The "traditions" to which Król refers— the heritage of Polish nationalism—had, despite the unwillingness of both the government and the leftist intelligentsia to countenance them, persisted within popular consciousness. The events of 1968 can be said to have marked, therefore, the first step in discarding a discourse entirely out of touch with most Poles for one that attempted to speak directly to them. It should come as no surprise that prominent among the "traditions" uncovered in the new discourse were the conflicting claims of the exclusivist and pluralist worldviews, nor that these two perspectives began to compete in the quest for a useable past, and above all in the task of shaping an acceptable narrative of the war years. This process could not avoid summoning into public awareness, in various incarnations, for better and for worse, the death-tainted image of the Jew.

The first stage of this process, one that was unambiguously for the worse, was the work of General Moczar and his Partisans. Moczar's links to the Soviet Union and especially to the NKVD dated to the war years. His influence began to grow after October 1956, when as a member of the right-wing faction in the PZPR, the so-called Chamy or boors, he helped rebuild the weakened security apparatus and transformed it into his personal power base. Moczar himself, of Ukrainian origin, was a rather enigmatic figure who may primarily have been a careerist for whom ideology figured as a card in the game of intraparty intrigue. Yet it was Moczar who transformed the dalliance between chauvinist nationalism and authoritarian communism into the formidable political force that became Endo-Communism. This sort of development was not unique to Poland, but was characteristic of declining communism elsewhere in the Soviet bloc, and especially in the Soviet Union itself. Many observers of Moczar and his followers have stressed the influence of the Soviet Union and the supposed Soviet model for the Polish anti-Zionist campaign. Certainly, from Stalin to Brezhnev, Soviet manipulation of the "Jewish question" played a role in Polish party intrigue. Yet one can no longer maintain that Polish anti-Zionism was made in Moscow, for recent research has shown that the Polish campaign preceded its Soviet counterpart. In other words, if one insists on tracing influences, it may be more fruitful to investigate the effect of the Polish campaign on the Soviets than the other way around.[6]

Beyond the issue of influences, the strategy chosen by Moczar and his followers to advance their political ambitions reveals a logic that transcends, or better, underlies, politics. The Moczarites tapped into attitudes and needs centered in the exclusivist vision of Polish national identity as it was shaped, and deformed, by the war years and two decades of Communist rule. Although Moczar himself had been a member of the KPP before the war, some of his associates had roots in the prewar Endecja and its radical offshoots. This connection was most spectacular in the case of Bolesław Piasecki, who had begun his political career in the 1930s as leader of the Fascist and rabidly anti-Semitic ONR-Falanga, then resurfaced in Poland after the war, with strong Soviet connections, to found PAX, a government-sponsored Catholic organization.

Moczar rose to power, moreover, not just by controlling the police apparatus but also by allying himself with the institutions specifically responsible for elaborating the memory of the war years. Securely linked to Moczar by the late 1960s were the Warsaw office of the International Auschwitz Committee and the High Commission to Investigate Nazi Crimes in Poland. Most important of all was Moczar's leadership of the veterans' association, ZBoWiD. This organization, with a membership of three hundred thousand, claimed to speak for all Polish veterans of the Second World War regardless of their politics. For the first time ever, tens of thousands of former members of the AK found it possible to come out of the closet, so to speak, and step proudly into the public arena. Moczar transformed them from outcasts into freedom fighters, and thereby assured himself their undying allegiance. The support of ZBoWiD, in turn, gave Moczar and his associates popular legitimation to appropriate the entire heritage of anti-Nazi resistance. Moczar could speak in the name of the generation most closely identified with the war years, those who had come of age during the war and immediately after. ZBoWiD, which hinted that it represented, better than the party, the interests of all Poles, became Moczar's ideological base, the driving force of the anti-Jewish campaign and after March 1968, of the assault on the students and intelligentsia as well. Moczar, finally, also built himself personally into a symbol, the incarnation of the Polish anti-Nazi underground. His war memoirs, *Barwy walki* (Colors of struggle), appeared during the 1960s in hundreds of thousands of copies, making it one of the most widely available books in postwar Poland. Required reading in secondary schools, it was translated into six languages and also made into a movie.[7]

Thus situated, Moczar was in a perfect position to lead a populist-style anti-intellectual campaign in the name of all "fighting Poles," all those, regardless of political allegiance, who had sacrificed for the fatherland during the World War, and now confronted a crafty and implacable foe that once again sought Poland's humiliation and defeat. Who was this adversary? Poland, according to the Partisans, was under siege by an international conspiracy that was overseen by American imperialism, but implemented by enemies much closer to home: Germans and Jews. The ultimate nature of the threat was always somewhat nebulous; it doubtless included the restoration of capitalism, but most of what was said turned on two other issues. The first was West German "revanchism," the supposed German desire to regain the territories that Poland had annexed after the war. The second was the alleged effort by Jews, both in Poland and abroad, to disfigure the memory of the war years.

Beginning in the mid-1960s, Moczar and his followers began to cultivate the image of a Poland reeling under a western propaganda attack directed at Polish attitudes to Jews during the war. Works such as Leon Uris's *Exodus* and *Mila 18* and Jerzy Kosinski's *Painted Bird* were accused of defaming the honor of the Polish nation. The kernel of truth in the Polish allegations was the western stereotype of Poles as "eternal anti-Semites" who had welcomed the murder of Jews on their soil. These accusations included the commonly held notion, widely discredited by historians, that it was Polish anti-Semitism that accounted for Hitler's choice of Poland as the site of the death camps.[8] Such beliefs, a product of the traumatic memories of Holocaust survivors interacting with the needs of western Jews and the western mass media, merit a thoroughgoing analysis of their own. For our purposes it is enough to imagine the acute sensitivity of Poles to such accusations. Polish reaction to these charges, which would henceforth play a role in all Polish efforts to grapple with the memory of the Holocaust, would be greatly exacerbated, beginning during this period, by their use in political intrigue. In this case, as official news of what was termed the "anti-Polish offensive" mounted, history began to be revised. References to Polish informing or indifference to the fate of the Jews during the war were increasingly censored, while accounts of Polish aid to Jews and "exposés" of Jewish collaboration with the Nazis proliferated.

All this came to a head during the campaign against the so-called Encyclopedists [*Encyklopedyści*]. At issue was an article on Nazi concentration camps that had appeared in the eighth volume of the prestigious *Wielka Encyklopedia Powszechna* (Great universal encyclopedia) published by the State Academic Publishing House (Państwowe Wydawnictwo Naukowe, PWN) in 1966.[9] The article differentiated between "concentration camps" [*obozy koncentracyjne*], where prisoners lived and worked albeit under conditions designed to hasten death, and "annihilation camps" [*obozy zagłady*], whose only purpose was murder and nearly all of whose victims were Jews. The commencement of a press attack against this article in August 1967 was shortly followed by "demonstrations" denouncing the Encyclopedists at commemorations of the start of World War II. By March 1968, the encyclopedia as a whole had been subjected to an analysis purporting to show that all the hitherto published volumes had slighted Polish martyrdom while emphasizing the suffering of Jews and Germans.[10] The agitation resulted in the dismissal of most of the encyclopedia's staff (some of whom happened to be of Jewish descent), and the addition of a "corrected" article to the volume. The new article denounced the idea that any distinction existed among Nazi camps and affirmed that they were all intended to exterminate everyone who passed through their gates, be they Poles or Jews.

During the following years, a host of other publications, both scholarly and popular, developed a greatly changed narrative about Poles and Jews during the war years. Though Moczar's influence waned after 1968, this new official narrative of Polish history persisted well into the 1980s. Thus, the edition of Wacław Poterański's pamphlet on the Warsaw Ghetto Uprising published on its twenty-fifth anniversary in 1968 begins with a new section on the prewar Jewish community, stressing its political and cultural attainments thanks to the Polish environment, and its control by "clerical," "bourgeois," and "Zionist elements." The German occupation, introduced as "the most tragic period in the history of the Polish nation," is characterized as follows: "The extermination plans of the Nazi occupier assumed the physical annihilation of the Polish population—Poles as well as national minorities: Jews, Ukrainians, Belorussians, Gypsies."[11] The victims of Nazi concentration and death camps are then discussed within this context. There are new sections on the *Judenrat* and the Jewish police, accusing them of collaboration with the Nazis, and much is made of Jewish demoralization and passivity.[12] Such material is counterposed to extended discussions of Polish aid to Jews; the list of the types of Poles who aided Jews is extended to the category "very many politically unaligned, patriotic Poles—people of good will."[13] The description of the uprising devotes three times as much space to Polish actions of support as to the Jewish fighting. The pamphlet no longer concludes on a note of internationalist heroism, but, amid quotes from Moczar and Gomułka warning against West Germans and Zionists, respectively, ends with a protest against "the anti-Polish propaganda of various historical institutes in Israel, as well as Zionist centers in Western Europe and the United States [which] accuses the Polish nation of anti-Semitism, of participation in the Nazi mass murder of the Jews during the Second World War, while ignoring Polish help to Jews in hiding and in battle, and falsifying the truth about the history of the Jews in Poland in order to whitewash and lessen the responsibility of Nazism and its heirs for genocide against Jews and other nations."[14] While in the 1973 edition of Poterański's pamphlet, Moczar and Gomułka are no longer cited, there is a new denial of the prevalence of prewar Polish anti-Semitism, along with, on one hand, new material on Jewish Gestapo agents, and on the other, details of the AK's efforts against the Polish blackmailers who preyed on Jews in hiding. Less space is devoted to the NSZ, who are described as anti-Semites and anti-Communists, but no longer as Fascists and Nazi collaborators.[15]

If Poterański's new narrative of the Warsaw Ghetto Uprising often has more to say about Poles than Jews, then in general accounts of the war years published from the late 1960s until the 1980s, the fate of the Jews is nearly indistinguishable from that of "the Polish nation." An excellent example is a volume jointly produced by the High Commission to Investigate Nazi Crimes and the Council for the Protection of Memorials to Struggle and Martyrdom entitled *Obozy hitlerowskie na ziemiach polskich, 1939–1945: Informator encyklopedyczny (Nazi camps on Polish soil, 1939–1945: Encyclopedic handbook)*.[16] This seven-hundred-page tome is a source of invaluable information about thousands of concentration, forced labor, transit, prisoner-of-war, and death camps; prisons; and ghettos established by the Nazis throughout Poland. However, edited and with a introductory essay by Czesław Pilichowski, a

member of the prewar ONR who took over as director of the High
Commission in 1968 and ran it until his death in 1984,[17] the volume is structured to function as a kind of rebuttal to the much-
maligned Encyclopedists by demonstrating that the many types
of Nazi camps were all directed to one end: "genocide and annihilation of the Polish nation."[18] Accordingly, in every category of
camp, Jewish victims are subsumed under Polish victims; Jews are
specifically discussed only in the context of ghettos. Perusing this
volume's otherwise reliable documentation, one can nevertheless
arrive at the conclusion that the Holocaust was something that
happened to Poles.

This is also the thrust of Polish history textbooks used in
secondary schools for at least two decades after the anti-Zionist
campaign. These books, first of all, scarcely mention Jews in any
context other than World War II. As a scholar writing in 1988 put
it: "If one asked a product of a secondary school, of whatever age,
what he was taught in history lessons about the Jews [aside from
their annihilation] the reply would probably be: nothing."[19] In a
textbook of the 1960s, the chapter on World War II includes a section headed "the annihilation [zagłada] of the Jews."[20] But beginning in 1969, the use of the word zagłada in relation to the Jews
becomes rare, and the distinction previously made between "concentration camps" and "mass death camps" vanishes; instead the
expression "exterminatory politics of the occupier" covers German
policies toward all Polish citizens. A textbook published in 1986
discusses the fate of the Jews in a chapter headed "Extermination
of the Polish, Jewish and Gypsy population," and suggests that all
of the "mass death camps" were mainly intended for Poles.[21] The
Warsaw Ghetto Uprising is discussed in 1969 primarily in the context of Polish aid to the Jewish fighters; in the textbook of 1986, the
account of the uprising begins as follows: "A specific kind of fighting of the Polish underground was the undertaking in 1943 of battle with the occupier by Polish Jews enclosed in ghettos."[22] The
latter text also includes the following inflation: "Of the 200,000
Jews saved by Polish society, the majority owe their survival to the
activities of Żegota."[23] There continued, however, to be one educational source that was largely unaffected by politics. Polish literature about the war and especially about Nazi atrocities, most

of it first published in the 1940s, remained required reading in Polish schools throughout the postwar period. Several generations of Polish schoolchildren were exposed to the horrific stories of Zofia Nałkowska, Tadeusz Borowski, and others. This literature included substantial material about the murder of Jews.[24]

Amid the wave of historical revision launched in the late 1960s, one portion of the new official narrative received support from an unexpected quarter. Władysław Bartoszewski, a founding member of Żegota, was a Catholic activist who had been imprisoned in Poland during the Stalinist period and remained a resolute opponent of the succeeding Communist governments. In 1963, citing as his motive western stereotypes of Poles as collaborators in the murder of Jews, Bartoszewski issued a call in the leading Polish Catholic and émigré press for material documenting Polish aid to Jews during the war.[25] Bartoszewski, who apparently did not experience the difficulties encountered by Michał Borwicz in assembling such material fifteen years previously, had two editions of collections of testimonies, *Ten jest z ojczyzny mojej* (He is of my fatherland), published by the Catholic publisher Znak (Sign).[26] But Bartoszewski was soon cited in the government press, and in 1970 the government publishing house Interpress issued a narrative by Bartoszewski, in English, French, and German editions, based on the testimonies.[27] This curious and temporary rapprochment between otherwise implacable enemies (by the 1980s Bartoszewski was again persona non grata in Poland) is another sign of the degree to which, as the generation of the war years came to power, issues connected with the Polish experience of the Holocaust, and indeed only these issues, had the power to transcend the most formidable political differences.

Although the rewriting of the history of Polish-Jewish relations during the war was hardly free of outright fabrications, for the most part it relied on distortions and exaggerations, on shifts of emphasis that could, in theory, be rationally debated. But this new narrative, which was to have the longest afterlife of any aspect of Moczar's campaign, was embedded in something larger: a comprehensive and magical worldview, a system of belief, woven of lies, that was entirely beyond disputation. It began to unfold in the mid-1960s, attained its fully developed form from March to

July 1968, and then exploded, as it were, with various of its pieces occasionally resurfacing over the next several decades.

In the fully elaborated belief system of Moczar and the Partisans, we confront a paranoid vision of reality: the notion of a worldwide conspiracy against Poles and Poland whose agents are West Germans and Zionists. Their weapons are revanchism and historical revisionism, their goals the mutilation of the nation's borders and memory, its body and soul. Although they have particular interests, each supports the work of the other. These notions were developed in a best-selling book by Tadeusz Walichnowski entitled *Izrael a NRF* (Israel and West Germany) and in scores of other publications.[28] One such article bears the title "Alliance Between Victims and Executioners," a phrase that epitomizes the thrust of the entire campaign: in a host of contexts, victims and victimizers, as well as past and present, are conflated.[29] Not only is Germany said to support Israel's "genocide" in the Middle East, not only are the Israelis *like* Nazis, they *are* Nazis. The public was informed that one thousand former Nazis were advising the Israeli army,[30] that Moshe Dayan was a disguised Nazi war criminal, that Martin Bormann was hiding in Golda Meir's apartment,[31] and that Dayan's daughter Yael "reminds us" of Ilse Koch, the Buchenwald commandant's wife reputed to have had lampshades made of human skin.[32] Moreover, this alliance between Nazis and Jews extended back into the past. Zionists, it was alleged, who needed the Holocaust to build support for a Jewish state, collaborated with the Nazis, as did Jewish communal leaders in the ghettos.[33] Who then within this labyrinth are the real victims? Clearly, Poles, and doubly so, in the present and in the past. For the current conspiracy of Germans and Jews against Poland is intended to deny Polish victimhood in the past, to deny the martyrdom of the Polish nation during the war, and more: to exonerate the Germans of the murder of the Jews and pin the blame for it on the Poles.

The Holocaust, in other words, has been transformed affectively into a German-Jewish conspiracy against Poles. In this extraordinary reversal, we recognize the unacceptable, unmasterable substratum of guilt connected to Polish witnessing of the Holocaust. This was an anguish most powerfully rooted precisely in those who had come of age during the war years, whose identity was directly shaped by them. Festering for twenty years, repressed psychologically in the individual psyche and politically in the public arena, this anguish was now channeled by Moczar and his followers into a system of belief that denied facts but not feelings. Twenty years after the event, the anti-Zionist campaign, in all its irrationality, suggested that the murder of the Jews had become an obstacle that stood between Poles and their past, preventing them from repossessing that past as a narrative of their exemplary martyrdom. The meaning of the Holocaust had become Polish victimization *by* the Holocaust. And therefore the emergence of a solution, recalling Lifton, in which the passive victimized become active victimizers, while nevertheless retaining the image of themselves as victims. Once again, the solution did not require the development of any new "totalism." Frozen into timeless availability was the model of exclusivist nationalism, the ideology of the prewar Endecja, complete with specific and eternal enemies: Germans and Jews.

Although in fantasy Poles became the victims, reality suggested the workings of a "repetition compulsion": Jews again were victimized, and extraordinarily, in a manner reminiscent of the Nuremberg Laws. Jews were "exposed" on the basis of a card index, assembled by Tadeusz Walichnowski in the Interior Ministry, which adopted racial criteria sometimes even more stringent than Nazi legislation. Those with a Jewish parent, occasionally even a grandparent, great-grandparent or spouse, found themselves stigmatized, while the accused often responded by trying to prove the purity of their blood. But bona fide "Aryans" could be "Zionists" as well. As a contemporary observer noted, one's descent, surname, physical appearance, position and place of work, career history, party membership, and degree of religious observance were all relevant; in other words: "The Jew was the one who, in social perception, was supposed to be a Jew."[34]

Unlike the Holocaust and unlike the immediate postwar years in Poland, however, the onslaught did not involve physical violence. Beginning in March 1968, at workplaces throughout the country, amid mass meetings and demonstrations called to denounce Zionism, "Jewish" employees were "unmasked" and dismissed from their positions. Although most of those affected were professionals in the big cities—doctors, engineers, academics, journalists, and above all, government functionaries—the purge extended to smaller towns and to those employed in lower-level positions as well, even to factory workers. All these individuals, unable to find work and subjected to the crudest anti-Semitic propaganda, were forbidden to leave Poland except under one condition: they surrender their Polish citizenship for an exit permit valid only for travel to Israel. In this fashion, over two years, some twenty thousand Poles of Jewish descent "proved" their allegiance to Israel through what was a forced expulsion. Having surrendered their citizenship, no Communist regime would ever readmit them into Poland. Ironically, relatively few of this final emigration, most of whom had spent their lives indifferent or hostile to Zionism, settled in Israel; most moved to the Scandinavian countries and to the United States.

What was the effect of the anti-Zionist campaign on Polish society? Here again, as with all such assessments of popular beliefs under communism, what is possible is informed speculation. Endek rhetoric in the mouths of party officials doubtless inspired confusion, some of it rather naïve. Much has been made, for example, of the slogan, apparently noted on workers' banners during this period, which, on the model of the prewar demand that Jews leave Poland, "Żydzi do Palestyny" (Jews to Palestine), now proclaimed, encouraged by the homonymic possibilities in Polish, "Syjoniści do Syjamu" (Zionists to Siam).[35] More to the point is that the figure of the persecuted Jew inspired fear, a fear doubtless intensified by memories of the war years. Should one come to the aid of a victimized friend or colleague and risk repression against oneself and one's family? Some of the intelligentsia, certainly, responded with an outpouring of compassion for individual victims of the campaign, observable at train stations in the larger cities, as old friends were forced to part over an accident of birth. More commonly, however, victims became nonpersons overnight to coworkers and even friends. Although some observers noted widespread indifference, the feeling that what was being played out was party business, an affair concerning the rulers and not the ruled, it would be a mistake to exaggerate this division. The officially inspired paroxysm that swept Poland, however irrational, played on issues, after all, to which all Poles were profoundly sensitive. The anti-

Zionist campaign, moreover, hardly developed in a vacuum, but making full use of stereotypes rooted in Polish history and above all in their well-tested postwar incarnation, the *Żydokomuna*. The desire for revenge against "Jewish Stalinists" reinforced by the lure of professional advancement was doubtless a powerful stimulus to voluntary denunciations of "Zionists"; the number of Poles who did not understand that "Zionist" meant Jew was surely rather limited.[36] There was scarcely any protest in Poland against the campaign. When the Polish episcopate finally released a pastoral letter on the subject in May 1968, the letter condemned both anti-Semitism and the "anti-Polish campaign" abroad.[37] Even the Catholic press, skilled in political commentary designed to skirt the censor's pencil, was silent.

The last years of the 1960s may be viewed from several perspectives: as a struggle for power within the Polish Communist Party climaxed by a police provocation; as an attack on independent culture and thinking of the post-Stalinist era; as the final gasp of a hopelessly outmoded ideology; but also as an attempted exorcism of the worst demons of Polish national memory. This exorcism, a turning point both in the history of the "Jewish question" and the history of postwar Poland, initiated the process of bringing back into view, beneath the fading rhetoric of class struggle, a more fundamental dynamic of modern Polish history, and indeed, of modern history as a whole. This is the struggle between chauvinism and pluralism, the forces that former Solidarity leader Adam Michnik (who began his political career in the 1960s as a *bananowiec* and "Zionist") recently termed the two faces of Europe.[38] Behind the remnants of Marxist posturing in 1968, emerged the discourse and often the representatives of prewar chauvinist nationalism. The failure of these forces to seize political power set the stage for the coming revolution, which would unfold under a very different sign: that of optimism, inclusiveness, and multiplicity. Fundamental to the new era would be a quest to restructure the values and symbols of the Polish psyche, a quest intimately connected to the effort to integrate into national memory the image of the murdered Jew. The freedoms to which the new era would aspire would include, perhaps, indeed, depend on, "emancipation from bondage to the deceased."[39]

6

Memory Reconstructed
1970–1989

While Gomułka weathered March 68, he did not survive the massive worker protests that, apparently unrelated, followed it. Centered in the Baltic shipyards of Gdańsk, Gdynia, and Szczecin in December 1970, provoked by an increase in food prices, events climaxed with street fighting between workers and the police and army, the burning of party headquarters in Gdańsk, and, according to government sources, the death of forty-five workers (the actual number may have been several hundred). With Gomułka's fall, Polish communism assumed its terminal configuration. This was a system in whose legitimacy even the rulers now scarcely believed, but in which, using contemporary euphemisms, "reasons of state" or "geopolitics" made it necessary to continue playing the game. It was staffed by a generation of younger apparatchiks, many of them supporters of General Moczar. Like its counterparts elsewhere, this generation of 68 was postideological too, but here that meant not the transcendance of ideology but its subservience to opportunism. Corruption, already widespread in every corner of the system and therefore in every corner of daily life outside the home, became even more pervasive.

The first to be entrusted with this system, for the first half of its remaining life, was Edward Gierek, a former miner from Silesia with a reputation as a strong manager. Announcing a new era of "dynamic growth" intended to smother politics with consumer goods, Gierek rolled back the price increases that had toppled his predecessor, then expanded trade and secured loans from the West.[1] For several years, while projecting a liberal image westward, particularly appealing in the era of détente, Gierek presided over something of an economic boom in Poland. He also oversaw a crucial political and symbolic breakthrough: West German ratification of a treaty declaring Poland's western borders to be inviolable. At home, references to patriotism predominated over socialism; the Church and other "nonparty" forces were briefly courted. But Gierek's economic initiatives began to flounder, particularly when western markets shrank after the oil crisis of 1973. The turning point was 1976, when another increase in food prices sparked another round of demonstrations, strikes, and riots by workers. Gierek revoked the price increases, then increased both political repression and loans from the West. By 1980, the year of Gierek's ouster, Poland's debt totaled $23 billion.

On the surface, the decade seemed to reflect yet another of the postwar cycles beginning with economic and political liberalization and ending with crisis and repression. It was commonly and hopelessly believed that such cycles, signs, like the demoralization of daily life, of membership in the Soviet empire, were destined to go on indefinitely. Nevertheless, during these relatively uneventful years, in certain corners of Polish society unprecedented changes in thinking began to point to a way out of this cul-de-sac. Perhaps the most important of these transformations was the gradual realization, by elements of the Church and the secular intelligentsia, that they had a great deal in common. What was involved was much more than a marriage of convenience, much more, that is, than "politics," and therefore precisely its chance of ultimate success.

In his influential essay *Kościół, lewica, dialog* (The church, the left, dialog), first published in Paris in 1977 but widely available in Poland through the growing clandestine press, Adam Michnik cited the poet Antoni Słonimski to account for what it was that had begun to bring, not unproblematically, Catholic and "progressive secular" thinking together. It was not a reconciling of worldviews, declared Słonimski, but the "intensified feeling of responsibility for human dignity [*człowieczeństwo*] threatened today in its very existence."[2] The ground of agreement, in other words, was the perception that the fundamental issue under the system of decomposing communism was not ideological but moral. The root of the system's evil was precisely the dualism that Henryk Grynberg, among many others, had described: the split between private and public realms, the acceptance of lying as a way of life. This approach bore a clear affinity to the "politics of 68" throughout the world, which typically developed critiques of established political and social systems from moral perspectives that were antipolitical. It also had roots in Polish history, in the universalism of the insurrectionists and the tradition of independent socialism of the PPS. In the Church, the secular intelligentsia discovered a bastion that resisted the split between public and private, a perspective that insisted that the essence of European civilization, as of Christianity, was belief in "the autonomous value of truth and human solidarity."[3] In contrast, what the enemy intended, by means of what Michnik, citing Leszek Kołakowski, called "sovietization," was to destroy the basis of European civilization in general and Polish culture in particular. The goal was to transform Poles into "a nation of broken backbones, captive minds, ravaged consciences . . . [for whom] every thought of changing the existing state of things would appear to be an irrational absurdity." The method proceeded in two stages: first was the destruction of tradition, the consignment to oblivion of huge areas of the Polish past; second was the replacement of tradition by a counterfeit notion of the past and therefore of the present, a "castrated" history whose only function was to legitimize the existing order.[4]

What emerges from this analysis is the possibility of two sorts of rehumanizing activity. The first is to begin to rediscover the history that had been silenced, to restore the broken connection to tradition. But which tradition? And what was the relation of this tradition to Catholicism? Was Catholicism its primary attribute or, as the Church along with the Endecja had insisted before the war, its only attribute? Here Michnik argued that since the interwar period, when it had allied with national chauvinism, the Polish Church, tempered by oppression and the ecumenical spirit of Vatican Council II, had greatly changed, that it was prepared to accept a credo comparable to Michnik's "profound conviction that the strength of our culture, what determines its richness and beauty, is pluralism, diversity, multiplicity of hue."[5] Michnik approvingly cites the teaching of Polish bishops in the 1970s: "Thanks to love of our own Fatherland, we attain to love of the entire human family. . . . True love of fatherland is linked to profound respect for everything that constitutes the value of other nations."[6] In this respect and many others, Michnik and his colleagues found a hospitable reception among the Catholic intelligentsia. Since the 1940s, these circles had gradually evolved into the closest thing possible to forums for independent liberal thought. Their publications, *Tygodnik Powszechny* (Universal weekly) and the monthly *Znak* (Sign) in Kraków, the monthly *Więź* (Link) in Warsaw, though subject to censorship, were not organs of the state; similarly, the Clubs of the Catholic Intelligentsia [Kluby Inteligencji Katolickiej, KIK] undertook the discussion of many otherwise taboo issues.[7]

Redeveloping links to the past was only half of the new program; the other involved reforging social bonds in the present. In 1968, workers had remained aloof from the student protests; two years later, students and intelligentsia, still licking their wounds, had ignored the workers' appeal for their support. But amid yet another worker confrontation with the state in 1976, a group of Polish intelligentsia founded an organization called the Workers' Defense Committee (Komitet Obrony Robotników, KOR). The members of KOR included Michnik and his colleagues, representatives of the generation of 68, as well as those of an older generation rooted in the PPS and liberal factions of the Home Army. Their immediate activities centered on providing financial, legal, and, where necessary, medical help for workers and their families who were being persecuted for their protests. Their longer-term strategy was not to confront the state in battles they could only lose, but to attempt to avoid it and instead stimulate the creation of centers of autonomous social activity, organizations built from the ground up. The goal was to begin to restore the "social glue," the human solidarity, that the system had gone far toward eradicating. Key to this work were notions linked to a Christian ethos; for example, work for the good of others seen as a transcendent ethical value; nonviolence and forgiveness toward one's enemies.

KOR activists and their friends also began to develop an un-censored clandestine press and founded an educational network known as the Flying University [Uniwersytet Latający], which or-ganized independent courses on history and culture. The name Flying University, which suggested the need for the classes to keep changing their location to avoid the police, linked this institution to one established under the same name and for similar purposes by the Warsaw intelligentsia in czarist times.[8]

After the anti-Zionist campaign of the late 1960s, a profound and nearly universal silence descended on the "Jewish question." The subject of Jews, indeed the very word, was avoided in public discourse; silence even commonly reigned in private conversation among intimates.[9] Abroad, it was believed that the history of the Jews in Poland had come to an ultimate conclusion; it was com-mon to speak of "the end of a thousand years."[10] The *American Jewish Year Book,* which published news of the tiniest Jewish com-munities throughout the world, ceased reporting on Poland for most of the 1970s. In Israel, the perception was marked by a sym-bolic transfer of Holocaust memory; in 1975, a smaller version of Rapoport's Warsaw Ghetto monument was installed at Yad Vashem, the Holocaust memorial center in Jerusalem, "where its Jewish na-tional spirit would be preserved."[11] Nevertheless, albeit tiny, aging, demoralized, and submissive, an official Jewish community, or-ganized in a handful of secular associations and religious congre-gations, managed to continue, as did such institutions as the Jewish Historical Institute, the State Yiddish Theater, and the Yiddish newspaper. Nor did the silence about Jewish matters prevent KOR activists, in their increasing contacts with the police, from being abused as "Trotskyist Jews" and "garlic-eaters."[12] More impor-tant, here and there in the circles of the emerging opposition, there were signs of an entirely new approach to the "Jewish question" and everything connected to it.[13]

The earliest such stirrings occurred within the Catholic intelli-gentsia. During the 1970s, the Warsaw Club of Catholic Intelli-gentsia began to organize annual Weeks of Jewish Culture. In the mornings, members of KIK would visit the huge, devastated Jew-ish cemetery in Warsaw and work at restoring the tombstones; in the evenings, they would attend lectures on Jewish culture. Mean-

while, outside Warsaw in the summer of 1979, at a therapy workshop with the American psychologist Carl Rogers organized by
his Polish disciples, one of the participants suddenly began to act
strangely. Pressed to talk about himself, this young Polish psychologist of Jewish descent, born a decade after the Holocaust, whose
father had held a high position under Polish Stalinism, in whose
family the word Jew had long been unmentioned, started to rave
about concentration camps. He and several other participants
agreed to continue to meet to explore such feelings. What most of
them had in common, besides having been born after the war and
raised in entirely assimilated Jewish families, was the trauma of
first confronting their Jewish origins in 1968. Several months after
the Rogers workshop, along with some members of KIK, they began
to organize gatherings for exploring Jewish identity and culture;
the resulting group, with fewer than a hundred members, became
known as the Jewish Flying University.[14]

These young "Jews," "half-Jews," spouses of Jews, and sympathetic non-Jews were above all Poles whose primary identification
was with the emerging opposition movement. They knew nothing of Jewish religious practices, languages, or history. They were
entirely cut off from the official Jewish community in Poland, whose
elderly members might have served as a link to Jewish tradition,
however attenuated; so long as communism reigned, they would
remain cut off from them, regarding the official community as
hopelessly compromised. Their increasing involvement in Jewish
culture could therefore assume the form of a voyage of pure discovery, the exploration of a lost continent. It was an approach
premised on discontinuity and silence, an approach that was possible only in the aftermath of the anti-Zionist paroxysm. For this
small group of seekers and the many more that would follow in
the 1980s, the expulsion of the "last" Jews of Poland was indeed
an exorcism that enabled them, as representatives of the postwar
generation, to begin to reinvent a Jewish past. This Jewish quest
was profoundly Polish, for it was an integral part of the larger
movement to regain the Polish past. But as part of the larger Polish enterprise it marked it in a crucial way, confirming it as inher-
ently pluralist. The Jew would increasingly appear as a legitimate
and even honored representative of the new Polish past.

If these developments bore an elitist character, involving only handfuls of the intelligentsia, they were not to remain that way for long. In October 1978, Karol Wojtyła, the archbishop of Kraków, an important member of the Catholic intelligentsia, became Pope John Paul II. His first encyclical, *Redemptor Hominis,* was about human dignity and the struggle for human rights. In June 1979, he visited Poland. About this visit, Jan Józef Lipski, one of the founders of KOR, has written: "Spiritually, Poland before June 1979 and Poland after June 1979 seemed to be two different countries. Who knows whether the breakthrough that occurred then was not deeper and more essential than the one that took place [with the emergence of Solidarity] in August 1980?"[15] For nine days the pope's presence transformed human relations. Millions of people, and above all youth, found themselves acting in a manner that the system had heretofore thwarted: "kinder to one another, disciplined yet free and relaxed, as they enjoyed these few days of internal, shared freedom."[16] John Paul's message, moreover, spoke to the very issues addressed by the emerging workers' movement: "Christ will never approve that man be considered, or that man consider himself *merely instruments of production. . . .* This must be remembered by the worker and the employer and the system of work," he announced in Nowa Huta. And he concluded his pilgrimage in Kraków before a crowd of one million people with the following words: "I ask you to accept . . . the whole of the spiritual legacy which goes with the name 'Poland,'" and added: "May you never despair, never grow weary, never become disheartened . . . never lose *that spiritual freedom* to which He 'calls' humanity."[17]

John Paul also visited Auschwitz. His words at a mass, widely reprinted and hailed in Poland as marking a new stage in the Church's relationship to the memory of the Holocaust, offered a foretaste of the reconciliations but also of the new conflicts that the new era would inspire. Noting the plaques at the foot of the International Memorial at Birkenau, John Paul asked his listeners to

pause . . . for a moment *at the plaque with an inscription in the Hebrew language.* This inscription evokes the memory of the nation whose sons and daughters were intended for complete extermination. This nation originates with Abraham, who is the "father of our faith"

(Romans 4:12), as Paul of Tarsus expressed it. This nation, which received from God Jahweh the commandment "Thou shalt not kill," itself experienced killing in special measure. It is not permissible for anyone to pass this plaque with indifference.[18]

The ideas expressed in this statement, the uniqueness of Jews by virtue of the Holocaust and by virtue of their role as "elder brother" to Christianity, would become the focus for expanding interest in Judaism within the Polish Church and among lay Catholics and would also inspire dialogue between Poles and Jews, both in Poland and abroad. But this Polish Catholic approach to Jews was hardly unproblematic, as the context for John Paul's words illustrates. His statement about Jews came after remarks dedicated to Maximilian Kolbe, a Franciscan priest imprisoned at Auschwitz who exchanged his life for that of another prisoner he did not know. John Paul's eulogy of Father Kolbe's "victory through faith and love" hinted that the meaning of Auschwitz could be encompassed by a Catholic paradigm. This "exclusivist" vision, along with the discovery that Father Kolbe, whom the pope canonized in 1982, had been the publisher of an anti-Semitic newspaper before the war,[19] would fuel growing hostility toward the Church among Jews throughout the world, hostility that would finally erupt in the bitter controversy over the establishment of a Carmelite convent at Auschwitz.

For the moment, however, not division but unity, indeed Solidarity, was the order of the day.[20] Its emergence was a result of a new wave of strikes responding to new price increases in the summer of 1980. The climax was a seventeen-day sit-in at the Lenin Shipyards in Gdańsk in August 1980, which produced a negotiated settlement and an extraordinary document, the Gdańsk Accords, that included the right of Polish workers to be represented by an independent trade union, the first in the Communist bloc. Although both the intelligentsia and the Church were indispensable to its emergence, Solidarity was above all the creation of Polish workers, of a generation raised in People's Poland that took the notion of its own historical mission more seriously than its teachers. It then proceeded to turn the tables on them, jettisoning the class struggle for the Polish insurrectionary tradition. Unlike the nineteenth century, however, this time the Polish initiative would indeed breach the walls of empire.

Solidarity was immediately much more than a trade union; during the sixteen months of its legal existence, it vastly expanded on the transformation that the pope's visit had achieved for nine days. Masks and persona, the duplicity and corruption of daily life, fell away. The public game that Henryk Grynberg had decried was no longer played. Instead, "people opened their lips," as one worker recalled, "and sincerely began to say what they had been forbidden to say before."[21] By the end of these months, with 10 million members, Solidarity, both as an organization and as a spirit that allowed people finally to look each other in the eyes, had penetrated into every corner of civil society, indeed, it had become that society.

Fundamental to Solidarity's "truth-telling" was an explosion of activity relating to the past, an attempt to repossess and use what the system had silenced for decades. The most immediate result was a proliferation of commemorative activity in a great variety of forms and contexts, beginning, certainly, with the tradition of Polish workers' struggles. One of the original demands of the Gdańsk strikers was for a memorial to those killed in Gdańsk in 1970; during the Solidarity era, workers throughout Poland put up plaques and statues at their factory gates, inevitably bedecked with flowers and wreaths, in memory of their own and previous strikes. But the symbolism of all this activity far transcended any conventional "proletarian" context, and entwined these workers' struggles with Polish national traditions. The Gdańsk memorial, for example, unveiled in December 1980, consisted of three 139-foot-high crosses surmounted by huge anchors. Beyond its universal and Christian connotations, the sign of the anchor, formed out of the letters P and W for Polska Walcząca (Fighting Poland), had been widely used as a symbol of the anti-Nazi underground and the Warsaw Uprising.[22] After the banning of Solidarity, the anchor, now constructed out of the letters S and W for Solidarność Walcząca (Fighting Solidarity), became ever present on Polish walls.

Solidarity also transformed the Polish calendar, filling it with unofficial commemorations typically celebrated with special masses and solemn gatherings at appropriate sites; the dates marked moments of martyrdom and victory throughout Polish history. Here too, the Second World War was strongly represented. The anniversary of the outbreak of the Warsaw Uprising, for example, was commemorated in 1980 at the Warsaw Catholic cemetery with homage to the victims of Katyń. Increasingly, the history of Solidarity itself was commemorated. After the banning of Solidarity and the declaration of martial law on December 13, 1981, the thirteenth of every month was dedicated to political prisoners. On these days priests would address strongly political sermons, masses would conclude with patriotic hymns, and silk-screened Solidarity logos or other leaflets would often flutter down upon the worshipers. As the calendar began to bulge with the weight of history, a popular joke suggested that Poles would soon run out of dates to commemorate their martyrdom.

A world of mass participation in the re-creation of national memory was ideally suited to wresting "Jews" and the "Jewish question" out of silence and into public discourse. A special supplement of an independent newsletter published shortly after the Gdańsk Accords provides a characteristic expression of this development. The occasion for the publication, entitled "Jews and Poles," is the fortieth anniversary of the sealing of the ghettos.[23] The editors' statement begins by citing the pope's words about Jews during his visit to Auschwitz the previous year, and then continues: "We have recalled the crime of Katyń and the crime perpetrated [by the Soviets] on the Baltic nations. We should perhaps also have remembered Palmiry [a forest near Warsaw where the Germans murdered masses of Poles]. WE MUST remember the beginning of the annihilation of the Jews of Europe." This memory must be cultivated, first of all, as "a turning point in human history. . . . Humanity [*Ludzkość*] reached the frontiers of the human [*człowieczeństwo*] and did not hesitate to cross them. This time toward its own shame." But the editors continue:

> Let us lay aside the general problem. Let us look at Polish Jews. And not only in order to honor their martyrdom, but because, though Jews themselves are no longer among us, the subject of Jews constitutes a problem for us. The problem is the very language with

which we speak of them—that very THEY. But they were a part of US, of our society (regardless of their degree of integration into that society). We say that they lived on our lands. But those lands were also their lands. They lived, quite simply, at home [*Żyli po prostu u siebie*].

With this recognition, rooted in an unambiguously pluralist conception of Polish history, as a basis, the editors then raise a number of "problems" that prefigure the explorations of the years to come. First is "the problem of our lack of knowledge . . . of the richness of the cultural, religious, social life of Jews in the old lands of the Polish Commonwealth," of their modern history, and of their annihilation. Second is the problem of

> outdated quarrels and (mutual) slanders unexamined for decades. Despite the beautiful stance of many Poles during the occupation years, who came forth to defend the tormented Jews, there is also the problem of our conscience—weighted with the anti-Jewish excesses of the prewar years, the bench ghettos in the universities. And there is the problem of the indifference of part of society during their annihilation.

Finally, there is the problem of the persistence of anti-Semitism in the present, its extent unclear, but with "someone always using it to advance their own interests." The statement concludes:

> Yes, there is a whole tangle of problems that silence continues to knot. Meanwhile—we must speak! Sometimes we must even shout. We must ask in order to find answers. We must understand in order to forgive, and ask for forgiveness in order to gain it.
>
> On the fortieth anniversary of the sealing of the ghettos, in the year of the bombing of European synagogues, but also in the year of our moral and social renewal, IT IS NOT PERMISSIBLE TO BE SILENT.[24]

The remaining twenty pages of this mimeographed newsletter are devoted to a collection of texts that, in their ensemble, preview the coming "Jewish revival." There is a brief chronology of a thousand years of Jewish history in Poland; recollections of the Warsaw Ghetto from the memoirs of the Home Army courier Jan Karski;

excerpts from the suicide note of Szmuel Zygielbojm, the Jewish representative to the Polish government-in-exile who killed himself to draw world attention to the Ghetto Uprising; an eyewitness account of the Kielce pogrom (suggesting Soviet involvement); an interview with Władysław Bartoszewski on postwar Polish-Jewish relations; an early version of an important essay on Jews and communism, written by one of the founders of the Jewish Flying University;[25] and several literary texts, Polish and translations from Yiddish. These include an essay introducing I. B. Singer to a Polish audience; excerpts from the writings of Stanisław Vincenz, an émigré Polish writer whose work evokes the vanished multicultural world of the *kresy;* from Yitzhak Katzenelson's lamentation *Lid fun oysgehargetn yidishn folk* (Song of the murdered Jewish people); and from Tadeusz Borowski's story "Proszę państwa do gazu" (This way to the gas, ladies and gentlemen); as well as a poem by Jerzy Ficowski that would be widely reprinted in the years to come.

> I did not manage to save
> a single life
>
> I did not know how to stop
> a single bullet
>
> and I wander round cemeteries
> which are not there
> I look for words
> which are not there
> I run
>
> to help where no one called
> to rescue after the event
>
> I want to be on time
> even if I am too late[26]

Ficowski's poem heralds an era in which the word "Jew" would begin to signify less a threat than an absence.

Yet the Solidarity era, dedicated to the breaking of a multitude of silences, was often inappropriate to exploring what thereby emerged, particularly the "Jewish question." In December 1980, for example, with press censorship greatly loosened, a letter appeared in a leading Warsaw weekly, signed by Władysław Bartoszewski, Jan Józef Lipski, and young members of the Jewish Flying University, among others.[27] The letter begins with the need for breaking the silence about "the problem of Polish-Jewish relations," describes "the history of Polish Jews [as] an integral part of the history of Poland," and "the so-called 'Jewish question'" as, above all, a Polish problem. It then specifically addresses the "anti-Semitic campaign" that erupted in March 1968, calling for the rehabilitation of its victims, and the gathering of accounts by participants and witnesses. It concludes: "It is our hope that in the present times, when truth, though bitter, comes to light, the honest presentation of Polish-Jewish relations, including their most sensitive aspects, will become possible." The editor's response, however, insisted that "the March events should not be reduced to—let us call it—the Jewish aspect." And in March 1981, when, for the first time, the events of the late 1960s were publicly aired during a series of lectures and colloquiums at the University of Warsaw, the emphasis, understandably, was on the state's crushing of the student movement, not on the "sensitive aspects" of Polish-Jewish relations.[28]

For sixteen months, under the apparatchik Stanisław Kania, the state countenanced a breach in its monopoly of power. Much was made of Solidarity's "non-political" goals, of its "self-limiting revolution," but in this case the state soon understood, better than the opposition, that what Solidarity represented could not be limited and constituted an absolute challenge to its authority. In December 1981, the state finally reacted as many Poles had long feared it would.[29] Assuming the positions of minister of defense, premier, and first secretary of the PZPR, and installing a handful of military cronies in other key positions, Gen. Wojciech Jaruzelski proclaimed martial law. Jaruzelski, who considered himself a Polish patriot and claimed that he acted to avoid a far more sanguinary Soviet "solution," had nothing new to propose beyond smashing Solidarity and "restoring order." Poland slid into a never-ending economic crisis; waiting in line for hours for every daily necessity became a way of life. No longer capable of even claiming to deliver the goods, the system's only remaining raison d'être became the raison d'état: the crude threat of Soviet invasion.

The imposition of martial law spilled comparatively little blood, but many thousands of activists were taken into custody and imprisoned without trial for months. A handful managed to elude capture and, aided by an apparently endless supply of fresh volunteers, established a clandestine organization that soon became the most elaborate underground in the Communist bloc. The struggle against the authorities was waged on a variety of fronts, symbolic above all. Characteristic of the period of martial law (ended in July 1983) was the appearance at public sites of giant flower crosses. Interspersed among the flowers were leaflets, communiqués, patriotic symbols, and religious icons of every sort; the crowds surrounding them would often break into religious or patriotic hymns. At night police would dismantle the crosses; in the morning they would reappear at the same or different sites. Also under martial law, with stringent censorship reimposed, the underground developed a superbly organized clandestine press. Even when, attempting to gain respectability, the government subsequently relaxed censorship, the clandestine press continued to expand, eventually publishing a full range of Polish and world literature, which was often produced more quickly and in better quality than through the government press. Side by side with the underground press, the legal Catholic press, especially that of the Catholic intelligentsia, greatly expanded its influence.

Poland after the banning of Solidarity was thus a profoundly contradictory place: on one hand, a visible daily public life of deprivation, decay, and frustration; on the other hand, an invisible private life, lived "underground," of emotional warmth, intellectual and spiritual energy. Such an atmosphere was well suited to giving up on the "real world," and, for those so inclined, often alongside various forms of clandestine activism, to the pursuit of study, reflection, and personal exploration. For young people it was first of all the Church that attracted, a Church involved in various alternative social, cultural, and quasi-political activities; during this period the number of young people entering monastic orders soared. Eastern religions and philosophies also proved attractive; ashrams multiplied. Simultaneously, there continued to evolve, at first primarily among students and intelligentsia but gradually involving larger circles, a growing interest, indeed a fascination with Jews, Judaism, and the Jewish past in Poland.

The locus of this interest was the postwar generation, which had neither seen a "real Jew" nor witnessed the Holocaust. Raised in a monochromatic world of cultural and ethnic uniformity, they sifted the Polish past for a myth of diversity and color. There they discovered the image of the bearded, black-garbed Jew, supremely exotic yet nevertheless an immemorial neighbor, rooted in the prewar landscape of a Poland that, like the Jew, no longer existed. The Nazis, everyone knew, had destroyed the Jews, but their absence in contemporary Poland became yet another affective indictment against the Communist system. For many young Poles as a whole, as for the "new Jews," the new image of the Jew arose out of silence, but a silence that not only was the aftermath of 1968 but also infused all of the postwar years. This new image of the Jew could thereby begin to perform a new symbolic function as a focus of longing for a many-hued Old Poland, a Poland of the multinational Commonwealth, of the *kresy* and the *shtetl*. Rooted in the needs of the young, the image also permitted older Poles a nostalgic return to an idealized prewar youth. These were the sources of the "fashion for Jews" increasingly noted by contemporary observers, the popularity of Jewish songs and music, of *Fiddler on the Roof*, even of Jewish food. *Ryba po żydowsku* ("fish Jewish-style," that is, sweetened carp or gefilte fish) became a restaurant staple.

For some, the image of the Jew was linked to a moral imperative, the responsibility to uncover and preserve the remaining physical remnants of the Jewish past. Hunting for old Jewish books, discovering ruined synagogues and cemeteries redeemed the past from oblivion and therefore, in the Poland of the 1980s, were also acts of resistance. Led by several of the "new Jews," an independent Citizens' Committee for the Protection of Jewish Cemeteries and Cultural Monuments in Poland was founded. At the same time, here and there throughout Poland, at sites where there was little or nothing to document or restore, monuments began to be raised commemorating Jewish communities and their annihilation. In the immediate postwar years, Holocaust survivors had done this work before leaving Poland; in this new round of construction the initiative often came from local Poles, sometimes with the help of survivors living abroad. These memorials, commonly erected at the site of ruined cemeteries, often consist of fragments of tombstones, an iconography of rupture, discontinuity, and loss.[30] Forty years after the Holocaust, amid a world of unprecedented possibilities, it also became possible for Poles to begin to mourn for the Jews. Antoni Słonimski's poem, "Elegia miasteczek żydowskich" (Elegy for the little Jewish towns), first published in 1950 but reprinted and recited throughout the 1980s, begins:

> They are gone, gone from Poland, the little Jewish towns,
> In Hrubieszów, Karczew, Brody, Falenica.
> In vain you would search in windows for lighted candles,
> Or listen for song from a wooden synagogue.[31]

During this period as well a number of international scholarly initiatives began to draw Polish historians and intellectuals into contact with their western Jewish counterparts. The first of a series of international conferences dedicated to Polish-Jewish relations was held in 1983 in New York;[32] in that year as well an unofficial delegation of Israeli historians was received at Polish academic institutions.[33] Beginning in 1985, these efforts were coordinated from Oxford, where an annual publication, *Polin: A Journal of Polish-Jewish Studies*, began to appear.[34] New scholarship thereby emerged, as well as a forum in which the most controversial historical issues could be aired, above all, that of Polish-Jewish relations during the Holocaust. Gradually this activity came to the notice of the larger Jewish and Polish communities abroad (the latter now including recently emigrated former Solidarity activists). Even in these communities, where positions traditionally were particularly polarized, some dialogue began to occur.

In Poland the 1980s witnessed a wave of publications, dissertations, films, plays, concerts, and exhibitions devoted to Jewish subjects.[35] Some of the publications were products of the clandestine and Catholic press; this included a six-hundred-page double issue of *Znak* dedicated to the Jews in Poland and Catholic-Jewish relations, published for the fortieth anniversary of the Warsaw Ghetto

Uprising,[36] as well as new editions, the first to be published in Poland, of Aleksander Hertz's pioneering work, *Żydzi w kulturze polskiej* (The Jews in Polish culture).[37] The majority of publications, however, were issued by Polish state publishing houses. Alongside popular and scholarly works that continued to blur the difference between the fate of Poles and Jews during the war, there appeared Holocaust memoirs, local histories of Jewish communities before and during the Holocaust, monographs by young historians on Polish Jewish history and culture, and collections of Jewish jokes and recipes. Translations from western fiction, especially books by I. B. Singer, also began to find large audiences, as did Polish literature about the Holocaust. Of ground-breaking importance was an anthology of Holocaust poetry and prose edited by the literary critic Irena Maciejewska.[38] Assembled in one volume were recent writings along with material first published during and just after the war. The latter included two extraordinary poems by Czesław Miłosz, the 1980 Nobel laureate in literature, that would catalyze Polish discourse about the Holocaust.[39]

A significant portion of this literature was by Jewish authors. This included the work of an older generation—Adolf Rudnicki, Artur Sandauer, and especially Julian Stryjkowski—who remembered the prewar Jewish world and evoked it, as well as the Holocaust, in their fiction. Some of their early writings now found new readers, while they continued to publish new work. For example, Stryjkowski's *Głosy w ciemności* (Voices in the darkness), first published in 1956, and *Austeria* (The inn), first published in 1966, both about Jewish life in Galician *shtetlekh* during the second decade of the century, went through numerous editions in the 1970s and 1980s; in 1983, *Austeria* was made into a movie directed by Jerzy Kawalerowicz.[40] At the same time, a younger generation of writers, whose memory went back no further than the Holocaust, now found their work, some of it published officially and some by underground presses in Poland or abroad, soar in popularity. Among these writers are Bogdan Wojdowski, author of *Chleb rzucony umarłym* (Bread thrown to the dying), a hallucinatory narrative of the Warsaw Ghetto based on his memories as a child smuggler; Hanna Krall, who tracks Holocaust survivors, their stories and their ghosts, throughout the world; and the émigré writer

Henryk Grynberg, whose cycle of autobiographic novels moves from Polish forests to a Los Angeles pawnshop.[41] This, as the critic Jan Błoński has put it, is "the cruelest of paradoxes: never before in the novel—and perhaps even in Polish literature—has the Jewish presence been more visible than after the Holocaust!" Here was a "Jewish" literature in the Polish language that had flowered "most literally—in a cemetery."[42]

It was inevitable that the upsurge of "Jewish" publications shaped by the new Polish cultural politics would in turn leave its mark on the political arena. Once again the "Jewish question" reappeared in Polish political discourse. Ever opportunistic, the party leadership played both sides of the issue. The first involved quietly supporting forces that remained nostalgic for the days of General Moczar and Endo-Communism. In March 1981, while the University of Warsaw sponsored its symposium on the "March events," representatives of a new organization called the Grunwald Patriotic Union [Zjednoczenie Patriotyczne "Grunwald"], named after the site of a medieval battle in which Poles defeated the Teutonic Knights, demonstrated in front of the building that in Stalinist times had housed the Ministry of Public Security. They demanded that a plaque be affixed to the building to commemorate Polish patriots and Communists, victims of "Zionist terror" under Polish Stalinism.[43] Throughout the 1980s, Grunwald issued its own publications and became a fixture of the government's many-sided attempts to undermine the opposition, a source of rumors about the Jewish origins of Solidarity leaders and of anti-German and anti-Semitic disinformation.[44] Other initiatives included a ZBoWiD-sponsored reprint (prefaced with an introduction honoring its recently deceased author) of Poterański's 1968 pamphlet on the Warsaw Ghetto Uprising, in which the statements of Moczar and Gomułka were restored, as well as a book on Polish-Jewish relations that advanced the thesis that the Kielce pogrom had been fomented by Zionists.[45]

Hungry for international legitimation and economic aid, however, and apparently believing that Jews were rather influential in shaping world opinion, Jaruzelski and his generals began to flirt publicly with the so-called philosemitic trends. Key to this change was the elaborate commemoration of the fortieth anniversary of the Warsaw Ghetto Uprising, to which the government issued invitations to Jews and Jewish organizations throughout the world. But this project encountered growing opposition when Marek Edelman, the last survivor of the leadership of the uprising, published an open letter in the underground press, quickly reprinted in the West, calling for a boycott of the proceedings, scheduled to occur while the country was still under martial law.

Edelman, before and during the war a member of the Bund, had become a cardiologist after the war and remained out of politics until the Solidarity era, when he was chosen as a delegate to Solidarity's last national conference. He had already attracted attention as the subject of a book-length interview by Hanna Krall, *Zdążyć przed Panem Bogiem* (Beating God to the punch), first published in 1977.[46] This interview with Edelman not only reopened Polish discussion about the Holocaust but did so on an entirely new level, suggesting that its meaning could not be reduced to "martyrdom and resistance." Unlike Poles during the war, Edelman pointed out, Jews in the ghettos could not choose a "beautiful" or "aesthetic" death, but "died unimpressively: in terror and darkness." And he doubted whether any conventional moral categories and notions of heroism were adequate for coping with the impossible choices faced by Jews in that "other world." In particular he wondered about the ultimate importance of a handful of "boys and girls" deciding to shoot at Germans. Ironically but not uncharacteristically, in the Poland of the 1980s, Edelman, who was "no good at talking because he was unable to yell [and] no good as a hero because he lacked grandiloquence," emerged as spokesman for the moral significance of the Warsaw Ghetto Uprising.[47] Edelman's open letter to the world's Jews read, in part:

Forty years ago we fought not only for life, but for a life of dignity and freedom. Commemorating our anniversary here, where today degradation and coercion weigh upon the whole of social life, where words and gestures have been utterly falsified, is to be faithless to our struggle, to participate in something entirely the opposite, it is an act of cynicism and contempt. . . . Far from manipulated commemorations, in the silence of graves and hearts, will survive the true memory of victims and heroes, of the eternal human impulse toward freedom and truth.[48]

World Jewish response to Edelman's call for a boycott of the official ceremonies was mixed; some Jews stayed home, but several thousand nevertheless attended the official wreath laying by a military guard of honor in front of the ghetto memorial. Meanwhile, with Edelman's blessing, an unofficial ceremony was organized at the same site a few days before the official one. Several hundred people listened to some hurried speeches and watched as a small cross of daffodils was laid before the monument and several of the "new Jews," their heads covered with *kipot,* chanted the *Kaddish,* the Jewish prayer for the dead, before being dispersed by riot police. On another day, demonstrators at the site of the notorious *Umschlagplatz,* the "transfer point" where once the Nazis had herded the Jews of Warsaw onto the trains for Treblinka but now only a gas station stood, demanded that a memorial mark the location.[49]

In the years following, commemoration of the Warsaw Ghetto Uprising and of the Holocaust as a whole became ever more closely intertwined with the Polish political struggle. The underground, for example, issued "postage stamps," which were sold clandestinely, and sometimes affixed to letters (which, rumor had it, were occasionally delivered by sympathetic mail carriers). The iconography of these stamps included the Solidarity logo, a portrait of Lech Wałęsa, symbols of the 1944 uprising, as well as several readily recognizable "Jewish" images: a ghetto fighter rousted from a bunker during the Warsaw Ghetto Uprising, a terrified little boy with his hands raised over his head (particularly well known in the West), and a wall constructed of broken Jewish tombstones. Competition to appropriate the meaning of the uprising climaxed in 1988, for its forty-fifth anniversary. The government used the occasion to dedicate new monuments, developed with informal Israeli input, in the streets surrounding the ghetto memorial. These were a Memorial Route of Jewish Martyrdom and Struggle marked by stones bearing the names of persons linked with the uprising, leading from the ghetto memorial to a new monument, the work of architects connected to the opposition, that had finally been erected at the site of the *Umschlagplatz*.[50] Meanwhile, Solidarity sponsored an unofficial unveiling at the Warsaw Jewish cemetery of a monument in memory of Victor Alter and Henryk Ehrlich, leaders of the Bund who had been murdered in the Soviet Union after they fled Nazi-occupied Poland. Lech Wałęsa's letter to Marek Edelman on that occasion declared:

> This land, the Polish land, knows the truth about a struggle against slavery on behalf of freedom, against degradation on behalf of dignity, a struggle on behalf of hope fought without any chance of victory. The struggle of our Jewish brothers, the heroes of the Warsaw Ghetto, was such a struggle. We honor it today in a special manner. For in this land, the land of so many uprisings, the uprising of the Jewish fighters was the most Polish of all Polish uprisings.[51]

A Poland in which an audience could cheer a popular entertainer for donning a *kipa* and performing a "Jewish" song about a *shtetl* [52] and the Warsaw Ghetto Uprising could be assimilated into the Polish insurrectionary tradition was well suited to confronting more problematic aspects of the "Jewish question" as well. During the Solidarity era, opposition leaders devoted considerable energy to attacking anti-Semitism, which was seen as an embarrassment, particularly discredited since it had become a tool of the state. When internal polemics occasionally evoked anti-Semitic slurs (typically directed against the "non-working" intelligentsia), immediate denunciations followed. When Solidarity went underground, such efforts began to be directed inwardly. In the introduction to the special "Jewish" issue of his periodical, the editor of *Znak*, Stefan Wilkanowicz, spoke in the name of a "wise patriotism," at home in a pluralist world, that required Poles "to make a national or social accounting of their conscience and to cleanse wounds—in order for time to heal them."[53]

In the endeavor of "national accounting," one of the most influential texts was Jan Józef Lipski's essay "Dwie ojczyzny—dwa patriotyzmy (Uwagi o megalomanii narodowej i ksenofobii Polaków)" (Two fatherlands, two patriotisms: remarks on Polish national megalomania and xenophobia). Lipski defines two traditions in Polish historical thinking: one that "serves national megalomania," the assumption, that is, that Poles can do no wrong; and another that he calls a "bitter tradition of reckoning" capable of national self-assessment and moral judgment. "The struggle for the shape of Polish patriotism," declares Lipski, "will determine the fate of our nation—its moral, cultural and political fate."[54] He then devotes the rest of the essay to a harsh indictment of Polish historical injustices toward Germans, Russians, Lithuanians, Belorussians, Ukrainians, Czechs, and finally, in greatest detail, toward Jews. He describes the wave of prewar Polish anti-Semitism, in the face of which "unfortunately, resistance in society was too weak," criticizes the role of the Church, and continues: "In this situation the war and the occupation arrived, as well as the horrendous extermination of the Jews by the occupier. An assessment of the test undergone by Poles in this situation cannot, unfortunately, be straightforward and unambiguous."[55] The Holocaust, that is, is seen to have represented a moral test for Poles, different perhaps in severity but not in kind from those faced by Poles in relation to other non-Poles. Underlying this self-examination, though only implicit in Lipski's comments about Poles and Jews, is a Christian model: the goal is to confess one's sins and ask those sinned against for forgiveness.

Lipski's essay and similar writings primarily circulated clandestinely among the intelligentsia. Simultaneously, however, two noisy polemics suddenly thrust the issue of Polish-Jewish relations during the Holocaust into the center of public discourse. In both cases, the catalyst was a profoundly disturbing work of art. The first was Claude Lanzmann's film *Shoah*, which premiered in Paris in April 1985. Nine and a half hours long, eleven years in the making, the film contains no documentary images, but consists nearly entirely of footage of Holocaust witnesses—Jews, Germans, and Poles—interviewed by Lanzmann. This testimony, which Lanzmann managed to elicit from his subjects with astounding immediacy, allows us, in the words of Shoshana Felman, "to see *three different performances of the act of seeing*." We see Jews who see but do not understand what they see, refusing to accept that their destination is death. We see Germans who speak in euphemisms; in place of their human victims they see "disembodied verbal substitutes." And we see Polish bystanders who see, but "do not quite *look*, they

avoid looking directly, and thus they *overlook* at once their responsibility and their complicity as witnesses."[56] The bystanders that
Lanzmann presents are nearly all peasants and residents of small
towns who lived near death camps and transports; except for Jan
Karski, no intelligentsia and no heroes are among them. They sometimes express sympathy for the Jews, but also repeat common anti-
Semitic stereotypes. In one remarkable scene, the only Jewish
survivor of a small town, whom Lanzmann brought back to Poland
from Israel, stands on the church steps among his well-wishing
former neighbors. A procession of white-clad young girls emerges
from the church, in which, we have just learned, Jews during the
war were locked before being gassed. Suddenly one of the people
on the steps recounts a story implying that the fate of the Jews was
just punishment for their betrayal of God, and the camera focuses
on the survivor's face, now bereft of its smile. This juxtaposition,
an extraordinary epiphany of a millennium of Christian-Jewish
relations, exemplifies the film's art. Its goal is not to accuse, but ultimately to make whole, to begin to move, through silences and
fragments, toward an adequate witnessing of the Holocaust.

Poles, unfortunately, first encountered the film in another way:
as the headline "Poland Accused" in a Paris newspaper. The situation was exacerbated by Lanzmann himself, whose public statements, unlike his film, were filled with accusations against Poles,
suggesting, for example, that concentration camps had been built
in Poland because of Polish anti-Semitism. Such provocations were
sufficient for the Polish press to slip into the musty rhetoric of conspiracy, describing the film as "yet another attempt to justify Nazi
crimes and erase from European memory German plans for the
biological annihilation also of the Polish nation."[57] Such statements
were coupled with an official Polish protest to the French government about the film's "insulting . . . insinuation of [Polish] complicity in Nazi genocide," a demand that the film be banned from
French television, and even a threat of breaking off French language teaching in Poland. By the end of the year, however, the
government had moderated its rhetoric. The "Polish" parts of *Shoah*
(about one-third of the film), followed by a discussion by "experts,"
were shown on Polish television; subsequently the entire film was
released in several theaters. Meanwhile the government began to

reestablish relations with Israel, broken off twenty years previously, and General Jaruzelski met in New York with Edgar Bronfman, president of the World Jewish Congress.[58] In typical Socialist bloc fashion, much energy was devoted to discerning in all this the government's hidden design, but it is more probable that here, finally, was a Polish government reacting to events in knee-jerk western style.

Shoah provoked impassioned and unprecedented discussion in Poland not only in the official, Catholic, and underground presses "but also in hundreds of thousands of Polish homes."[59] This response was due to the role of television, which gave the entire nation direct access to the disputed images; as in the West, the complete film had only a limited audience when it was shown in theaters. For perhaps the first time in postwar Poland, an issue received thoroughgoing public exposure in a manner, like the government's response, more reminiscent of western than of Communist societies. That this issue concerned Polish-Jewish relations during the Holocaust was hardly a coincidence.

Occasionally, the film met with approval and understanding; thus the Solidarity leader Jacek Kuroń wrote:

> Jews were condemned to death because they were Jews. In other words, people were condemned because they were people. And this changed human history in a fundamental way. All of us who lived here in these killing grounds emerged maimed, and this the film *Shoah* shows very well. . . . What was the difference between Poles and Jews during the occupation? It was the following: that on a trolley through the ghetto on my way to a swimming pool I watched people dying on the other side of the wall.[60]

The great majority of responses, however, denounced the film as "anti-Polish," as an unjust accusation against Poles that required a defense of Polish national honor and morality. Here the differences among the official, Catholic, and underground press tended to be minimal, although the tone of the official press was certainly more strident.[61] The film was attacked for its choice of witnesses, "dirty" and "primitive," for its supposed manipulation of them, and for its omission of testimony from anyone involved in saving

Jews. Much energy was devoted to remembering Polish help to Jews during the war; the work of Władysław Bartoszewski was frequently cited. The unique dangers of trying to assist Jews in Poland were stressed, as was the great number of Poles awarded the Righteous Among Nations medal by the Israeli government for saving Jews. The attitude of Poles was contrasted to that of western bystanders and especially the French, who, it was re-called, had collaborated politically with the Germans and even participated in deporting Jews to death camps.[62] The complexity of Polish witnessing of the Holocaust tended to be reduced, in a word, to venality or heroism, guilt or innocence: the dualism of traditional Christian morality. Meanwhile, however, the notion that there had been no difference between the fate of Jews and Poles during the war slipped out of public discourse.

This polemic had just begun to recede from public awareness when another similar one exploded. It was occasioned by a poem by Czesław Miłosz, entitled "Biedny chrześcijanin patrzy na getto" (A poor Christian looks at the ghetto), and a response to it by the literary critic Jan Błoński entitled "Biedni Polacy patrzą na getto" (The poor Poles look at the ghetto), published in *Tygodnik Pow-szechny* in January 1987.[63] Błoński begins by citing an imaginary conversation typical of what ensued when Poles traveling abroad were inevitably asked why Poles were anti-Semites. After tracing characteristic volleys of accusation and rebuttal concerning events beginning in the Middle Ages and ending in 1968, he concludes: "And so on, endlessly. The debates of historians resemble this dis-cussion." To escape the cycle he turns to Miłosz's powerful, diffi-cult, claustrophobic poem, one of two that the poet wrote in 1943, as he watched the ghetto burn from the "Aryan" side of Warsaw. The other, "Campo dei Fiore," which has also been widely re-printed and discussed in Poland in recent years, is about the "happy throngs [that] laughed/on a beautiful Warsaw Sunday" as they played on a merry-go-round outside the ghetto walls, oblivious to "those dying alone, forgotten by the world."[64]

"A Poor Christian Looks at the Ghetto" begins with a descrip-tion of a terrible "tearing . . . trampling . . . breaking" followed by fire and the collapse of roofs and walls. Then, underground, the poet confronts a peculiar apparition: a "guardian mole . . . [w]ith a small red lamp fastened to his forehead," who counts burned bodies, "distinguishes human ashes." He concludes:

> I am afraid, so afraid of the guardian mole.
> He has swollen eyelids, like a Patriarch
> Who has sat much in the light of candles
> Reading the great book of the species.
>
> What will I tell him, I, a Jew of the New Testament,
> Waiting two thousand years for the second coming of Jesus?
> My broken body will deliver me to his sight
> And he will count me among the helpers of death:
> The uncircumcised.[65]

Błoński interprets:

> This mole burrows underground but also underneath our conscious-
> ness. This is the feeling of guilt [wina] which we do not want to
> admit. Buried under the rubble, among the bodies of the Jews, the
> "uncircumcised" fears that he may be counted among the murder-
> ers. . . . [The poem] makes tangible something which is not fully
> comprehended, something that was, and perhaps still is, in other
> people's as much as in the poet's own psyche, but in an obscure,
> blurred, muffled shape. When we read such a poem, we understand
> ourselves better, since that which had been evading us until now is
> made palpable.[66]

What Błoński is pointing to in the Polish psyche, "blurred" and "muffled" under strata of rationalization and denial, is the her-itage of unacceptable, unmasterable guilt born of witnessing the Holocaust. It is the memory of guilt that resulted not from having committed any crime, but from the catastrophic intersection of two sets of conditions: witnessing the Holocaust in the context of the unique history of Polish-Jewish relations. Błoński expresses this by speaking first of all of the Jew as someone who "shared our home, lived on our soil, [whose] blood has remained in the walls, seeped into the soil, [and] has also entered into ourselves, into our memory." But this Jew is simultaneously someone who, insofar as he "shared our home," was made to "live in the cellar."[67] And as a result:

> Eventually, when we lost our home, and when, within that home, the invaders set to murdering Jews, did we show solidarity towards them? How many of us decided that it was none of our business? There were also those (and I leave out of account common criminals) who were secretly pleased that Hitler had solved for us "the Jewish problem." We could not even welcome and honor the survivors, even if they were embittered, disoriented and perhaps sometimes tiresome.[68]

But Poles have blocked the memory of this part of their history because "when we consider the past, we want to derive moral advantages from it . . . we want to be *completely* clean. We want to be also—and only—victims." This desire, however, is "underpinned by fear," accompanied by "the horror," by "the mole who burrows in our subconscious." How to get rid of this mole? It may not, finally, be possible to do so. To the extent that it is, Błoński suggests that the only remedy is, first, to see the past fully, without defensiveness, and then to "acknowledge our own guilt, and ask for forgiveness." But forgiveness for what? Certainly not for participation in the Holocaust, but for what Błoński terms "shared responsibility" [*współ-wina*], and above all, for the Polish attitude toward Jews *before* the Holocaust.[69]

Błoński's article ignited a ferocious controversy. In the words of Jerzy Turowicz, the editor of *Tygodnik Powszechny:* "When we printed the article, I was, as were my colleagues, aware that it would be an event to which there would certainly be a strong reaction. The reaction was greater than anything known in the course of the 42 years during which I have edited that paper. I cannot remember any article which provoked such a strong reaction on the part of the readers."[70] As with *Shoah,* most of this reaction, published in the pages of *Tygodnik Powszechny* and throughout the Polish press, was negative. What was rejected above all was the notion that Poles needed forgiveness from Jews. First of all, Błoński was misread as affirming Polish participation in the Holocaust. This misreading was reinforced when Poles were informed in western accounts of the controversy that at last they were accepting joint responsibility with the Germans for the murder of the Jews. Błoński's article also made Polish-Jewish relations before the Holocaust a subject of intense public discussion. Here too, most writers rejected the notion that Poles had wronged Jews; many denied the existence of anti-Semitism in Poland altogether. In defending Polish attitudes, many writers drew on the full spectrum of prewar Endek discourse: Jews had exploited Poles economically, they had been hostile to Polish independence, they had overwhelmed Polish professions and cultural life, in short, they had constituted a "foreign element" at war with Poland, Poles, and Polishness. There were also allusions, often veiled, to the *Żydokomuna*. For Jerzy Turowicz, the nearly two hundred letters and articles received in response to Błoński's article, while in no way comparable to an opinion research poll, "disclosed the existence of anti-Semitism still in Poland, today more than forty years after the war." Although "one should not exaggerate the size of this phenomenon," his mail convinced him that it was "an attitude which cannot easily be uprooted or overcome, and one that even at times regenerates itself."[71]

Nevertheless, although few in numbers, the polemic also included voices of support for Błoński and even the refinement of his ideas. One young observer, Ewa Koźmińska, made the reaction to Błoński's article the subject of a master's dissertation. Among her conclusions was that Poles, having witnessed the Holocaust, were confronted by an unwanted sense of guilt resulting from the fact that regardless of whether they could have done more to save Jews, as a nation Poles had survived, but Polish Jews had not.[72] Andrzej Bryk, the scion of a family rooted in Home Army traditions, used the occasion to define the dilemma of Polish witnessing of the Holocaust as that of "a Polish community raised in a largely anti-semitic culture and subconsciously accepting Jews as aliens suddenly in a situation where its culture offered no moral means to resist an easy acceptance of the fact of the annihilation of the Jews by the Germans." The result, which has molded Polish consciousness since the Holocaust, is what Bryk terms "the hidden complex of the Polish mind"—the inability of Poles to to process the witnessing of the Holocaust, in contrast to other national memories and particularly those of the war years, according to any "clear-cut dichotomous model" of morality.[73]

The polemics around *Shoah* and Błoński's essay were both rooted in attempts at a direct confrontation, bereft of mediating systems of meaning, with the dilemma of witnessing the destruction of Jews on Polish soil. The difficulty of this endeavor was reflected in the polemics it evoked, in the repeated but frustrated attempts to return the experience of witnessing to accepted ideological and moral frameworks. These polemics also opened public discourse to an unprecedented variety of voices. Behind the "opportunism" of the state and the "morality" of the opposition, behind, that is, the polarity of public discourse as it had existed for over a decade, one began to distinguish a host of ordinary opinions, reflecting a range of "correctness." This was entirely appropriate considering that Poland in the late 1980s was a society on the verge of another critical transformation: from embattled totalitarianism to democracy. Shortly to swell into the cacophony well known in the West, such "voices of the people" began to emerge precisely in confronting the "hidden complex of the Polish mind."

Two years after Błoński's article was published, another, more explosive, controversy about Poland and the Holocaust burst into international attention. It pitted Poles and Jews against each other and escalated into the most serious crisis in Christian-Jewish relations since Vatican Council II. The dispute about the presence of a Carmelite convent at Auschwitz had been incubating for most of the 1980s.[74] It was fueled, first of all, by transformations in Polish national self-perception, by the movement away from the bankrupt narrative of internationalism and toward the "patriotic-symbolic-religious language" of reemerging "traditions." What this entailed at Auschwitz—or as it is known to Poles, Oświęcim (pronounced "oshvienchim")—was the emergence of a symbolic palimpsest: not the eradication of the old narrative with its marginalization of the memory of Jews, but the development of a new narrative layer that only partially covered the old. This new layer of meaning consisted of the proliferation of religiously sanctified sites of Polish martyrdom. These sites included the cell where Father Maximilian Kolbe awaited death;[75] a site connected to Edith Stein, a murdered Carmelite nun who had been a convert from Judaism; the bullet-scarred Wall of Death, before which thousands of Polish prisoners were shot. These sites, nearly all in the work camp area, marked by plaques, often by crosses, and strewn with flowers, attained the status of national shrines, the objects of pilgrimage and prayer by millions of Poles. To bear witness to the "victory of faith and love," as the pope had described Father Kolbe's martyrdom, and to pray for "all the victims" of Auschwitz, in 1984 a group of Carmelite nuns moved into a building abutting its walls and raised a twenty-foot cross in front of their new home.

The controversy that was to erupt depended as well on developments in western perception. To the rest of the world and to Jews above all, the place that Poles called "Oświęcim" was known as "Auschwitz," a word with a very different signification.[76] Because of its scale and probably also because of its twofold function as both death camp and slave labor camp—as a result of which most camp survivors and testimonies emerged from Auschwitz and not from Bełżec, Sobibór, Majdanek, or Treblinka—by the 1980s Auschwitz and its chimneys had come to represent the universe of absolute evil associated with the word "Holocaust." For Jews and for the West, Auschwitz became a symbol of unassimilable, unfathomable evil, "a black hole of meaning,"[77] a place before which even language crumbles, and to which the most authentic response, as Elie Wiesel has insisted, is silence. So long as Poland, in western eyes, continued to exist in a never-never land behind the Iron Curtain, there was little inclination to connect the word Auschwitz with the place called Oświęcim. In the 1980s, this isolation began to be broken, and when westerners started to look, they discovered a site visited annually by hundreds of thousands of people, most of them Polish tourists and secondary school students, containing ruins, restored barracks, watchtowers and barbed wire, a museum, offices, parking lot, souvenir shops, and snack bar. This place, moreover, scarcely referred to Jews, but bore the signs of forty years of Communist and Polish Catholic commemorative activity, climaxed by a new addition: the convent and the cross.

Jewish protests about the inappropriateness of a Catholic place of worship at Auschwitz did not begin, nevertheless, until the existence of the convent was rather inappropriately publicized by

Catholics themselves. In 1985, a Belgian Catholic organization issued an appeal for support of the convent, "which will become a spiritual fortress and a guarantee of the conversion of strayed brothers from our countries as well as proof of our desire to erase the outrages so often done to the Vicar of Christ."[78] This example of "Catholic triumphalism," widely publicized in European Jewish circles, coming on the heels of the pope's canonization of Father Kolbe, led Edgar Bronfman to raise the issue of the convent with Polish authorities later that year. Direct negotiations between representatives of European Jews and Polish and Western European Catholics began at Geneva in 1986 and ended in an agreement signed the following year to move the convent to a new Catholic center to be built near Auschwitz within two years. When the deadline arrived, however, ground breaking on the new center had not even begun and considerable opposition to the agreement had developed in the Polish Church and among lay Catholics.

Amid accelerating Jewish protests, in July 1989, a group of American Jews wrapped in prayer shawls, led by Rabbi Avi Weiss of New York, climbed over the convent fence and staged a noisy demonstration in front of the convent. They were roughed up and expelled from the grounds by local workers. This small event, echoing at this site, triggered a remarkable fallout of historical memory entirely incommensurable with the event itself. *Newsweek*, for example, described the event as "one of the worst cases of antisemitism in Poland since the Communist Party forced thousands of Jews to leave the country in 1968."[79] Referring to the failure of the nuns and a local priest to intervene with his attackers, Rabbi Weiss accused them of treating Jews "just like your Church did fifty years ago."[80] In Poland, the intrusion into the Camelite convent, whose regulations prohibited all contact with the outside world, was termed an "invasion," and was seen as the climax of an international Jewish campaign directed against the Church's work at Oświęcim. The actions of Rabbi Weiss and his group could thereby resonate through layers of popular stereotypes beginning with ritual-murder accusations and ending with the "memory" of Jewish Stalinists arresting priests and closing churches.

For Poles, moreover, the controversy erupted at yet another turning point in their history. In May 1988, a new generation of workers amid a new series of strikes demanded the relegalization of Solidarity. As a result of roundtable talks in early 1989 between the opposition and the weakening government, by July reports of Rabbi Weiss's "invasion" shared the front pages of Polish newspapers with accounts of the first free election campaign in sixty years. The victory of the opposition marked its obsolescence. Strains had already begun to develop between the Church and Solidarity as well as within Solidarity itself. Now, faced with the opportunities of electoral politics, the opposition began to fragment into competing factions. These would soon become political parties, which, despite predictions to the contrary, assumed a roughly traditional configuration of pluralist Left to chauvinist Right. In the new Poland, the Church would champion an agenda of religious education in the public schools and the banning of abortion. The birth of "normal" Polish politics was linked to a fundamental social transformation: the emergence into public discourse of a full spectrum of popular opinion. As elsewhere in Eastern Europe, this development included, especially at its beginnings, the expression of resentments and hatreds long suppressed by the system, but also, in its own way, by the opposition.

In the weeks that followed Rabbi Weiss's eviction from the convent, readers of the newly uncensored Polish press followed the unfolding controversy in unaccustomed detail. They read reports of subsequent, larger Jewish demonstrations and of their confrontation by angry crowds of local Poles, often expressing crudely anti-Semitic opinions.[81] Sister Teresa, the mother superior of the convent, interviewed in the Polish-American press, claimed, among other things, that because three of the Catholic negotiators at the Geneva Conference were actually Jews, "naturally" the outcome of the conference was "one-sided in favor of World Jewry." She concluded: "You can tell the Americans that we are not moving a single inch. And like the Pauline monks who bravely withstood the Swedish siege of their monastery at Częstochowa in 1655, we are here to stay!"[82] Meanwhile Cardinal Franciszek Macharski of Kraków, in whose diocese Auschwitz was located, citing "a violent campaign of accusations and insinuations on the part of some Jewish circles in the West . . . insulting aggression expressed not only in words," called for the abrogation of the Geneva accord.[83] This was followed by a homily delivered by Cardinal Józef Glemp, the primate of Poland, at the national shrine of the Black Madonna of Często-chowa, in which the cardinal spoke of making peace "with those nations towards whom resentment has remained because of the war . . . Germans and Jews." Implying that Rabbi Weiss's group had planned to murder the nuns, and accusing Jews in general, among other things, of controlling the world's media, Cardinal Glemp concluded: "If there is no antipolonism, there will be no antisemitism in us."[84] Glemp, appointed to his position by the pope, but whose sympathies lay less with the Catholic intelligentsia than with Endek ideologues, outraged many in the opposition and was criticized in the newly legalized Solidarity press. In Israel, Prime Minister Yitzhak Shamir responded to Glemp's remarks by declaring that Poles "suck [anti-Semitism] in with their mother's milk."[85] The controversy began to subside only with direct pressure from the Vatican; in February 1990, construction commenced on the Catholic center to which the nuns were expected to move. But three years later, with the new building completed, the nuns were still in their convent and there continued to be considerable sentiment in the Church and among lay Catholics against their moving. The resolution of the issue required direct papal intervention. In April 1993, as Jewish groups threatened to boycott the commemorations of the fiftieth anniversary of the Warsaw Ghetto Uprising, a letter from the pope to the nuns specifically asked them to move.[86] Two years later, while the nuns were gone, the twenty-foot cross still remained.

7

Memory Regained?
1989–1995

Besieging the most widely accepted Polish understanding of the war years with a notion of the Holocaust developed in the "free world," the convent controversy accompanied the Polish entry into that world. In Poland, as throughout Eastern Europe, this entry has wrought overwhelmingly rapid change whose meaning it is still difficult to assess. The establishment of a democratic political system and a capitalist economy on the ruins of forty years of Polish "people's democracy" has led to phenomena that are by turns comfortably predictable, unexpectedly hopeful, and darkly ominous. Such variety certainly applies to matters connected to the "Jewish question" and the memory of the Holocaust.

As throughout Eastern Europe, the fall of communism immediately released swarms of petty traders and primitive commerce into the streets of Polish cities. In the bazaarlike atmosphere of the first months of freedom, as hoodlums flourished and the police seemed to vanish, vicious anti-Semitic graffiti proliferated and remained untouched for months, Jewish cemeteries and institutions were vandalized, and amid stalls, trucks, card tables, and blankets overflowing with a dizzying assortment of tawdry goods, anti-Semitic tracts were prominently displayed. In the first election campaigns, candidates representing liberal views were often attacked as Jews. The most notorious case occurred during the first presidential elections in 1990 when Lech Wałęsa ran against his erstwhile ally, Tadeusz Mazowiecki. Mazowiecki, a member of the Catholic intelligentsia and of *szlachta* descent, whose base of support was in Solidarity's left wing, was believed by a significant portion of the electorate to be a Jew. Wałęsa found it politically expedient to wonder out loud during the campaign why some of his opponents "conceal their origins." Succeeding governments as well have been perceived by many Poles as filled with Jews, as have liberal political parties and newspapers.[1]

Over the following years, nevertheless, as Polish streets began to look more "European" and the new political and economic system maintained its balance, both anti-Semitic graffiti and the use of the "Jewish question" in Polish politics began to fade. Despite many fears to the contrary, and unlike elsewhere in Europe, overtly anti-Semitic political parties gained little following. Bolesław Tejkowski, whose entire political program consists of the struggle against Jews, whom he accuses of running both the Polish government and the Vatican, became the subject of criminal and psychiatric investigations. In October 1994, he was convicted of slander and "promoting national strife" and given a one-year suspended prison sentence. He awaits another trial for circulating anti-Semitic leaflets in Polish schools.[2] Poland has developed few skinheads. Hooliganism directed against Jews has been substantially lower than that reported in Germany and France, for example. The only incident of mass ethnic violence, termed a "pogrom" by the press, occurred in June 1991 in the eastern town of Mława, when, after a car accident in which a young Gypsy driver severely injured several Poles, Polish residents destroyed the Gypsy section of the town.

For the first time in postwar history, anti-Semitism has been frequently and publicly discussed, with particular attention devoted to the previously taboo subject of the immediate postwar years. Excerpts from Krystyna Kersten's research on the postwar roots of anti-Jewish stereotypes were published in the daily press, as were polemics sparked by issues ranging from demands for the rehabilitation of the Fascist NSZ as heroes of the anti-Communist resistance[3] to government attempts to ban publication of the *Protocols of the Elders of Zion* and *Mein Kampf*.[4] At the same time, the first public opinion polls made it possible to assess attitudes to Jews in contemporary Polish society. These polls revealed higher levels of anti-Jewish sentiment in Poland than elsewhere in Europe except Slovakia. Antipathy to Jews, however, was dwarfed by hostility to numerous other groups. Figures for 1990–91, for example, show 19.5 percent of respondents declaring a dislike for Jews, 21 percent disliking Blacks, 23 percent Rumanians, 28 percent Russians, 29.5 percent Arabs, 38.5 percent Ukrainians, 39 percent Germans, and 45.5 percent disliking Gypsies.[5] One poll revealed that when asked with whom they would prefer to share a seat in class, secondary school students ranked Jews as slightly less desirable than Germans and the children of Communists, slightly more desirable than Russians, and much more desirable than those infected with HIV, Gypsies, homosexuals, or the mentally ill.[6] Yet Poles' attitudes toward Jews at least in one respect seem qualitatively different from their attitudes toward other groups; if positive and indifferent responses are tabulated as well, it emerges that attitudes toward Jews are the most "emotionally loaded." In contemporary Poland, in the words of sociologist Alina Cała, "Jews can be liked or hated; it is hard to be indifferent to them."[7]

To probe this "emotional load," in May 1992, a detailed questionnaire entitled "Poles, Jews, and Other Nationalities" was administered to a carefully selected sampling of subjects. The results were then analyzed by a team of sociologists from the Jewish Historical Insitute (ŻIH).[8] How, first of all, do Poles learn about Jews? Fifty-nine percent of respondents mentioned television, film, and radio; 48 percent mentioned books, newspapers, and magazines. The great proponderance of this media exposure has only come in the last several years. In contrast, the two other major sources of information mentioned by respondents have been a constant: discussions with family (48 percent) and friends (30 percent). Comparatively unimportant, the study shows, has been the influence of educational institutions; only 14 percent of respondents mentioned school and only 11 percent mentioned the Church as a source of knowledge about Jews. The legacy of forty years of communism is apparent; for better and for worse, it is above all personal narrative, transmitted behind closed doors by family and friends, that has been relied upon for making sense of the world.

Analyzing the nature of anti-Jewish feeling in contemporary Poland, the study suggests the necessity for distinguishing between "traditional" and "modern" anti-Semitism.[9] Although the former, primarily religiously based and local in perspective, appeared rather weak, the latter, a "political-ideological" worldview that has varied little throughout the world over the past hundred years, proved rather strong. Thus 55 percent of respondents believed that Jews have too much influence internationally, and 58 percent agreed that Jews control most of the world's finances. In all, 60 percent of the subjects chose at least one response that can be considered anti-Jewish.[10] Many responses were contradictory, characteristic of what the researchers term "neurotic attitudes." For example, most respondents affirmed that Polish society as a whole "does not like Jews," but an even greater number denied that Poles should be considered anti-Semites.[11]

Although the study found relatively little correlation between attitudes toward Jews and education or income, age turned out to be highly significant. As expected, the youngest respondents evinced the least antipathy to Jews. On the other hand, the oldest respondents were not those who most disliked Jews. For the generation of Poles over seventy, with strong memories of prewar Jewish life, anti-Semitic attitudes proved to be primarily of the "traditional" variety and were accompanied by a relatively high degree of sympathy for Jews as well. Rather, antipathy to Jews in the form of modern anti-Semitic beliefs appeared strongest in those born between 1924 and 1940, that is, those who came to maturity during World War II and immediately after. Could this response be linked to their experience of the imposition of Communist rule in the years just after the war? The study undercuts this hypothesis, for relatively few Poles, even of the generation in question, continue to associate Jews with communism.[12] One is left, therefore, with the conclusion, startling to the researchers, that it is precisely those who were "young witnesses of the Nazi crimes [who] manifest the greatest antipathy to Jews!"[13]

When asked directly about the Holocaust, nearly 90 percent of the respondents affirmed that Poles had done all they could to save Jews, and nearly 70 percent, that Poles had no reason to feel guilty about Jewish accusations that Poles had not helped them during the war. Ten percent of respondents felt that Poles did have reason to feel guilty, 12 percent felt it was hard to say, and another 10 percent replied that they could not answer such a question. Although nearly half agreed that Jews had suffered more than Poles during the war, one-third of the respondents stated that both had suffered equally and 6 percent replied that Poles had suffered more.[14] The interviewers encountered particular reticence when they tried to elicit information about Jews that had been passed down from older family members. Difficulties multiplied when the subject was the Holocaust. Such recollections were not only rare but, in the words of one interviewer, "banal and vague." "One is constantly struck by the enigmatic nature of the information and the [respondents'] emotional distance from its content," he continues and wonders: "Do family narratives, therefore, conceal memories of the Holocaust, and why?"[15] From the perspective we have developed in these pages, both this paradox and the preceding one, that the most powerful aversion to Jews is to be found precisely among those who witnessed the Holocaust in their youth, emerge as the traces in contemporary Poland of half a century's repression of the memory of the murdered Jew.

There are other, very different, traces as well. Existing side by side with the anti-Jewish sentiment that polls have revealed, the "Jewish revival" that began in the 1980s shows no sign of abating and, indeed, continues to grow. The interest in Jews, Judaism, and Jewish culture, it is important to note, has entirely transcended the political context in which it was rooted and that was partly used to explain it. Festivals of Jewish culture, modeled on the highly successful annual spring festival in Kazimierz, the old Jewish quarter of Kraków, are increasingly popular, as are "Jewish" restaurants, cafés, shops, and souvenirs, as well as competing brands of "kosher" vodka. Although Jewish travel to Poland has greatly expanded and there is a joke about German tourists paying to see Poles disguised as Jews, much of the interest and market for Judaica remains Polish and includes a new middle class with disposable income.

The first half of the 1990s has also witnessed a wave of "Jewish" publications that has already far surpassed the output of the entire preceding decade. One example is the phenomenal growth of interest in the work of I. B. Singer. Ten years ago, it was considered remarkable when four works by Singer were published in Poland. But in post-Communist Poland, with publishing finally geared to a market, resulting in hard times for many literary authors, the first half of the 1990s have witnessed the publication of twenty-one books by Singer![16] With the Jewish Historical Institute under new leadership and the establishment of new centers of scholarship at other Polish institutions, the study of Polish Jewish history, in various contexts, has also blossomed. On one hand, Polish secondary school teachers have been attending seminars organized by the Jewish Historical Institute on Jewish history and the Holocaust. On the other hand, an international conference entitled "Czy obojętność może zabić?" (Can indifference kill?), dedicated to Christian-Jewish relations during the Holocaust, was held in Warsaw in July 1993. Three months later in Warsaw, the first international conference on the history of Yiddish theater was organized amid a festival of Jewish films, art exhibitions, concerts, and theater.[17] In the same month, the privately funded Shalom Foundation announced the winners of a contest among Polish secondary school students for the best essays on the subject of Jewish culture in Poland. There had been four thousand entries.

Belying the popular western conception that there are no Jews left in Poland, an organized Jewish community has also revived. According to official statistics, in 1993 this community numbered 4,415; those involved in Jewish affairs most often cite the figures 5 to 10,000.[18] Much of the leadership of the organized community consists of the "new Jews" of the 1980s, now more comfortable with their identity. Alongside the old organizations, they have been active in new ones, ranging from Jewish day-care centers and schools to a President's Council on Polish-Jewish Relations and a Polish-Israeli Friendship Society, the latter particularly active since Poland's exchange of ambassadors with Israel. Joint Polish-Israeli projects include the revision of school textbooks in Poland and Israel dealing with the history of Polish-Jewish relations.[19] Perhaps most surprising has been the emergence of a generation in their twenties and younger, claiming to be Polish Jews. They are often the children or grandchildren of "hidden Jews" who remained in Poland after the war, typically with a non-Jewish spouse, but continued to hide their origins. Some of their descendants now study Jewish religion and culture, attend Jewish summer camp, and among other things, have founded a Maccabi sports club and a periodical audaciously entitled *Jidełe* (The little Jew, recalling the Polish word *żydek*). Much of their activity is funded by the American philanthropist Ronald Lauder, who also supports Poland's two rabbis, Pinchas Joskowicz and Michael Schudrich.

The years since the fall of communism have also witnessed an expansion of the Holocaust-related commemorative activity initiated in the 1980s. At the sites of death camps and ghettos, often with the participation of Holocaust survivors from abroad, new tablets and monuments have risen and many kinds of gatherings have been organized. The fading of the meaning of such activity as political resistance seems in no way to have diminished the urge to commemorate—just the opposite. In the absence of opposition from the state, indeed with its support, such commemorations now also celebrate their own possibility; commemorating the Holocaust becomes an affirmation of the victory over communism and the emergence of historical truth. This was the case at Sobibór, for example, where a tablet referring to 250,000 murdered "Soviet prisoners of war, Jews, Poles, and Gypsies" was replaced by one commemorating "over 250,000 Jews and about 1,000 Poles." Similarly, a March of Death in 1992 that traced the steps of Jews herded by the Nazis from the town of Rembertów to Falenica (and thence by train to Treblinka) fifty years previously also echoed the first such symbolic march, organized clandestinely by a handful of "new Jews" eight years earlier. This time the marchers did not have to tread so lightly and, in collaboration with the local Solidarity committee, dedicated a monument at the march's terminus.[20]

On the occasion of the republication of Jan Błoński's essay "The Poor Poles Look at the Ghetto," a reviewer hailed the author for laying the foundation for the "contemporary history of our conscience," but wondered how far the discussion had progressed in eight years. "When, without fear of anyone's hysterical reaction, will it be possible . . . to learn the whole truth about the *szmalcownicy,* about the trade called *pożydowski* [in abandoned Jewish possessions], about the sometimes tragic fate of Jews already after the war."[21] There have, nevertheless, been explorations that have begun to plumb these depths as well. These include Barbara Engelking's pioneering study of the Holocaust based on the oral testimony of survivors still living in Poland; Piotr Matywiecki's attempt to wrestle into speech the "nothingness" of the Warsaw Ghetto, where he was conceived; and the memoirs of Calel Perechodnik, a Jewish policeman in the Otwock ghetto. These memoirs, whose author did not survive the war, lay unpublished for nearly half a century in the Jewish Historical Institute. They offer a unique and disturbing vision of an unheroic, morally compromised world. We learn of Poles greedily awaiting the possessions of their Jewish neighbors ("You won't need them where you're going") and later stripping the bodies of the dead, of Jews expelling their own family members from crowded hiding places, and of Perechodnik himself who, tricked by his German superiors, brought his wife and daughter to a death transport, which he, however, managed to avoid.[22]

There was also Paweł Łoziński's documentary film *Miejsce urodzenia* (Birthplace). It follows the writer Henryk Grynberg, a child survivor of the Holocaust, as he returns from America in 1992 to the countryside of his birth to investigate the circumstances of his father's death during the war. The film not only documents Grynberg's confrontation with a peasant who probably helped murder his father but also Grynberg's astonishing discovery of his father's remains. When the film was shown on Polish television, a scene in which a witness identifies the murderers was deleted and replaced by a statement explaining the need to protect the witness. In an interview about the making of the film, the director speaks of meeting a peasant woman who continues to conceal the fact that she had hidden Jews during the war. "I'm afraid," she told him. "What if someone breaks into my house to look for gold under the floor?"[23] This comment, suggesting the ongoing life of fifty-year-old fears, recalls the words of an old peasant, spoken to one of the ŻIH interviewers: "In Międzyrzec many houses were Jewish but no one today comes [for them]. People have settled in these houses and live there. How it will be in the future, we still don't know; maybe they'll still ask for them back."[24]

A different kind of settling of accounts involved the controversy over Jerzy Kosinski's celebrated novel, *The Painted Bird*. First published in the United States in 1965 (in Poland not until two decades later), it chronicles the horrific odyssey of a young boy attempting to survive the Holocaust amid inconceivably brutish and vengeful peasants in an unspecified corner of Eastern Europe. Partly because of Kosinski's comments, the book was treated as autobiographic, a fact that contributed to its stunning success precisely as, on the heels of the Eichmann trial, western attention began to focus on the Holocaust. In Poland in the late 1960s, immediately read as a narrative about the *kresy*, *The Painted Bird* figured as an element in the alleged western conspiracy to blame the Holocaust on the Poles. Twenty-nine years after the novel's publication and three years after Kosinski's suicide in New York, a book by Joanna Siedlecka appeared in Poland entitled *Czarny Ptasior* (The ugly black bird) that was based on interviews with peasants who had, at great risk and apparently with great decency, hidden young Kosinski along with his parents during the war.[25] In the United States, the news that Kosinski's novel was indeed fiction inspired reflections, of the sort Kosinski would doubtless have appreciated, on the relationship between writing and reality. In Poland the news functioned in a different context. The enigmatic Kosinski, who lived his life in the company of jet-setting celebrities and the New York demimonde, served as an object lesson in a certain narrative about Poles and Jews. Here was the supremely perfidious Jew who, saved from the Holocaust by simple, good-hearted Poles, based his considerable worldly success on betraying them. Siedlecka's exposé ends, ironically and triumphally, with a Catholic prayer for the salvation of his sinful, tormented soul.[26]

But in Poland over the last several years, as elsewhere in the world, public awareness of the Holocaust has been most strongly linked to a series of commemorations of the fiftieth anniversary of World War II. Fiftieth anniversaries of historical events have a unique character. Although they are the last major ceremonies in which those who participated in the events can still play a role of some importance, their presence no longer dominates the commemoration, and the needs and values of the succeeding generation are usually clearly evident. Ideally there is a sense of one generation "passing the torch" to another. In Poland, however, the significance of these commemorations was much more ambiguous.

The fiftieth anniversary of the Warsaw Ghetto Uprising in April 1993 was the occasion for the most elaborate Holocaust commemoration in Polish history. The vanguard of the commemoration was the Polish media, newly freed to emulate their western counterparts. For a week, newspapers, magazines, television, and radio were filled with news of the ceremonies as well as features examining numerous aspects of Polish Jewish history and the Holocaust. Images of the ghetto wall and of Rabbi Joskowicz, the white-bearded, black-garbed chief rabbi of Poland, were ever present icons on posters, newsstands, and TV screens. Here and there within the media barrage, there were attempts to tap memory. Among the more interesting was a feature published in the leading weekly, *Polityka*, entitled "A Scene I Cannot Forget," consisting of selections from more than a hundred responses to an appeal, jointly sponsored by the Society of Children of the Holocaust, for "unforgettable" memories of the Holocaust. When this feature was repeated a year later, this time with selections from 225 submissions, editor Marian Turski noted the "curious and significant" fact that among the writers who were survivors of the Holocaust and among those who helped Jews survive, "a significant portion (about thirty) wanted to remain anonymous."[27]

The ceremonies included an ecumenical memorial service at the Warsaw synagogue with the unprecedented presence of Church officials, and climaxed with an official wreath-laying ceremony at the ghetto monument that included President Lech Wałęsa; Marek Edelman; the Israeli prime minister, Yitzhak Rabin; and the U.S. vice president, Al Gore. Thousands of Jews from all over the world were present as well. These included elderly Holocaust survivors but also many young Israelis who surrounded the monument in a sea of Israeli flags. Most Poles, lacking the special passes required to approach the monument, watched the proceedings from a great distance behind police barricades. For most of the Jews of the world, the Warsaw ceremonies were hardly central; in the United States that role was filled by the opening of the Holocaust Memorial Museum in Washington, D.C.

Prime Minister Rabin's presence at the ghetto monument was doubtless linked to President Wałęsa's trip to Israel in May 1991, when his speech before the Israeli parliament included the apparently extemporaneous addition "Please forgive us." These words triggered considerable outrage in Poland. Yet they came on the heels of a pastoral letter from Polish bishops, read in all parishes in January 1991, that reaffirmed, on its twenty-fifth anniversary, Vatican II's historic revocation of the charge of deicide against Jews (*Nostra Aetate*) and included the following on the Holocaust and Polish-Jewish relations:

> In spite of so many heroic examples of help on the part of Polish Christians, there were also people who remained indifferent to this incomprehensible tragedy. We are especially disheartened by those among Catholics who in some way were the cause of the death of Jews. If only one Christian could have helped and did not stretch out a helping hand to a Jew during the time of danger or caused his death, we must ask for forgiveness of our Jewish brothers and sisters. We are aware that many of our compatriots still remember the injustices and injuries committed by the postwar communist authorities, in which people of Jewish origin also took part. We must acknowledge, however, that the source of inspiration for their activity was clearly neither their origin nor religion, but the communist ideology, from which the Jews themselves, in fact, suffered many injustices. . . . We express our sincere regret for all the incidents of antisemitism which were committed at any time or by anyone on Polish soil. . . . In expressing our sorrow for all the injustices and harm done to Jews, we cannot forget that we consider untrue and deeply harmful the use by many of the concept of what is called "Polish antisemitism" as an especially threatening form of antisemitism; and in addition, frequently connecting the concentration camps not with those who were actually involved with them, but with Poles in a Poland occupied by the Germans.[28]

With the commemoration of the Jewish uprising pronounced a success by the Polish media, it was expected that the fiftieth anniversary of the Polish uprising, in August 1994, would be the occasion for at least as unambiguous an observance. But in the months before the commemoration, a bitter polemic about Polish-Jewish relations during the Warsaw Uprising suddenly erupted and cast a pall over the preparations. The affair began with an unfortunately worded remark in a review of Calel Perechodnik's memoirs, published in *Gazeta Wyborcza* and written by its chief cultural affairs correspondent, Michał Cichy. Perechodnik, wrote Cichy, survived the death of his family by two years and "even lived through the Warsaw Uprising, when the AK and the NSZ wiped out [*wytłukli*] many survivors of the ghetto."[29] This line, which reached hundreds of thousands of readers, sparked numerous angry letters. One correspondent noted, not unreasonably, that someone with little knowledge of history might conclude that the Warsaw Uprising had been an insurrection of Jews crushed by the AK and NSZ. Another letter, from the World Union of Soldiers of the Home Army, protested "the editorial oversight that permitted a citizen living in Poland to join the foreign attacks of groups abroad hostile to Poland and to defile the history of his own nest."[30]

Admitting that Cichy's words had been an "an inadmissable generalization," *Gazeta Wyborcza* responded by publishing Cichy's documention of Jews murdered by "people in the uniforms of insurrectionists."[31] The article, entitled "Polacy-Żydzi: Czarne karty powstania" (Poles and Jews: black pages of the uprising), weighed the limited available evidence and established with a fair amount of certainty that, at a time when the Nazis murdered two hundred thousand Warsaw residents, twenty to thirty Jews were murdered by soldiers of the AK. The article was prefaced by an introduction written by *Gazeta Wyborcza's* editor-in-chief, Adam Michnik. Michnik hailed the heroism of the uprising, recognized the importance for Poles of this ultimate "lost cause," particularly after the decades-long suppression of its very memory, but affirmed that even the insurrectionists were "ordinary people" with their share of sins. Should one recall their sins now, however, as the fiftieth anniversary of their heroism approached? Michnik concludes: "I believe nevertheless that the ability to confront the dark episodes of one's own heritage is for each nation a test of its democratic maturity. I affirm that Poles have matured to democracy, which means they have the right to the full truth about their own past."[32]

Announcing that few writings had provoked, even before publication, such editorial controversy as Cichy's "Black Pages,"[33] *Gazeta* opened its pages to a debate that lasted several months on whether the article should have been published. Some responses fully supported Michnik's position, but most, including letter writers and those polled by telephone, did not.[34] Many respondents wove together familiar accusations covering the past fifty years of Polish history, implying, more or less openly, that *Gazeta Wyborcza,* established during the roundtable talks in 1989 as the first legal independent newspaper in Poland, was run by Jews. One writer, for example, addressed Michnik as follows:

> Mr. Editor
>
> *Gazeta* has adopted a curious method for the commemoration of the fiftieth anniversary of the Warsaw Uprising. The text "Poles and Jews: Black Pages of the Uprising" is a supplement to the slogan "AK—spit-flecked reactionary dwarf." . . . How would you react— or that group, so thinned by the twists of history, of "Poles of Jewish origin" (I apologize for this tasteless and undignified formulation)—if preceding the ceremonies commemorating half a century since the Ghetto Uprising, there appeared an article, covering five pages in a mass circulation newspaper, condemning Jewish *ubecy* [political police] for torturing and murdering Poles in the years 1944–56? Only Jews. Or another text, for instance enumerating the misdeeds of the so-called Jewish auxiliary police in the ghettos or describing Jewish Gestapo agents. For they existed too. I believe that you would find such materials to be anti-Semitic and provocative. And you would be correct . . . I have, unfortunately, the right to suspect that both Cichy's first "review" as well as the succeeding article did not appear by accident. These are writings with a goal, that of undermining the legend of the Home Army.[35]

Another furious letter, addressed to "Msrs. Michnik, Cichy, or whatever your real names are," and advising them to move to Israel if they hated Poland so much, included a remarkable memory of the war years. The writer recounts how her family helped Jews during the war and then recalls the following incident:

> I was walking in the street with my mother when a group of pitiful Jews under German guard passed by. Mother gave me bread and said: "Give it to those poor wretches; you're little, the soldiers won't notice you." That in fact is what happened. The woman to whom I gave the bundle passed near my mother and said: "Remember, Polish women, when they finish with us, they'll start in on you." As if

they weren't at us every day. I asked Mother: "Why is that lady mad at us?" But I don't remember her answer.[36]

Congealed, layer upon layer, in this dense narrative, rooted in a child's witnessing of the Holocaust, are most of the Polish defenses that, for half a century, have been summoned against the memory of that witnessing. First, there is the conviction that "we did our best to help them"; then, the retort "Didn't we suffer as well?"; and finally, the bitter "lesson," recalling Zofia Kossak: "No matter what we do, they hate us."

The glorious "lost cause" of the Warsaw Uprising has been embraced by Poles above all as a statement about the steadfastness of human values. This is how one veteran described its meaning soon after the anniversary commemoration: "To everything [the Germans] brought to our land: contempt for humanity [człowieczeństwo], hatred, crime as a principle, to nihilism as an 'anti-value' we counterposed what we had succeeded in preserving in our hearts: the value of love of fatherland, the value of always responding to a cry for help, the value of human brotherhood."[37] Into this purest expression of Polish historical identity, it required only a poorly phrased sentence to summon the image of the murdered Jew. The commemoration of the Warsaw Uprising, successful in the eyes of the Polish media, was nevertheless haunted by an apparition. It was an apparition that not only undermined particular values—for example, that of "always responding to a cry for help"—but also carried the terrifying potential of nullifying all values, all attempts at discovering meaning at the heart of so much death.

In January 1995, Poland observed the fiftieth anniversary of the liberation of Auschwitz. During the years preceding the commemoration, Auschwitz/Oświęcim had begun to show signs of overcoming the strife it had provoked in the past. First of all, the composition of its visitors began to change. While only 5 of the 22 million people who visited Auschwitz over the past fifty years came from outside Poland, since the fall of communism half the visitors have been non-Polish, primarily Germans and Jews from all over the world, including eleven thousand young Israelis annually.[38] In response to the new visitors and in the aftermath of the bitterness inspired by the convent controversy, post-Communist governments consulted with Jews from Poland and abroad and initiated a number of changes at Auschwitz. These included the recaptioning of photographic displays with information about Jewish victims, the translation of captions into Hebrew alongside European languages, and the retraining of some of the guides.[39] In 1990, responding to new studies, including one by the historian of the State Auschwitz Museum, greatly reducing the estimated number of victims of Auschwitz and greatly altering the proportion between Polish and Jewish victims (roughly 1 million Jews to 75,000 Poles), the new Polish government acted to remove the inscriptions at the International Memorial referring to 4 million victims.[40] For two years, while decisions were repeatedly postponed, visitors encountered the monument surrounded by empty tablets. In 1992, the following was finally inscribed in nineteen languages: "Let this place remain for eternity as a cry of despair and a warning to humanity. About one and a half million men, women, children, and infants, mainly Jews from different countries of Europe, were murdered here. The world was silent. Auschwitz-Birkenau, 1940–1945." Nearby a larger tablet was inscribed with a quotation from the Book of Job (16:18): "O Earth, hide not my blood / And let my cry never cease."[41]

These attempts to tell the truth and reduce the strife surrounding Auschwitz were insufficient, however, to spare the fiftieth-anniversary commemoration from confusion and discord. The turmoil began several months before the commemoration, when it was noted that Yasser Arafat, as part of a delegation of Nobel Peace Prize laureates, might be an honored guest at the ceremonies.[42] This dispute (resolved by limiting the Nobel laureates to those who had already officially received the prize, thereby excluding Yitzhak Rabin as well) was succeeded by complaints, first from the International Auschwitz Committee, then from the European Jewish Congress and the World Jewish Congress, about the Polish government's plans for the commemoration. The planning was called haphazard; invitations to heads of state were apparently not sent until the month before the ceremonies. Criticism also focused on the alleged "polonization" of the commemoration: on one hand, plans for several speeches by President Wałęsa, on the other, the lack of an officially scheduled time for the *Kaddish*, the Jewish prayer for the dead. According to one set of plans, prayers were to be confined to an ecumenical service after the end of the official ceremonies, at which Rabbi Joskowicz would be given a somewhat longer microphone cord so he could stand, according to his request, somewhat apart from the Christian and Muslim participants.[43]

Three Jewish leaders announced they would not attend the ceremonies: Elie Wiesel; Simone Veil, French minister of social affairs and also an Auschwitz survivor; and Edgar Bronfman, president of the World Jewish Congress. In the end, only Bronfman failed to appear, but talk began about "alternative" Jewish ceremonies at Auschwitz. The Union of Combatants of the Russian Federation announced that, contrary to expectations, representatives of the liberators of Auschwitz would not appear at the ceremonies. On the other hand, a number of uninvited guests promised to be on hand, chief among them Rabbi Avi Weiss.[44]

In the days before the commemoration, a rift developed between Polish and German Catholics occasioned by the refusal of the Poles to agree with their German counterparts on a long-planned joint statement on Auschwitz and the Holocaust. This refusal, criticized by some Polish Catholics as a "lack of courage or prophetic spirit," was best explained by Jerzy Turowicz in *Tygodnik Powszechny*.[45] The Polish episcopate decided to issue a separate statement, declares Turowicz, because "there was not the least doubt that world media would have announced, not without a certain satisfaction, that here finally Polish and German Catholics had acknowledged their common guilt or even common responsibility for the annihilation of millions of European Jews." Turowicz distinguishes between guilt or fault [*wina*] and responsibility [*odpowiedzialność*]: "responsibility for the annihilation of the Jews rests solely with those who decided on the plan for their annihilation and carried it out." He admits that the roots of anti-Semitism were "first of all religious, Christian," but then also distinguishes between the guilt of the Polish Church and the German. The latter, shielded by Hitler's concordat with the Vatican and with relative freedom of action, chose to remain silent; meanwhile many of its members actively participated in the Holocaust. But the guilt of the "persecuted and repressed" Polish Church was of an entirely different order. To approach it, Turowicz recalls Jan Błoński's celebrated article and continues: "We were powerless and helpless witnesses of the crime committed on our soil. Our only fault [*wina*] was the indifference of a significant portion of this society toward the horrible fate of the Jews."

As a result of the Polish decision, two separate statements appeared in the days preceding the ceremonies. The document released by the German Conference of Bishops refers to Auschwitz as "the symbol of the annihilation of European Jews, designated as the Holocaust or by the Hebrew word Shoah." The document assigns to the German Church and German Catholics "numerous sins" connected to the Holocaust and asks Jews to accept "this word of repentance and desire for renewal."[46] Unlike the German document, which was hailed in the *New York Times* as "an unusually blunt admission,"[47] the corresponding Polish statement offered little that was new. The declaration of the Polish Episcopal Commission for Dialogue with Judaism begins by reviewing the new figures concerning the nationality of the victims of Auschwitz and then carefully states: "The annihilation, defined by the term Shoah, has painfully burdened not only relations between Germans and Jews, but also to a great degree relations between Jews and Poles, who in common, but not in equal measure, were victims of Nazi ideology and as a result of physical proximity became unwilling witnesses of the extermination of the Jews." The document then presents a somewhat idealized summary of Polish-Jewish relations in history, recalls those who helped save Jews during the Holocaust as well as, citing from the 1991 pastoral letter, those who helped destroy them. The statement ends by defining the responsibility incumbent upon Poles fifty years after the liberation of Auschwitz "to combat all forms of trampling on human dignity, racism, anti-Semitism, xenophobia, and antipolonism." In commentary appended to the statement in *Gazeta Wyborcza*, Stanisław Krajewski notes the "unfortunate" coupling of anti-Semitism and antipolonism in the context of Auschwitz: only one of these led to mass murder.[48]

Despite last-minute changes by Polish authorities, the message of the two-day commemoration itself, as transmitted by the media, was essentially that of discord. In Kraków on January 26, Lech Wałęsa presided over morning ceremonies at Jagiellonian University, whose faculty had been decimated by the Nazis. His speech was followed by those of numerous Jewish leaders. In the afternoon, he presided over a gathering of Nobel Peace Prize laureates at the Wawel palace. In neither of his speeches did Wałęsa make specific reference to Jews or employ the word Holocaust. In a separate ceremony at Birkenau, held during the lunch break at the official ceremonies, Jews prayed at the crematorium ruins and heard speeches by Elie Wiesel; Shevah Weiss, the speaker of the Israeli parliament and an Auschwitz survivor; and Jean Kahn, president of the European Jewish Congress. Kahn rebuked Wałęsa for organizing a "nationalist" ceremony. The presence at this gathering of Roman Herzog, the president of Germany, was widely noted.[49] Television cameras at the official ceremonies focused on the empty seats of Herzog, Wiesel, and other participants in the unofficial gathering.

On the following day, the official ceremonies moved to Auschwitz, first to the Wall of Death and then to the "disembarkation ramp" at Birkenau. At the Wall of Death, flanked by Elie Wiesel and Simone Veil, representing the United States and France, respectively, and apparently as a result of protracted negotiations with Jewish leaders, President Wałęsa amended his prepared remarks and, after the phrase "the suffering of many nations," inserted the clause "especially the Jewish nation."[50] The peculiar "clumsiness" of Wałęsa, otherwise celebrated for his political craft, was much discussed but never satisfactorily explained. As one columnist put it, doubtless somewhat overoptimistic about Polish public opinion: "Why did the respected anti-Communist Lech Wałęsa, on the occasion of the fiftieth anniversary of the liberation of Auschwitz, decide to revive the Communist myth, instead of renouncing it once and for all and gaining the sympathy of both Jews and all of Polish and foreign public opinion? This I simply don't understand."[51]

Television cameras and fifteen hundred reporters swarming over the Auschwitz grounds also attracted demonstrators with a variety of connections to the site. There was Sigmund Sobolewski, Auschwitz prisoner number 88, a Polish Catholic who had survived five years of imprisonment. Representing a group of Canadian Christians and Jews, for years Sobolewski has been protesting what he terms the "christianization of Jewish suffering at Auschwitz." Dressed in his striped camp uniform with a placard in English hanging from his neck that read "We the Christians are also guilty of the Holocaust of the Jews," Sobolewski passed out leaflets and gave scores of interviews. On the anniversary of the greatest slaughter in history, there were also groups protesting contemporary slaughter in Chechnya and Bosnia. "Concentration camps are not the past," declared a leaflet distributed by Bosnian supporters. A handful of members of the Spartakus Group of Poland, Germany, and Russia, members of a "Fourth Communist International," demonstrated against Zionism and Catholicism. Before and during the ceremonies, Rabbi Weiss and several supporters, whose demands included transferring authority over Auschwitz into Jewish hands, demonstrated at several sites. Among them were the presidential palace in Warsaw; the vestibule of a church in Brzezinka near the site of the camp, from which they were removed by police; and the cross still standing before the former Carmelite convent, where they scuffled with Poles who held a banner declaring their defense of the cross against Jews and Freemasons.[52]

In contrast, the aging Polish former prisoners of Auschwitz who revisited the site of their torment seemed marginalized at the ceremonies. "Twenty-five years ago they were the center of attention, [but] today they are convinced that they are only an addendum," notes one journalist and cites a young Pole: "When I looked at the cordoned-off celebrities and at these shriveled prisoners assembled off on the side, I was ashamed." A former prisoner reflects: "Now they tell us that only 75,000 of us died here. Too little. Certainly, in comparison to the Jews it's little. But this number on my arm hurts as much as it did fifty years ago."[53] "We're unneeded," comments another. "It grieves us that there was so little about us here. That so little was said about Poles. For there weren't only Jews here. There were also Frenchmen and others." Rooted in the memory of the slave labor camp, the notion of Auschwitz as a great equalizer and therefore internationalizer persists. "I didn't sense a division into nationalities," remarks another former prisoner. "It didn't matter whether one was a Jew, a Gypsy, a Pole or a Russian. In the camp everyone worked equally, was beaten, stood for roll call." Another adds: "The path we're walking on is soaked with blood, not only Jewish, but the blood of all nations." And another draws the traditional conclusion: "One national group wants to place itself above all others. I mean the Jews. Let them put up a synagogue next to the church in Brzezinka. And if they don't want to, then too bad."[54]

Though the former prisoners may have been marginalized in the context of the ceremonies, a public opinion survey taken in the weeks before the commemoration revealed that many Poles still identified with much of what this older generation represented. Forty-seven percent of those polled believed that Auschwitz was primarily a place of Polish martyrdom, while only 8 percent believed that most of its victims were Jews. More than half stated that they had visited Auschwitz; nearly all said that remembering Auschwitz was important to them. "For many Poles," the authors of the survey conclude, "Oświęcim bears the dimension of a personal family tragedy and is an element of Polish tradition and Polish experience."[55] However "awkward" in an international context, President Wałęsa's remarks were well suited to his domestic audience.

One week later, Elie Wiesel praised the Polish government for the ceremonies and for helping to reduce the tensions between Poles and Jews.[56] But in Poland there was little sense of satisfaction and much of the reaction was defensive. Polish fragility had already been evident on the eve of the ceremonies, when an article on French Jewish children murdered at Auschwitz that appeared on the op-ed page of the *New York Times* used the phrase "the Polish concentration camp" as a synonym for Auschwitz. The article drew an immediate protest from the Polish embassy in Washington and was widely discussed in the Polish press.[57] In the weeks after the ceremonies, the Catholic nationalist press responded to criticism that Poles wanted to "own" [*zawłaszczyć*] Auschwitz by reversing the accusation. "The conflict broke out," writes one columnist, "not because Poles wanted to 'own' Oświęcim, but because the Jewish side . . . wanted the anniversary ceremonies to have a purely Jewish character." Moreover, according to the writer, this Jewish perspective assigns a revised role to the Poles: "Half a century after the war, the true image of the Nazi crimes gradually fades, and its place is taken by a new media-created chain of associations. Auschwitz is ever more rarely associated with the Germans or Nazism—it is transformed into a symbol of Polish anti-Semitism."[58] The writer is apparently unaware that this "danger" had already been denounced twenty-five years earlier during the anti-Zionist campaign.

Ironically, even *Gazeta Wyborcza* and its editor found it necessary to enter the fray on the Polish side, albeit using rather different rhetoric. In an interview in *Le Monde* that was subsequently reprinted in his paper, Adam Michnik defends Lech Wałęsa against the charge of anti-Semitism and declares himself, as a francophile, "ashamed" of French accusations of Polish "shared responsibility" [*współodpowiedzialność*] for the Holocaust, and, as a "Pole of Jewish origin," wounded by the assumption that every Pole is born an anti-Semite.[59] In the ensuing polemic, a remarkably fruitless exchange that amounted to little more than name-calling, Michnik accused his antagonists of antipolonism and was in turn accused of using his Jewish origins to serve Polish nationalism, and wanting to "erase the memory" of events such as the Kielce pogrom and the anti-Zionist campaign.[60] The pages of *Gazeta Wyborcza* that contained these exchanges, however, also contained the results of an opinion poll taken just after the Auschwitz ceremonies. In the new survey, the remarkable educational effects of the free media are apparent: those associating Auschwitz chiefly with Polish suffering dropped from 47 to 32 percent, while those identifying it with the Holocaust more than doubled.[61]

But beyond the polarized alternatives of polemics and opinion polls, the anniversary ceremonies also evoked more complex responses. "Who was the host and who was the guest?" asked one journalist, and another posed two unanswered questions: "For what purpose?" and "For whom?"[62] In the pages of *Tygodnik Powszechny*, Marek Frysztacki begins an article entitled "Questions about Auschwitz" as follows:

> In the big parking lot colored buses stand in a row. One hears the multilingual buzz of groups waiting for their guides. Taking advantage of a free moment, tourists line up to change money or buy

ice cream or address postcards. Tired travelers stretch out on the lawn. A teacher scolds some overly noisy children. A group of young Israelis unfurl national flags. Several Germans emerge from the flower shop with wreaths. A bright red truck with a Coca-Cola sign arrives at the restaurant, just behind it a green bus marked [in English] "Kraków—Wieliczka—Auschwitz. Every day at 6 p.m."

We are in Auschwitz—a real place on the earth. Thirty kilometers from Katowice, sixty from Kraków. We find ourselves in a place that is exceptionally problematic.[63]

Frysztacki presents an Auschwitz that is fully in our world in a way that it was not for decades under Communist rule. Then, for Poles, it had been a concrete place linked to a distinct national narrative. For the West it barely existed as a place, its reality purely symbolic, purely about meaning (or its lack). But now fully open to the world, Auschwitz strains against a flood of meanings, evoking the "problems" [kłopoty] that Frysztacki addresses.

First are "problems of conception" based on the fact that the meaning of the site varies depending on one's cultural context. Therefore the differing meanings of Auschwitz for Poles, Germans, Jews, Gypsies, Armenians, Bosnians, Kurds, and Japanese; the Japanese, for example, naturally bracket the site with Hiroshima. Then there are "problems of authenticity," linked to attempts to conserve a site that has already undergone an assortment of changes, planned and unplanned. "Problems of imagination" concern the inability to conceive of the torment that once rose from what visitors today often described as an "idyllic" site. "Problems of knowledge" arise from "a museum that explains nothing" because it cannot help visitors understand how a gas chamber was possible, "not technically, but morally." As a result, visitors emerge only with "sorrow, fear, and despair." Finally, there are the "problems of a cemetery" in which no one was ever buried, a site where Jews and Christians each pray in their own way over ashes that are inextricably mixed, while around them stroll those who came "because you can't miss it." And meanwhile:

The undefined sense of unrest and sorrow that visitors take from this place has been translated by the local market into a ready-made aesthetic proposition. Not only candles and wreaths are available, but also stylized postcards. The ramp seen from under a cattle car. Birkenau at sunset. Auschwitz "by night." A broken rose hanging from barbed wire. Soft colors. Black borders of mourning. The sweetness of sorrow and reverie. The *anus mundi* discovers its contemporary aesthetic expression in the company of an advertising folder.[64]

For better and for worse, not only Auschwitz but Poland now fully belongs in our world, with all its attendant freedoms and ambiguities. It is a world in which grand myths give way to "points of view," magisterial authority to the evening news, a world in which Karl Marx seems to have, if nothing else, the last word: "All that is solid melts into air."[65] In this world of vapors and fragments, Poles, like many of us, will nevertheless attempt to continue to weave the narrative of a collective past. In this attempt, they will unavoidably encounter, in ever-new contexts, the imprint of their most agonizing historical memory, the image of the Jew destroyed before their eyes and those of their parents and grandparents. What they will do with this memory, how it will shape Polish history and consciousness, is unpredictable. One can only hope that it will be used in the service of renewal rather than repression.

Notes

Index

Notes

Preface

1. Emmanuel Ringelblum, *Polish-Jewish Relations During the Second World War* (Evanston, Ill.: Northwestern Univ. Press, 1992), 1.

2. Here it is appropriate to note several recent studies that probe comparable issues for other nations: Charles S. Maier, *The Unmasterable Past: History, Holocaust, and German National Identity* (Cambridge, Mass: Harvard Univ. Press, 1988); Henry Rousso, *The Vichy Syndrome: History and Memory in France since 1944* (Cambridge, Mass.: Harvard Univ. Press, 1991); Saul Friedländer, *Memory, History, and the Extermination of the Jews of Europe* (Bloomington, Ind.: Indiana Univ. Press, 1993); Tom Segev, *The Seventh Million: The Israelis and the Holocaust* (New York: Hill and Wang, 1993); David Wyman, ed., *The World Reacts to the Holocaust: 1945–1992* (Baltimore: Johns Hopkins Univ. Press, 1996). See also the important theoretical essay by Pierre Nora, "Between Memory and History: *Les Lieux de Mémoire.*" *Representations*, no. 26 (Spring 1989): 7–25.

1. Poles and Jews Before the Holocaust

1. Norman Davies, *God's Playground: A History of Poland* (New York: Columbia Univ. Press, 1982), vol. 1, 3–4.

2. On Jewish civilization in the Polish Commonwealth, standard works in English are Salo Wittmayer Baron, *A Social and Religious History of the Jews*, vol. 16, *Poland-Lithuania, 1500–1650* (New York: Columbia Univ. Press, 1976); Bernard D. Weinryb, *The Jews of Poland: A Social and Economic History of the Jewish Community in Poland from 1100–1800* (Philadelphia: Jewish Publication Society, 1972). Important new studies are M. J. Rosman, *The Lord's Jews: Magnate-Jewish Relations in the Polish-Lithuanian Commonwealth During the 18th Century* (Cambridge, Mass.: Harvard

Univ. Press, 1990); Gershon David Hundert, *The Jews in a Polish Private Town: The Case of Opatów in the Eighteenth Century* (Baltimore: Johns Hopkins Univ. Press, 1992).

3. Strictly speaking, the term *Rzeczpospolita*, designating the formal political union of Poland and Lithuania, applies to the period 1569 to 1795. From 1385 to 1569, the union was a personal one incarnated in the Jagiellonian dynasty of Lithuanian origin. The best English-language history of the Polish Commonwealth is in Davies, *God's Playground*, vol. 1, 159–469. This otherwise excellent historian is unfortunately entirely unreliable on matters concerning Polish Jews.

4. Davies, *God's Playground*, vol. 1, 199–200. For the relevant text of the Act of the General Confederation of Warsaw, see Manfred Kridl, Władysław Malinowski, and Józef Wittlin, eds., *For Your Freedom and Ours: Polish Progressive Spirit Through the Ages* (New York: Frederick Ungar, 1943), 32–33. See also Janusz Tazbir, *A State Without Stakes: Polish Religious Toleration in the Sixteenth and Seventeenth Centuries* (Warsaw: Państwowy Instytut Wydawniczy, 1973).

5. See, for example, "Być Żydem w Polsce," *Tygodnik Solidarność* 50 (117), Dec. 14, 1990.

6. *The Earth Is the Lord's: The Inner World of the Jew in East Europe* (New York: Farrar, Straus Giroux, 1978), 10.

7. The Council of the Four (Polish) Lands began to meet formally in 1580, the Lithuanian Council in 1623. The system of intercommunal councils was abolished by Polish authorities in 1764.

8. As another example of the problems of writing the history of these regions, it should be noted that among Ukrainians, Bogdan Khmelnytsky, the leader of the Cossack uprising, is considered a national hero. Among Jews his name for centuries occupied a place supplanted in modern times only by that of Hitler. Jewish estimates of his Jewish victims have ranged from 100,000 to 250,000 and higher; recent Jewish scholars still speak of tens of thousands, while a recent Ukrainian scholar suggests ten thousand. See Jaroslaw Pelenski, "The Cossack Insurrections in Jewish-Ukrainian Relations," in Peter J. Potichnyj and Howard Aster, eds., *Ukrainian-Jewish Relations in Historical Perspective* (Edmonton, Canada: Canadian Institute of Ukrainian Studies, 1987), 31–42.

9. Evyatar Friesel, *Atlas of Modern Jewish History* (Oxford: Oxford Univ. Press, 1990), 30; Hundert, *The Jews in a Polish Private Town*, xi.

10. On *szlachta* stereotypes of the Jew in Old Poland, see Eugenia Prokopówna, "Śmiech szlachecki w satyrycznych obrazach żydowskiego świata," in *Studenckie zeszyty naukowe Uniwersytetu Jagiellońskiego: Studenckie zeszyty polonistyczne* (Kraków), vol. 7 (1988), no. 3, *Ironja, parodia, satyra*, 131–51. On Polish stereotypes of the Jew in the nineteenth century, see Aleksander Hertz, *The Jews in Polish Culture* (Evanston, Ill.: Northwestern Univ. Press, 1988); Michael C. Steinlauf, "Mr. Geldhab and Sambo in *Peyes*: Images of the Jew on the Polish Stage, 1863–1905," *Polin: A Journal of Polish-Jewish Studies* 4 (1989): 110–18. On the stereotype of the Jew among Polish peasants in the 1970s, see Alina Cała, *Wizerunek Żyda w polskiej kulturze ludowej* (Warsaw: Wydawnictwo Uniwersytetu Warszawskiego, 1992).

11. Two good sources for the history of this period are Norman Davies, *God's Playground: A History of Poland* (New York: Columbia Univ. Press, 1982), vol. 2, 3–392; Piotr Wandycz, *The Lands of Partitioned Poland, 1795–1918* (Seattle: Univ. of Washington Press, 1974).

12. Cited in Michael T. Kaufman, *Mad Dreams, Saving Graces; Poland: A Nation in Conspiracy* (New York: Random House, 1989), ix.

13. On the history of the Jews in the lands of partitioned Poland, there as yet exists no comprehensive work.

14. Salo Baron, *The Russian Jew under Tsars and Soviets* (New York: Macmillan, 1976), 64.

15. On this important era in Polish-Jewish relations, see Magdalena Opalski and Israel Bartal, *Poles and Jews: A Failed Brotherhood* (Hanover, N. H.: Univ. Press of New England, 1992).

16. According to a recent study, a significant factor even in contemporary Polish attitudes toward Jews is the Polish preoccupation with "moral superiority," which includes a competitive religious component: "Which nation is not only chosen, but is truly faithful to God?" See Ireneusz Kremiński, "Wprowadzenie: Polacy i Żydzi w świetle socjologicznego badania," separately paginated chapter of typescript *Czy Polacy są antysemitamy?* (Are Poles anti-Semites?), 13; for more on this study, see pp. 124–26 above.

17. At the end of the nineteenth century, Aleksander Świętochowski, the dean of the Positivists, could still laugh at the notion of a Polish factory owner; see the citation (originally published in *Nowiny* [Warsaw], no. 134, May 4, 1880) In Steinlauf, "Mr. Geldhab and Sambo in *Peyes*," 103–4.

18. The standard work is Jonathan Frankel, *Prophecy and Politics: Socialism, Nationalism, and the Russian Jews, 1862–1917* (Cambridge: Cambridge Univ. Press, 1981).

19. *Canonicus cracoviensis, natione Polonus, gente Ruthenus, origine Judaeus;* see Davies, *God's Playground,* vol. 2, 12–13.

20. For the persistence of this saying into the 1980s, see Anna Sawisz, "Obraz Żydów i stosunków polsko-żydowskich w listach telewidzów po emisji filmu *Shoah,*" in Aleksandra Jasińska-Kania, ed., *Bliscy i dalecy,* Studia nad postawami wobec innych narodów, ras i grup etnicznych, vol. 2 (Warsaw: Uniwersytet Warszawski, Instytut Socjologii, 1992), 160. See also Maria Kamińska, "References to Polish-Jewish Coexistence in the Memoirs of Łódź Workers: A Linguistic Analysis," *Polin: A Journal of Polish-Jewish Studies* 6 (1991): 207–22.

21. On interwar Poland, see Davies, *God's Playground,* vol. 2, 393–434; and Antony Polonsky, *Politics in Independent Poland, 1921–1939: The Crisis of Constitutional Government* (Oxford: Clarendon Press, 1972). On minorities in interwar Poland, see the important work by Jerzy Tomaszewski, *Rzeczpospolita wielu narodów* (Warsaw: Czytelnik, 1985).

22. On the Jews of interwar Poland, an excellent survey is the first chapter of Ezra Mendelsohn, *The Jews of East Central Europe Between the World Wars* (Bloomington, Ind.: Indiana Univ. Press, 1983), 11–83. See also Joseph Marcus, *Social and Political History of the Jews in Poland, 1919–1939* (Berlin: Mouton, 1983); Yisrael Gut-

man, Ezra Mendelsohn, Jehuda Reinharz, and Chone Shmeruk, eds., *The Jews of Poland Between Two World Wars* (Hanover, N.H.: Univ. Press of New England, 1989); and Jerzy Tomaszewski, "Niepodległa rzeczpospolita," in Jerzy Tomaszewski, ed., *Najnowsze dzieje Żydów w Polsce w zarysie (do 1950 roku)* (Warsaw: Wydawnictwo Naukowe PWN, 1993).

23. Szyja Bronsztejn, *Ludność żydowska w Polsce w okresie międzywojennym: Studium statystyczne* (Wrocław: Zakład Narodowy im. Ossolińskich, 1963), 126–27; Mendelsohn, *The Jews of East Central Europe Between the World Wars*, 24–25, 26–27; Marcus, *Social and Political History of the Jews in Poland*, 113, 116, 120.

24. Mendelsohn, *The Jews of East Central Europe Between the World Wars*, 35.

25. Ibid., 29–32.

26. Thus Bernard Johnpoll entitles his study of the interwar Bund that focuses exclusively on such issues: *The Politics of Futility* (Ithaca, N. Y.: Cornell Univ. Press, 1967).

27. In 1936, Tarbut and Yavneh schools, where instruction was primarily in Hebrew, had an enrollment of 60,703 students (33.7 percent of all children in Jewish elementary schools); the Central Yiddish School Organization (TsYShO) enrolled 16,486 students (9.2 percent); while the various Orthodox schools had 100,649 students (55.9 percent). To keep these figures in perspective, it should be stressed that more than half of all Jewish elementary school students attended Polish public schools, though a substantial portion of these attended additional Jewish classes after school. See Chone Shmeruk, "Hebrew-Yiddish-Polish: A Trilingual Jewish Culture," in Gutman et al., *The Jews of Poland Between Two World Wars*, 291–93.

28. Moyshe Kligsberg, "Di yidishe yugnt-bavegung in Poyln tsvishn beyde velt-milkhomes (a sotsyologishe shtudye)," in Joshua A. Fishman, ed., *Studies on Polish Jewry, 1919–1939* (New York: YIVO Institute for Jewish Research, 1974), 137–228.

29. Rafał Żebrowski and Zofia Borzymińska, *Po-lin: Kultura Żydów polskich w XX wieku (Zarys)* (Warsaw: Wydawnictwo Amarant, 1993), 84.

30. Ephraim E. Urbach, "The History of Polish Jews after World War I as Reflected in the Traditional Literature," in Gutman et al., *The Jews of Poland Between Two World Wars*, 223–46; Ben-Zion Gold, "Religious Education in Poland: A Personal Perspective," in ibid., 272–82; Żebrowski and Borzymińska, *Po-lin*, 74–90.

31. Michael C. Steinlauf, "The Polish Jewish Daily Press," in Antony Polonsky, ed., *From Shtetl to Socialism: Studies from Polin* (London: Littman Library of Jewish Civilization, 1993), 332–58; Yechiel Szeintuch, *Preliminary Inventory of Yiddish Dailies and Periodicals Published in Poland Between the Two World Wars* (Jerusalem: Hebrew University, Center for Research on the History and Culture of Polish Jews, 1986).

32. See Z. Segalovitsh, *Tlomatskie 13: Fun farbrentn nekhtn* (Buenos Aires: Tsentral-farband fun poylishe yidn in Argentine, 1946); Ber Y. Rozen, *Tlomatskie 13* (Buenos Aires: Tsentral-farband fun poylishe yidn in Argentine, 1950); B. Kutsher, *Geven amol Varshe: Zikhroynes* (Paris: Kultur opteylung baym Dzhoynt in Frankraykh, 1955).

33. The camp was at Jabłonna. For sources, see Celia Heller, *On the Edge of Destruction: Jews of Poland Between the Two World Wars* (New York: Columbia Univ. Press, 1977), 302, n. 5.

34. See Joshua Rothenberg, "The Przytyk Pogrom," *Soviet Jewish Affairs*, 16, no. 2 (1986): 29–46.

35. August Hlond, *Na straży sumienia narodu* (Ramsey, N.J.: Don Bosco, 1951); cited in Ronald Modras, *The Catholic Church and Antisemitism: Poland, 1933–1939* (Chur, Switzerland: Harwood, 1994), 346. This important study, which documents the strongly anti-Semitic stance of the Polish Church during this period, argues that its teachings were not exceptional, but were entirely in line with those of the Church elsewhere in Europe and with the rhetoric of the Vatican. But nowhere else in Europe did the Church confront 3.5 million Jews.

36. See Edward Wynot, "'A Necessary Cruelty': The Emergence of Official Anti-Semitism in Poland, 1936–39," *American Historical Review* 76 (1971): 1035–58.

37. *Gazeta Polska*, December 4, 1938; cited in Heller, *On the Edge of Destruction*, 137. Simultaneously with Hitler's occupation of the Sudetenland, and with his permission, Poland seized Teschen (Zaolzie), a portion of Silesia it had claimed since 1919.

38. Marcus, *Social and Political History of the Jews in Poland*, 358.

2. Poles and Jews During the Holocaust: 1939–1944

1. An enlightening study of the occupation is Jan Tomasz Gross, *Polish Society under German Occupation: The Generalgouvernement, 1939–1944* (Princeton, N. J.: Princeton Univ. Press, 1979). See also Richard C. Lukas, *Forgotten Holocaust: The Poles under German Occupation, 1939–1944* (New York: Hippocrene Books, 1990); and Davies, *God's Playground*, vol. 2, 435–91. By the end of 1944, most of the territory of prewar Poland had been freed of the Nazis and occupied by the Red Army; it is most accurate to date the end of the Holocaust and the beginning of the postwar period in Poland from that year.

2. After the German invasion of the Soviet Union, the territory of eastern Galicia, including Lwów, was added to the Generalgouvernement.

3. Treblinka, Sobibór, Majdanek, and Bełżec were in the Generalgouvernement; Auschwitz-Birkenau was on its western border in German-annexed Silesia; Chełmno was west of the Generalgouvernement in another annexed portion of Poland, the so-called Wartheland.

4. *Obozy hitlerowskie na ziemiach polskich 1939–1945: Informator encyklopedyczny* (Warsaw: Państwowe Wydawnictwo Naukowe, 1979). This important source must, however, be used with care; see pp. 82–83 above

5. On this issue in the concentration camp setting, see the essay by Primo Levi, "Useless Violence," in *The Drowned and the Saved* (New York: Summit Books, 1988), 105–26.

6. Antoni Szcześniak and Wiesław Szota, *Droga do nikąd: Działalność organizacji ukraińskich nacjonalistów i jej likwidacja w Polsce* (Warsaw: Wydawnictwo Ministerstwa Obrony Narodowej, 1973), 166–67, 170; Ryszard Torzecki, *Kwestia ukraińska w polityce III Rzeszy (1933–1945)* (Warsaw: Książka i Wiedza, 1972), 328–30; both cited in Gross, *Polish Society under German Occupation*, 193.

7. Franciszek Skalniak, *Bank emisyjny w Polsce, 1939–1945* (Warsaw: Państwowe Wydawnictwo Ekonomiczne, 1966), 133; cited in Gross, *Polish Society under German*

Occupation, 109. See also the important essay by Kazimierz Wyka, first published just after the war, "Gospodarka wyłączona," in *Życie na niby; Pamiętnik po klęsce* (Kraków: Wydawnictwo Literackie, 1984), 138–75. It has been translated as "The Excluded Economy," in Janine Wedel, ed., *The Unplanned Society: Poland During and After Communism* (New York: Columbia Univ. Press, 1992), 23–61.

8. Gross, *Polish Society under German Occupation*, 256–58, 283–306.

9. Other groups that remained outside the Home Army were the Peasant Battalions [Bataliony Chłopskie] and a portion of the forces organized by the PPS.

10. Gross, *Polish Society under German Occupation*, 281.

11. Ibid., 283–86.

12. Ibid., 160–83.

13. The long-accepted figure of three million Poles killed is no longer tenable. Studies published since the fall of communism, although not definitive, particularly for eastern Poland, have established that two million is an upper limit. But the accepted figure of three million Polish Jews murdered has been confirmed. See Czesław Łuczak, "Szanse i trudności bilansu demograficznego Polski w latach 1939–1945," *Dzieje najnowsze* (Warsaw) 26, no. 2 (1994): 12–14; see also Krystyna Kersten, "Szacunek strat osobowych w Polsce Wschodniej," ibid., 41–50.

14. On the development of this policy, see Raul Hilberg, *The Destruction of the European Jews*, 3 vols., rev. and definitive ed. (New York: Holmes and Meier, 1985). For a summary of the course of the Holocaust in Poland, including Jewish responses, see Lucy Dawidowicz, *The War Against the Jews, 1933–1945*, 10th anniv. ed. (New York: Bantam Books, 1986), 197–340. See also Yisrael Gutman, *The Jews of Warsaw, 1939–1943: Ghetto, Underground, Revolt* (Bloomington, Ind.: Indiana Univ. Press, 1982). A major work on the Warsaw ghetto, Ruta Sakowska's *Ludzie z dzielnicy zamkniętej*, 2nd ed., rev. and exp. (Warsaw: Wydawnictwo Naukowe PWN, 1993), awaits translation into English.

15. The average Polish ration was 669 calories, the German 2,613. See Eugeniusz Duraczyński, *Wojna i okupacja: Wrzesień 1939-kwiecień 1943* (Warsaw: Wiedza Powszechna, 1974), 69; cited in Lukas, *Forgotten Holocaust*, 30. For slightly different figures, see Yisrael Gutman and Shmuel Krakowski, *Unequal Victims: Poles and Jews During World War Two* (New York: Holocaust Library, 1986), 45.

16. Gutman, *The Jews of Warsaw*, 64.

17. Ber Mark, *Powstanie w Getcie Warszawskim* (Warsaw: Wydawnictwo "Idisz Bukh," 1963), 41; cited in Lukas, *Forgotten Holocaust*, 178. The numbers follow Gutman, *The Jews of Warsaw*; previous estimates have suggested up to two thousand Jewish fighters and a surviving ghetto population of seventy thousand.

18. For some studies in English, see Michael Borwicz, "Factors Influencing the Relations Between the General Polish Underground and the Jewish Underground," in *Jewish Resistance During the Holocaust: Proceedings of the Conference on Manifestations of Jewish Resistance, Jerusalem, April 7–11, 1968* (Jerusalem: Yad Vashem, 1971), 343–64; Emmanuel Ringelblum, *Polish-Jewish Relations During the Second World War* (Evanston, Ill.: Northwestern Univ. Press, 1992); Shmuel Krakowski, "Holocaust in the Polish Underground Press," *Yad Vashem Studies* 16 (1984): 241–70; Gutman and Krakowski, *Unequal Victims*; David Engel, *In the Shadow of Auschwitz: The Pol-*

ish Government-in-Exile and the Jews, 1939–1942 (Chapel Hill, N. C.: Univ. of North Carolina Press, 1987), and *Facing the Holocaust: The Polish Government-in-Exile and the Jews, 1943–1945* (Chapel Hill, N.C.: Univ. of North Carolina Press, 1993). Krakowski's work suffers from a deliberately provocative tone; on this see the exchange "Polemic as History" between Krakowski and Stanislaus A. Blejwas, *Polin: A Journal of Polish-Jewish Studies* 4 (1989): 354–69. A substantial portion of Richard Lukas's work, *Forgotten Holocaust*, is devoted to a defense of Polish behavior against Jewish "accusations"; see esp. 117–81. Lukas seriously underestimates Polish anti-Semitism, and tends to blur the distinction between Nazi policies toward Jews and Poles. In a subsequent book, *Out of the Inferno: Poles Remember the Holocaust* (Lexington, Ky.: Univ. Press of Kentucky, 1989), this author appropriates the word Holocaust without any modifier to designate the Polish experience of the war. Davies too fails to grasp the crucial distinction between the fate of Jews and Poles during the war; in *God's Playground* he makes the extraordinary statement: "To ask why the Poles did little to help the Jews is rather like asking why the Jews did not nothing to assist the Poles" (vol. 2, 264).

19. Ringelblum, *Polish-Jewish Relations,* 29.

20. See, for example, Gross, *Polish Society under German Occupation,* 185–86.

21. Wyka, "Gospodarka wyłączona," 155–60.

22. Ringelblum, *Polish-Jewish Relations,* 257.

23. A good source is Jan Rzepecki, "Organizacja i działanie Biura Informacji i Propagandy (BIP) Komendy Głównej AK: Zakończenie," *Wojskowy Przegląd Historyczny,* 1971, no. 4: 147–53.

24. See the important study by Jan T. Gross, *Revolution from Abroad: The Soviet Conquest of Poland's Western Ukraine and Western Belorussia* (Princeton, N. J.: Princeton Univ. Press, 1988).

25. Gross, *Revolution from Abroad,* 146.

26. Ibid., 194. The number of Polish citizens who moved, willingly or unwillingly, into the interior of the USSR during 1939–41 was estimated by the Polish Foreign Ministry as 1.25 million.

27. Davies, *God's Playground,* vol. 2, 545.

28. Jaff Schatz, *The Generation: The Rise and Fall of the Jewish Communists of Poland* (Berkeley, Calif: Univ. of California Press, 1991), 96–98. See also Gabriele Simoncini, "Ethnic and Social Diversity in the Membership of the Communist Party of Poland: 1918–1938," *Nationalities Papers* (New York) 22, Suppl. no. 1 (1994): 60.

29. On Jews and communism, see also the essay by A. Kainer [Stanisław Krajewski], "Żydzi a komunizm," *Krytyka* (London), 1983, no. 15: 214–47.

30. See Gross, *Revolution from Abroad,* 28–35; Paweł Korzec and Jean-Charles Szurek, "Jews and Poles under Soviet Occupation (1939–1941): Conflicting Interests," *Polin: A Journal of Polish-Jewish Studies* 4 (1989): 204–25; Ben-Cion Pinchuk, *Shtetl Jews under Soviet Rule: Eastern Poland on the Eve of the Holocaust* (Oxford: Basil Blackwell, 1991); Krystyna Kersten, *Polacy, Żydzi, Komunizm: Anatomia półprawd, 1939–1968* (Warsaw: Niezależna Oficyna Wydawnicza, 1992), 25–33; Dov Levin, *The Lesser of Two Evils: Eastern European Jewry under Soviet Rule, 1939–1941* (Philadelphia: Jewish Publication Society, 1995).

31. Gross, *Revolution from Abroad*, 29.

32. For one version, see Pinchuk, *Shtetl Jews under Soviet Rule*, 114; another version was told to me by Prof. Joshua Rothenberg in the 1980s.

33. Walter Lacqueur, *The Terrible Secret: Suppression of the Truth about Hitler's "Final Solution"* (Boston: Little, Brown, 1980), 109–10; Engel, *In the Shadow of Auschwitz*, 186–87.

34. See Jan Karski, *The Story of a Secret State* (Boston: Houghton Mifflin, 1944); E. Thomas Wood, *Karski: How One Man Tried to Stop the Holocaust* (New York: J. Wiley, 1994).

35. Engel, *In the Shadow of Auschwitz*, 173–202; Gutman and Krakowski, *Unequal Victims*, 65–74.

36. Engel, *In the Shadow of Auschwitz*, 196–97; Gutman and Krakowski, *Unequal Victims*, 88–89. The printed Polish version of his speech omitted the promise of equal rights for Jews.

37. The most well-known exception was a radio broadcast by Sikorski one month after the start of the Warsaw Ghetto Uprising. For the relevant text, see Władysław Bartoszewski and Zofia Lewin, eds., *The Samaritans: Heroes of the Holocaust* (New York: Twayne, 1970), 42.

38. See the important volume of material from the Polish underground press: Paweł Szapiro, ed., *Wojna żydowsko-niemiecka: Polska prasa konspiracyjna 1943–1944 o powstaniu w getcie Warszawy* (The Jewish-German war: The Polish underground press [1943–1944] on the uprising in the Warsaw ghetto) (London: Aneks, 1992).

39. Teresa Prekerowa, *Konspiracyjna Rada Pomocy Żydom w Warszawie 1942–1945* (Warsaw: Państwowy Instytut Wydawniczy, 1982), 112 (facing), emphasis in original; cited in Aleksander Smolar, "Tabu i Niewinność," *Aneks* (London), 1986, no. 41–42: 93–94. The text of the leaflet is also reproduced in Jan Błoński, "Polak-katolik i katolik-Polak," in *Biedni Polacy patrzą na ghetto* (Kraków: Wydawnictwo Literackie, 1994), 38–40. Kossak was a member of the Front Odrodzenia Polski (Front for the Rebirth of Poland).

40. Ewa Berberyusz, "'The Black Hole': Conversation with Stanisław Krajewski, 'A Pole and a Jew in One Person,'" in Antony Polonsky, ed., *My Brothers' Keeper? Recent Polish Debates on the Holocaust* (London: Routledge, 1990), 104.

41. Błoński, "Polak-katolik i katolik-Polak," 41. On Błoński, see pp. 113–17 above.

42. In 1943 and 1944, about twenty out of two thousand; see *Polskie Siły Zbrojne w Drugiej Wojnie Światowej* (London: Instytut Historyczny im. Gen. Sikorskiego, 1950), vol. 3, 472–73; Prekerowa, *Konspiracyjna Rada Pomocy Żydom*, 294–95; and her article, "The 'Just' and the 'Passive,'" *Yad Vashem Studies* 19 (1988): 369–77. Żegota also tried unsuccessfully to convince the Delegate's Bureau to publish a fictitious list of death sentences for crimes against Jews.

43. Ringelblum, *Polish-Jewish Relations*, 125–26.

44. The term "universe of obligation" was first employed in this context by Helen Fein; see *Accounting for Genocide: National Responses and Jewish Victimization During the Holocaust* (Chicago: Univ. of Chicago Press, 1979), 33.

45. See Wacław Bielawski, *Zbrodnie na Polakach dokonane przez hitlerowców za*

pomoc udzielaną Żydom (Warsaw: Główna Komisja Badania Zbrodni Hitlerowskich w Polsce, 1987).

46. See Nechama Tec, *When Light Pierced the Darkness: Christian Rescue of Jews in Nazi-Occupied Poland* (New York: Oxford Univ. Press, 1986).

3. Memory's Wounds: 1944–1948

1. Davies, *God's Playground*, vol. 2, 575–76. The major work on this period is Krystyna Kersten, *The Establishment of Communist Rule in Poland, 1943–1948* (Berkeley, Calif: Univ. of California Press, 1991).

2. This was argued by Józef Chałasiński, whose influential book *Przeszłość i pryszłość inteligencji polskiej* was first published in Rome in 1947.

3. The party was named the Social Democracy of the Kingdom of Poland and Lithuania [Socjał-demokracja Królestwa Polskiego i Litwy, SDKPiL], and was founded by Rosa Luxemburg and others at the turn of the century.

4. Józef Adelson, "W Polsce zwanej ludowej," in Jerzy Tomaszewski, ed., *Najnowsze dzieje Żydów w Polsce w zarysie (do 1950 roku)* (Warsaw: Wydawnictwo Naukowe PWN, 1993), 398; see also 387–91, 399–400. For other sources, see Lucjan Dobroszycki, "Restoring Jewish Life in Postwar Poland," *Soviet Jewish Affairs* (London) 3, no. 2 (1973): 58–60; Paul Glikson, "Jewish Population in the Polish People's Republic, 1944–1972," in *Papers in Jewish Demography, 1973: Proceedings of the Demographic Sessions Held at the 6th World Congress of Jewish Studies, Jerusalem, August 1973* (Jerusalem: Institute of Contemporary Jewry, Hebrew University, 1977), 237–39.

5. On the rebuilding of Jewish life in postwar Poland, see the sources in the previous note as well as Yisrael Gutman, *Ha-yehudim be-Folin aharei milhamat ha-olam ha-shniya* (Jerusalem: Zalman Shazar Center for the Furtherance of the Study of Jewish History, 1985); Bernard D. Weinryb, "Poland," in Peter Meyer et al., *The Jews in the Soviet Satellites* (Syracuse, N.Y.: Syracuse Univ. Press, 1953), 207–326; Sh. L. Shnayderman, *Between Fear and Hope* (New York: Arco, 1947).

6. Lucy Dawidowicz, *The Holocaust and the Historians* (Cambridge, Mass.: Harvard Univ. Press, 1981), 98; until the early 1950s, the institution was known as the Central Commission to Investigate German Crimes in Poland.

7. See Bernard Mark, *Męczeństwo i walka Żydów w latach okupacji: Poradnik bibliograficzny* (Warsaw: n.p., 1963).

8. *Biuletyn Żydowskiego Instytutu Historycznego* (Bulletin of the Jewish Historical Institute), a historical journal, has appeared quarterly since 1951; other publications, including the Yiddish historical journal *Bleter far geshikhte,* have appeared sporadically. See Abraham Wein, "The Jewish Historical Institute in Warsaw," *Yad Vashem Studies* 8 (1970): 203–13.

9. James E. Young, *The Texture of Memory: Holocaust Memorials and Meaning* (New Haven, Conn.: Yale Univ. Press, 1993), 120.

10. For this approach to the "Jewish problem" in postwar Poland, I am indebted to the work of Krystyna Kersten, *Polacy, Żydzi, Komunizm: Anatomia półprawd, 1939–1968* (Warsaw: Niezależna Oficyna Wydawnicza, 1992).

11. "Zagadnienie polskiego antysemityzmu," *Odrodzenie,* no. 28, July 14, 1946;

cited in Kersten, *The Establishment of Communist Rule in Poland*, 220. Another excellent example is *Nowe Widnokręgi* 5 (1945), no. 6. This issue of the newspaper, published throughout the war in Moscow, juxtaposes articles on the Ghetto Uprising and the new Polish democracy with a (somewhat censored) version of the poet Julian Tuwim's powerful Holocaust elegy "My, Żydzi polscy . . ." (We, Polish Jews . . .).

12. On the history of the monument, see Young, *The Texture of Memory*, 175–84.

13. See for example, "Problem antysemityzmu," *Kultura* (Paris), no. 1/111–2/112 (Jan.–Feb. 1957): 60. The first monument commemorating the Polish underground was raised in the 1960s and bore the vague inscription "To the heroes of Warsaw, 1939–1945." Not until 1989, and after enormous controversy, was a monument specifically dedicated to the Polish Uprising completed. For more on these monuments, see Young, *The Texture of Memory*, 176.

14. Anna Radziwiłł, "The Teaching of the History of the Jews in Secondary Schools in the Polish People's Republic, 1949–88," *Polin: A Journal of Polish-Jewish Studies* 4 (1989): 413, 414.

15. Kersten, *Polacy, Żydzi, Komunizm*, 108.

16. *Sublokatorka* (Paris: Libella, 1985), 64.

17. As Kersten correctly points out in *Polacy, Żydzi, Komunizm*, 76–78.

18. Although the figures were considerably more lopsided for the KPP than for the PPR and PZPR.

19. On Jews in the UB, see Kersten, *Polacy, Żydzi, Komunizm*, 83–84; Jaff Schatz, *The Generation: The Rise and Fall of the Jewish Communists of Poland* (Berkeley, Calif.: Univ. of California Press, 1991), 222–28; Raymond Taras, "Gomułka's 'Rightist-Nationalist Deviation,' the Postwar Jewish Communists, and the Stalinist Reaction in Poland, 1945–1950," *Nationalities Papers* (New York) 22, Suppl. no. 1 (1994): 114–23. On popular Polish conceptions about Jews in the government, see also the interesting report from Warsaw to the British Foreign Secretary of September 21, 1948, published in *Soviet Jewish Affairs* 10, no. 1 (1980): 64–68.

20. Dobroszycki, "Restoring Jewish Life," 66; Adelson, "W Polsce zwanej ludowej," 401. The hundreds of Yiddish and Hebrew memorial books [*yizker bikher*] published after the Holocaust by survivors of particular communities provide ample documentation of such attacks.

21. The most comprehensive documentation is in Bożena Szaynok, *Pogrom Żydów w Kielcach 4 VII 1956 r.* (Warsaw: Wydawnictwo Bellona, 1991).

22. Adelson, "W Polsce zwanej ludowej," 424.

23. Shnayderman, *Between Fear and Hope*, 181.

24. Kersten, *Polacy, Żydzi, Komunizm*, 113–38, summarizes the status of this theory, which, despite frequent rumors of impending revelations, remains unproven. Aside from its truth value is the separate question of its role in recent discussions of Polish-Jewish relations. To the extent that postwar violence against Jews has been addressed in Poland at all, the discussion has focused nearly exclusively on the Kielce pogrom, and most writers have assumed it was an NKVD provocation.

25. Kersten, *Polacy, Żydzi, Komunizm*, 152.

26. S. Łukasiewicz, *Okupacja* (Warsaw: Czytelnik, 1978), 246; cited in Józef Wróbel, *Tematy żydowskie w prozie polskiej, 1939–1987* (Kraków: Towarzystwo Autorów

i Wydawców Prac Naukowych "Universitas", 1991), 117. Łukasiewicz's book was written in 1947 and first published in 1958.

27. Kersten, *Polacy, Żydzi, Komunizm*, 17–18; see pp. 39–40 above.

28. For some of the diverse material on these subjects see: David S. Wyman, *The Abandonment of the Jews: America and the Holocaust, 1941–1945* (New York: Pantheon, 1984); Deborah E. Lipstadt, *Beyond Belief: The American Press and the Coming of the Holocaust, 1933–1945* (New York: Free Press, 1986); Raul Hilberg, *The Destruction of the European Jews*, 3 vols., rev. and definitive ed. (New York: Holmes and Meier, 1985); Gutman, *The Jews of Warsaw*; Primo Levi, *The Drowned and the Saved* (New York: Summit Books, 1988).

29. Shoshana Felman, "The Return of the Voice: Claude Lanzmann's *Shoah*," in Shoshana Felman and Dori Laub, *Testimony: Crises of Witnessing in Literature, Psychoanalysis, and History* (New York: Routledge, 1992), 211, emphasis in the original. In this volume see also Dori Laub, "An Event Without a Witness: Truth, Testimony, and Survival," 75–92.

30. Memorial books for Jewish communities destroyed in the Holocaust contain many such accounts, as do Jewish memoirs. Among the latter, see Dovid Sfard, *Mit zikh un mit andere* (Jerusalem: Farlag Yerushelayimer Almanakh, 1984), 160; and Hersh Smoliar, *Oyf der letster pozitsye, mit der letster hofnung* (Tel Aviv: Farlag Y.L. Peretz, 1982), 29; both authors were leaders of the postwar Jewish community in Poland. For further sources, see David Engel, "Palestine in the Mind of the Remnants of Polish Jewry," *Journal of Israeli History* 16, no. 3 (1995): 229n. 34.

31. Aryeh Josef Kochavi, "The Catholic Church and Antisemitism in Poland Following World War II As Reflected in British Diplomatic Documents," *Gal-Ed: On the History of the Jews in Poland* (Tel Aviv) 11 (1989): 116–28.

32. Letter to the editor, *Kultura* (Paris), no. 11/133 (Nov. 1958): 147.

33. Ibid., 147; cited from Maria Hochberg-Mariańska, *Dzieci oskarżają* (Kraków: Centralna Żydowska Komisja Historyczna w Polsce, 1947), xxxii. This book has been translated as *The Children Accuse* (Portland, Ore.: Valentine Mitchell, 1996).

34. David Engel, "The Situation of Polish Jewry as Reflected in United States Diplomatic Documents, Dec. 1945-July 1946," *Gal-Ed: On the History of the Jews in Poland* 14 (1995): 120. The author of the memorandum was Samuel Margoshes, a former editor of the New York Yiddish daily, *Der Tog*.

35. "Problem antysemityzmu," *Kultura* (Paris), no. 1/111–2/112 (Jan.-Feb. 1957): 56–57.

36. Review of Irena Hurwic-Nowakowska, *A Social Analysis of Postwar Polish Jewry*, in *Polin: A Journal of Polish-Jewish Studies* 3 (1988): 440–41.

37. "History Beyond the Pleasure Principle: Some Thoughts on the Representation of Trauma," in Saul Friedländer, ed., *Probing the Limits of Representation: Nazism and the "Final Solution"* (Cambridge, Mass.: Harvard University Press, 1992), 151. Santner's context is an analysis of the German historians' polemic [*Historikerstreit*] of the late 1980s. See also Saul Friedländer, "Trauma, Memory, and Transference," in Geoffrey H. Hartman, ed., *Holocaust Remembrance: The Shapes of Memory* (Oxford: Basil Blackwell, 1994), 252–63.

38. Robert Jay Lifton, *The Broken Connection: On Death and the Continuity of Life*

(New York: Basic Books, 1979); see also Lifton's *Death in Life: Survivors of Hiroshima* (New York: Random House, 1967) and *The Nazi Doctors: Medical Killing and the Psychology of Genocide* (New York: Basic Books, 1986); see also Cathy Caruth, "Interview with Robert Jay Lifton," *American Imago* 48 (1991), no. 1: 153–75.

39. Lifton, *The Broken Connection,* 169, 171, 173, 175, 176, 177. Lifton cites the final phrase from Erich Lindemann, "Symptomology and Management of Acute Grief," *American Journal of Psychiatry* 101 (1944): 143. Freud discussed traumatic neurosis and the compulsion to repeat in *Beyond the Pleasure Principle* (New York: Liveright, 1950), 9–11, 38–42, first published as *Jenseits des Lustprinzips* (Leipzig: Internationaler Psychoanalytischer Verlag, 1920); see also Freud et al., *Psycho-Analysis and the War Neuroses* (Vienna: International Psychoanalytical Press, 1921), first published as *Zur Psychoanalyse der Kriegsneurosen* (Leipzig: Internationaler Psychoanalytischer Verlag, 1919).

40. Lifton, *The Broken Connection,* 295, 297, 299, 302–3.

41. "Polak-katolik i katolik-Polak," 51.

42. Kazimierz Wyka, "The Excluded Economy," in *The Unplanned Society: Poland During and After Communism,* ed. Janine Wedel (New York: Columbia Univ. Press, 1992), 41. Emphasis in the original. For the Polish text see "Gospodarka wyłączona," in *Życie na niby; Pamiętnik po klęsce* (Kraków: Wydawnictwo Literackie, 1984), 157; the essay bears the date 1945 and was first published in this version in 1959.

43. Some of the articles were reprinted in *Martwa fala: Zbiór artykułów o antisemityźmie* (Warsaw: Spółdzielnia Wydawnicza "Wiedza", 1947). An organization, Ogólnopolska Liga do Walki z Rasizmem (All-Polish Anti-Racist League), was also founded in 1946. It published a periodical, *Prawo Człowieka* (The rights of man), that appeared sporadically, as well as twenty books. On the League, see Władysław Bartoszewski, "The Founding of the All-Polish Anti-Racist League in 1946," *Polin: A Journal of Polish-Jewish Studies* 4 (1989): 243–54.

44. Kersten, *Polacy, Żydzi, Komunizm,* 102–3.

45. Shnayderman, 158; Kersten, *Polacy, Żydzi, Komunizm,* 114.

4. Memory Repressed: 1948–1968

1. On postwar Poland up to the rise of Solidarity, see Davies, *God's Playground,* vol. 2, 556–633.

2. See Andrej Micewski, *Cardinal Wyszynski: A Biography* (San Diego, Calif.: Harcourt Brace Jovanovich, 1984); this book, however, is primarily hagiography.

3. See Janine Wedel, *The Private Poland: An Anthropologist's Look at Everyday Life* (New York: Facts on File, 1986).

4. See, for example, Josef Banas, *The Scapegoats: The Exodus of the Remnants of Polish Jewry* (London: Weidenfeld and Nicholson, 1979).

5. See the important article by K[onstanty]. A. Jeleński, "White Eagle Today and Yesterday," *Soviet Survey* (London), no. 35 (Jan.–Mar. 1961): 12–25.

6. Michael Checinski, *Poland: Communism, Nationalism, Anti-Semitism* (New York: Karz-Cohl, 1982), 89–103; Raymond Taras, "Gomułka's 'Rightist-Nationalist Deviation,' the Postwar Jewish Communists, and the Stalinist Reaction in Poland, 1945–1950," *Nationalities Papers* (New York) 22, Suppl. no. 1 (1994): 123–24.

7. They were also known as the Puławy and Natolin factions, respectively, after locations in Warsaw with which they were associated.

8. For a summary, see *American Jewish Year Book* (Philadelphia) 59 (1958): 326; 60 (1959): 215.

9. "Problem antysemityzmu," *Kultura* (Paris), no. 1/111–2/112 (Jan.–Feb. 1957): 62. Another respondent from Poland expressed the opinion that "today anti-semitism, in distinction from the prewar period, has been embraced by broad masses of peasants and workers, while the participation of the intelligentsia has diminished" (62).

10. Hanka Szwarcman, "Kartki z pamiętnika," in *Po prostu, 1955–1956: Wybór artykułów* (Warsaw: Iskry, 1956), 153–59. In this collection of articles from a leading revisionist publication, Szwarcman's comments are followed by an article by Leszek Kołakowski, which reminds its readers that anti-Semitism inevitably means counter-revolution ("Antysemici—pięć tez nienowych i przestroga" [Anti-Semites—five theses which aren't new and a warning], 160–70). See also Paweł Machcewicz, "Anti-semitism in Poland in 1956," *Polin: Studies in Polish Jewry* (London) 9 (1996): 170–83.

11. Banas, *The Scapegoats*, 29–30.

12. *American Jewish Year Book* 62 (1961): 292.

13. *American Jewish Year Book* 60 (1959): 216; 61 (1960): 265; 64 (1963): 360; 69 (1968): 505; Paul Glikson, "Jewish Population in the Polish People's Republic, 1944–1972," in *Papers in Jewish Demography, 1973: Proceedings of the Demographic Sessions Held at the 6th World Congress of Jewish Studies, Jerusalem, August 1973* (Jerusalem: Institute of Contemporary Jewry, Hebrew Univ., 1977), 243–44.

14. The creation of such narratives has been termed "memory work" by some recent writers; see, for example, Iwona Irwin-Zarecka, *Neutralizing Memory: The Jew is Contemporary Poland* (New Brunswick: Transaction Publishers, 1989); and James E. Young, *The Texture of Memory: Holocaust Memorials and Meaning* (New Haven, Conn.: Yale Univ. Press, 1993).

15. Franciszek Piper, "Estimating the Number of Deportees to and Victims of the Auschwitz-Birkenau Camp," *Yad Vashem Studies* 21 (1991): 49–103; Piper is employed by the State Auschwitz Museum at Oświęcim. Based on somewhat earlier research, the Israeli historian Yehuda Bauer arrived at slightly higher figures: 83,000 Poles and 1,350,000 Jews; see "Auschwitz: The Dangers of Distortion," *Jerusalem Post*, September 30, 1989, reprinted in Carol Rittner and John K. Roth, eds., *Memory Offended: The Auschwitz Convent Controversy* (New York: Praeger, 1991), 251–53.

16. *Miejsca męczeństwa i walki Żydów na ziemiach polskich, 1939–1945* (Warsaw: Rada Ochrony Pomników Walki i Męczeństwa, 1978), text in Polish, Yiddish, English, French, Russian, and German, 5.

17. Young, *The Texture of Memory*, 139–40.

18. *Struggle, Death, Memory, 1939–1945: On the Twentieth Anniversary of the Rising in the Warsaw Ghetto, 1943–1963* (Warsaw: Council for the Preservation of the Monuments of Struggle and Martyrdom, 1963), unpaginated.

19. Wacław Poterański, *Walka Warszawskiego Ghetta* (Warsaw: Zarząd Główny Związku Bojowników o Wolność i Demokrację, 1963), 52.

20. Ibid., 28.

21. Ibid., 37.

22. (Warsaw: Iskry, 1957), unpaginated.

23. Janusz Gumkowski and Kazimierz Leszczyński, *Poland under Nazi Occupation* (Warsaw: Polonia, 1961), 16–17. For a review of Polish Holocaust historiography published until 1970, see Lucy Dawidowicz, "Appropriating the Holocaust: Polish Historical Revisionism," in *The Holocaust and the Historians* (Cambridge, Mass.: Harvard Univ. Press, 1981), 88–124. While nearly nothing about the Holocaust was published from 1949 to 1955, more than forty volumes of histories, memoirs, and literature appeared between 1956 and 1962; see Bernard Mark, *Męczeństwo i walka Żydów w latach okupacji: Poradnik bibliograficzny* (Warsaw: n.p., 1963).

24. "Musimy pamiętać, będziemy pamiętać," *Prawo i życie*, 1964, no. 11; cited in Young, *The Texture of Memory*, 363–64.

25. Henryk Grynberg, *Życie osobiste* (Personal life) (Warsaw: Oficyna Wydawnicza "Pokolenie", 1989), 56; the book was first published in London in 1979.

26. The ability to survive daily life psychologically demanded compromises, "the search for grains of truth, quarter-truths, half-truths, and three-quarter truths, and such could be found, thanks to which this world seemed more bearable" (Jerzy Halbersztadt, personal communication, January 23, 1995).

27. For memories of growing up in a "typical" patriotic Polish family in the 1950s and 1960s, see Marek Turbacz, "1968 and All That," in Abraham Brumberg, ed., *Poland: Genesis of a Revolution* (New York: Random House, 1983), 237–39.

28. *Życie osobiste*, 26.

5. Memory Expelled: 1968–1970

1. A typical example of this approach is the recent book by Jerzy Eisler, *Marzec 1968* (Warsaw: Państwowe Wydawnictwo Naukowe, 1991); an important exception is an article by Helena Poróg, "Spory o marzec," *Krytyka* (Warsaw), 1982, no. 10–11: 33–52.

2. English sources include: *The Anti-Jewish Campaign in Present-Day Poland: Facts, Documents, Press Reports* (London: Institute of Jewish Affairs in association with the World Jewish Congress, 1968); Paul Lendvai, *Anti-Semitism Without Jews: Communist Eastern Europe* (Garden City, N.Y.: Doubleday, 1971); Josef Banas, *The Scapegoats: The Exodus of the Remnants of Polish Jewry* (London: Weidenfeld and Nicholson, 1979); Michael Checinski, *Poland: Communism, Nationalism, Anti-Semitism* (New York: Karz-Cohl, 1982).

3. *The Anti-Jewish Campaign in Present-Day Poland*, 11.

4. "8 marca 1988 roku," *Krytyka* (Warsaw), 1988, no. 28–29:22.

5. "O marcu—dziś: Z rozmowy redakcyjnej (fragmenty)," *Res Publica* (Warsaw) 2 (1988), no. 3 (9): 6–7.

6. Those who have strongly argued for the influence of the Soviets on the Polish anti-Zionist campaign include M. K. Dziewanowski in his *Communist Party of Poland: An Outline of History* (Cambridge, Mass.: Harvard Univ. Press, 1976), 299–301. But the Soviet anti-Zionist campaign did not originate, as once assumed, immedi-

ately after the Six-Day War, but only as a response to the subsequent growth of the Jewish national movement in the Soviet Union. The "opening salvo" in this campaign was an article published in *Pravda* on Nov. 30, 1969. See Jonathan Frankel, "The Soviet Regime and Anti-Zionism: An Analysis," in Yaacov Ro'i and Avi Beker, eds., *Jewish Culture and Identity in the Soviet Union* (New York: New York Univ. Press, 1991), 332.

7. The first edition was *Barwy walki* (Warsaw: Wydawnictwo Ministerstwa Obrony Narodowej, 1961); see Checinski, 160.

8. See, for example, the comments of Yisrael Gutman, the Israeli historian of the Warsaw Ghetto Uprising, in "Polish-Jewish Relations During the Second World War: A Discussion," *Polin: A Journal of Polish-Jewish Studies* 2 (1987): 341.

9. The original article appeared on pp. 87–89 of vol. 8 (Warsaw: Państwowe Wydawnictwo Naukowe, 1966).

10. See Władysław Machejek, "Smutno mi, Boże . . . ," *Życie literackie* (Kraków), Aug. 6, 1967; Tadeusz Kur [Witold Jerzmanowski], "Encyklopedyści," *Prawo i życie*, Mar. 24, 1968; Adam Bromberg, "Encyklopedyści," *Kultura* (Paris), 1973, no. 7–8: 174–78; no. 9: 123–28; no. 10: 157–64.

11. Wacław Poterański, *Warszawskie ghetto: W 25-lecie walki zbrojnej w getcie w 1943 r.* (Warsaw: Książka i Wiedza, 1968) 6–7.

12. Hannah Arendt had first made such accusations in the West in 1963, when her reports on the Eichmann trial were serialized in *The New Yorker*. They were published in book form as *Eichmann in Jerusalem: A Report on the Banality of Evil* (New York: Viking, 1965).

13. Poterański, *Warszawskie ghetto: W 25-lecie*, 54.

14. Ibid., 77.

15. Wacław Poterański, *Warszawkie getto: W 30-lecie powstania zbrojnego w getcie w 1943 r.* (Warsaw: Wydawnictwo Interpress, 1973), 11, 29, 54.

16. Warsaw: Państwowe Wydawnictwo Naukowe, 1979.

17. Simon Wiesenthal, "Jew-Baiting in Poland: A Documentation about Prewar Fascists and Nazi Collaborators and Their Unity of Action with Anti-Semites from the Ranks of the Communist Party of Poland," mimeograph (Vienna, 1969); cited in Lendvai, *Anti-Semitism Without Jews*, 136, 357 n. 45. Pilichowski was succeeded as director of the High Commission by Kazimierz Kąkol, another of Moczar's Partisans.

18. Czesław Pilichowski, "Hitlerowskie obozy i ośrodki przymusowego odosobnienia oraz ich rola w realizacji programu ludobójstwa i zagłady narodu polskiego," in *Obozy hitlerowskie na ziemiach polskich*, 11. A similar perspective is adopted by Czesław Madajczyk in his influential history of the war years, *Polityka III Rzeszy w okupowanej Polsce*, 2 vols. (Warsaw: Państwowe Wydawnictwo Naukowe, 1970).

19. Anna Radziwiłł, "The Teaching of the History of the Jews in Secondary Schools in the Polish People's Republic, 1949–88," *Polin: A Journal of Polish-Jewish Studies* 4 (1989): 417–18.

20. H. Sędziwy, *Historia dla klasy XI* (Warsaw, 1968), 243–44.

21. R. Wapiński, *Historia dla kl. IV liceum ogólnokształcącego* (Warsaw, 1969); T. Siergiejczyk, *Dzieje najnowsze 1939–45: Historia dla szkół średnich* (Warsaw, 1986); Radziwiłł, 415.

22. Siergiejczyk, 199, cited in Radziwiłł, 416.

23. Ibid., 205.

24. See Zofia Nałkowska, *Medaliony* (Medallions) (Warsaw: Czytelnik, 1946); Tadeusz Borowski, *Pożegnanie z Marią* (Farewell to Maria) (Warsaw: Wiedza, 1948) and *Kamienny świat* (World of stone) (Warsaw, 1948); these stories were reprinted in numerous subequent editions. Borowski's work is well known in English; see *This Way for the Gas, Ladies and Gentlemen* (New York: Penguin, 1967).

25. "Polacy z pomocą Żydom, 1939–1944," *Tygodnik Powszechny* (Kraków), 1963, no. 12: 3; reprinted in *Kultura* (Paris), 1963, no. 5 (187): 93–95.

26. Władysław Bartoszewski and Zofia Lewinówna, eds., *Ten jest z ojczyzny mojej: Polacy z pomocą Żydom, 1939–1945* (Kraków: Znak, 1966); 2d enl. ed. (Kraków: Znak, 1969). There are two English versions, the first based on the second Polish edition, the other abridged: *Righteous among Nations: How the Poles Helped the Jews* (London: Earlscourt, 1969); *The Samaritans: Heroes of the Holocaust* (New York: Twayne, 1970). Polish aid to Jews during the war was also the subject of a monograph published several years earlier by scholars connected to the Jewish Historical Institute in Warsaw: Tatiana Berenstein and Adam Rutkowski, *Pomoc Żydom w Polsce, 1939–1945* (Warsaw: Polonia, 1963).

27. The English edition is Władysław Bartoszewski, *The Blood Shed Unites Us* (Warsaw: Interpress, 1970). The following year Interpress published another volume of documents, testimonies, and photographs: Stanisław Wroński and Maria Zwolakowa, eds., *Polacy i Żydzi, 1939–1945* (Warsaw: Interpress, 1971).

28. *Izrael a NRF* (Warsaw: Książka i Wiedza, 1967); the author reemerged twenty years later as a researcher of Soviet crimes against the Poles during World War II. See Tadeusz Walichnowski, ed., *Deportacje i przemieszczenia ludności polskiej w głąb ZSRR, 1939–1945: Przegląd piśmiennictwa* (Warsaw: Państwowe Wydawnictwo Naukowe, 1989).

29. Wojciech Zabrzeski, "Sojusz ofiar z katami," *Prawo i życie*, Nov. 21, 1967.

30. Banas, *The Scapegoats*, 83; the comment is attributed to Kazimierz Rusinek, deputy minister of culture and art, in the period just after the Six-Day War.

31. Piotr Goszczyński, *Głos Robotniczy*, May 12, 1968; cited in Lendvai, *Anti-Semitism Without Jews*, 159.

32. Lendvai, *Anti-Semitism Without Jews*, 159; the original source was apparently the Polish émigré periodical *Kultura*.

33. A characteristic work is Wacław Szafrański, *W sieci Szymona Wiesenthala* (In the net of Simon Wiesenthal) (Warsaw: Wydawnictwo Ministerstwa Obrony Narodowej, 1972), which "reveals" Wiesenthal's postwar ties to West Germany and the CIA alongside his wartime links to the Gestapo.

34. Pobóg, "Spory o marzec," 44.

35. See, for example, Banas, *The Scapegoats*, 57–58.

36. See Pobóg, "Spory o marzec," 46–49; Kersten, *Polacy, Żydzi, Komunizm*, 166–70.

37. Eisler, *Marzec 1968*, 328.

38. Adam Michnik, "The Two Faces of Europe," *New York Review of Books*, July 19, 1990.

39. Lifton, *The Broken Connection*, 177.

6. Memory Reconstructed: 1970–1989

1. See Keith John Lepak, *Prelude to Solidarity: Poland and the Politics of the Gierek Regime* (New York: Columbia Univ. Press, 1988); see also the useful chronology in Lawrence Weschler, *Solidarity: Poland in the Season of Its Passion* (New York: Simon and Schuster, 1982), 137–207.

2. *Kościół, lewica, dialog* (Paris: Instytut Literacki, 1977), 89; published in English as *The Church and the Left* (Chicago: Univ. of Chicago Press, 1993). Słonimski, to whom the book is dedicated, had been attacked during the interwar period, as was Michnik during the 1960s and after, for his Jewish origins.

3. *Kościół, lewica, dialog*, 91.

4. Ibid., 116–19.

5. Ibid., 114.

6. *Listy Pasterskie Episkopatu Polski, 1945–1974* (Paris: Editions du Dialogue, 1975), 707–8, cited in *Kościół, lewica, dialog*, 110.

7. *Tygodnik Powszechny*, ed. Jerzy Turowicz, and *Znak*, ed. Stefan Wilkanowicz, were published continuously since the 1940s except 1953–56; *Więź*, ed. Tadeusz Mazowiecki, began publication in the late 1950s. On the Catholic intelligentsia in Polish politics, see Andrzej Micewski, *Współrządzić czy nie kłamać? Pax i Znak w Polsce, 1945–1976* (Paris: Libella, 1978).

8. See Jan Józef Lipski, *KOR: A History of the Workers' Defense Committee in Poland, 1976–1981* (Berkeley, Calif.: Univ. of California Press, 1985), 62–78, 208–31.

9. See, for example, Kersten, *Polacy, Żydzi, Komunizm*, 144–45.

10. This was the title, for example, of a pamphlet published by left-wing Yiddish-speaking Jews: Itche Goldberg and Yuri Suhl, eds., *The End of a Thousand Years: The Recent Exodus of the Jews from Poland* (New York: Committee for Jews of Poland, 1971).

11. Young, *The Texture of Memory*, 182.

12. Lipski, *KOR: A History*, 139–40.

13. On Jews and the memory of the Holocaust in Poland in the 1980s, see Iwona Irwin-Zarecka, *Neutralizing Memory: The Jew in Contemporary Poland* (New Brunswick N.J.: Transaction Publishers, 1989), and "Poland, after the Holocaust," in Yehuda Bauer et al., eds., *Remembering for the Future: Working Papers and Addenda* (Oxford: Pergamon Press, 1989), vol. 1, 143–55; Antony Polonsky, "Polish-Jewish Relations and the Holocaust," *Polin: A Journal of Polish-Jewish Studies* 4 (1989): 226–42; Andrzej Bryk, "Polish Society Today and the Memory of the Holocaust," *Gal-Ed: On the History of the Jews in Poland* (Tel Aviv) 12 (1991): 107–29; and Young, *The Texture of Memory*, 113–208.

14. Michel Wieviorka, *Les Juifs, la Pologne et Solidarność* (Paris: Denoël, 1984), 175–85. For an interview with one of the organizers of the Jewish Flying University, see Małgorzata Niezabitowska, "Finding It (an Interview with Stanisław Krajewski)," *Moment* (Boston), Apr. 1984.

15. Lipski, *KOR: A History*, 331.

16. Ibid., 337–38.

17. "Budowałem razem z wami na fundamencie chrystusowego krzyża," June 9, 1979, and "Bierzmowanie dziejów," June 10, 1979, in *Jan Paweł II na Ziemi Pol-*

skiej (Vatican City: Libreria Editrice Vaticana, 1979), 248, 268; emphasis in the original.

18. "Zwycięstwo przez wiarę i miłość: Homilia Ojca świętego Jana Pawła II," June 7, 1979, in *Jan Pawel II na Ziemi Polskiej,* 207; emphasis in the original.

19. From 1935 to 1939, Kolbe was the publisher of the virulently anti-Semitic Catholic tabloid, *Mały Dziennik* (Little daily), the largest circulation daily newspaper in Poland. On Kolbe and *Mały Dziennik,* see Ronald Modras, *The Catholic Church and Antisemitism: Poland, 1933–1939* (Chur, Switzerland: Harwood, 1994); on Kolbe, see also Jan Józef Szczepański, "Święty," in *Przed nieznanym trybunałem* (Warsaw: Czytelnik, 1975), 31–58.

20. There is a large literature in English on Solidarity. Excellent journalistic accounts of its origins are Neal Ascherson, *The Polish August: The Self-Limiting Revolution* (New York: Viking, 1982); Weschler, *Solidarity: Poland in the Season of Its Passion;* Timothy Garton Ash, *The Polish Revolution: Solidarity* (New York: Scribner, 1984). See also Abraham Brumberg, ed., *Poland: Genesis of a Revolution* (New York: Random House, 1983), and the studies by David Ost, *Solidarity and the Politics of Anti-Politics: Opposition and Reform in Poland since 1968* (Philadelphia: Temple Univ. Press, 1990), and Roman Laba, *The Roots of Solidarity: A Political Sociology of Poland's Working-Class Democratization* (Princeton, N. J.: Princeton Univ. Press, 1991).

21. Józef Przybylski, "Wspomnienia," *Kontakt* (Paris), 1, 21 (Jan. 1984): 32, cited in Laba, *The Roots of Solidarity,* 131.

22. On the history of the Gdańsk monument, see Laba, *The Roots of Solidarity,* 135–38. For documentation of the use of the anchor as a symbol during the war years, see Stanisław Kopf, *Lata okupacji: Kronika fotograficzna walczącej Warszawy* (Warsaw: Instytut Wydawniczy Pax, 1989), 286, 289, 385.

23. *Biuletyn Dolnośląski* (Lower Silesian bulletin), "Żydzi i Polacy, Dodatek specjalny," no. 11/18, Nov.–Dec. 1980; the Hebrew date is also given: "Kislew-Teweth 5741." The Warsaw Ghetto was sealed in Nov. 1940; other ghettos were closed during this or the following year.

24. *Biuletyn Dolnośląski,* 1–2; emphases in the original.

25. A. Kainer [Stanisław Krajewski], "Żydzi a komunizm," *Krytyka* (London), 1983, no. 15: 214–47.

26. The original appeared in *Odczytanie popiołów: Wiersze* (London: Niezależna Oficyna Wydawnicza, 1979), the translation in *A Reading of Ashes,* trans. Keith Bosley with Krystyna Wandycz (London: Menard Press, 1981), 2. Ficowski has also written about the prewar Polish-Jewish writer and artist Bruno Schultz and about Polish Gypsies.

27. "Listy do redakcji: Marzec 1968," *Polityka,* no. 50, Dec. 12, 1980.

28. See the comments of Stanisław Krajewski in a collection of contemporary documents: Towarzystwo Kursów Naukowych, *Marzec 1968* (Warsaw: Niezależna Oficyna Wydawnicza, 1981), 38–39; another such collection is *Post Factum: Biuletyn specjalny* (Warsaw: NSZ Uniwersytet Warszawski, March 1981).

29. On the final years of Polish communism, see Michael T. Kaufman, *Mad Dreams, Saving Graces: Poland—A Nation in Conspiracy* (New York: Random House, 1989); Maciej Łopiński, Marcin Moskit, and Mariusz Wilk, eds., *Konspira: Solidarity Un-*

derground (Berkeley: Univ. of California Press, 1990); Ost, *Solidarity and the Politics of Anti-Politics*, 149–222.

30. James Young uses the term "broken tablets"; see *The Texture of Memory*, 185–208.

31. Antoni Słonimski, "Elegia miasteczek żydowskich," in Jan Winczakiewicz, ed., *Izrael w poezji polskiej: Antologia* (Paris: Instytut Literacki, 1958), 239.

32. The conference was appropriately titled: "Poles and Jews: Myth and Reality in the Historical Context." See *Proceedings of the Conference on Poles and Jews— Myth and Reality in the Historical Context, Held at Columbia University, March 6–10, 1983* (New York: Institute on East Central Europe, Columbia Univ., 1986). Subsequent conferences have been held in the United States, England, Israel, and Poland.

33. The delegation's official status was that of tourists; it was headed by Prof. Chone Shmeruk of the Hebrew University.

34. As of 1996, nine volumes of *Polin* have appeared; the editor is Antony Polonsky. Beginning with vol. 8, its subtitle has been changed to *Studies in Polish Jewry*.

35. The only comparable period, and only with respect to publications about the Holocaust, was 1945–48. But more than half of the new "Jewish" publications were not directly about the Holocaust. This wave of publications, moreover, kept growing; there were 171 "Jewish" books published during 1980–86, 123 during the subsequent two years. See "Judaica: Bibliografia publikacji polskich za lata 1980– 1986" and "Judaica . . . za lata 1987–1988," unpublished typescripts available through the Jewish Historical Institute in Warsaw. In English, see also Natan Gross, "Requiem for the Jewish People (Polish Literary Judaica in the Years 1987–1989)," *Polin: A Journal of Polish-Jewish Studies* 6 (1991): 295–308.

36. *Znak* 35 (1983), nos. 2–3.

37. *Żydzi w kulturze polskiej* appeared in an edition published by Więż (Warsaw, 1988) and also in an underground edition (Oficyna Wydawnicza Margines, 1987). It was first published in Paris (Instytut Literacki) in 1961; an English translation by Richard Lourie appeared in 1988: *The Jews in Polish Culture* (Evanston, Ill.: Northwestern Univ. Press). On Hertz, see Michael C. Steinlauf, "Whose Poland? Returning to Aleksander Hertz," *Gal-Ed: On the History of the Jews in Poland* (Tel Aviv) 12 (1991): 131–42.

38. *Męczeństwo i zagłada Żydów w zapisach literatury polskiej* (The martyrdom and annihilation of the Jews as recorded in Polish literature) (Warsaw: Krajowa Agencja Wydawnicza, 1988). Maciejewska's volume is prefaced by an essay reviewing Polish literature on the Holocaust (5–33); see also her "Poezja polska wobec powstania w getcie warszawskim" (Polish poetry on the Warsaw Ghetto Uprising), *Kronika Warszawy* (1989), no. 1:77–98. On Polish Holocaust literature, see also the recent study by Natan Gross, *Poeci i Szoa: Obraz Zagłady Żydów w poezji polskiej* (Poets and the Shoah: The image of the annihilation of the Jews in Polish poetry) (Sosnowiec: Offmax, 1993). For surveys in English, see Madeleine G. Levine, "Polish Literature and the Holocaust," *Holocaust Studies Annual* 3 (1987): 189–202; Monika Adamczyk-Garbowska, "A New Generation of Voices in Polish Holocaust Literature," *Prooftexts* (1989), no. 3: 273–87. See also Madeleine G. Levine, "The Ambiguity of Moral Outrage in Jerzy Andrzejewski's *Wielki Tydzień*," *Polish Review* 32 (1987), no. 4: 385–99.

39. On these poems, see pp. 113–17 above. Older publications on which Maciejewska drew include the clandestinely published booklet *Z otchłani* (Out of the abyss) (Warsaw, 1944), republished as *Poezje ghetta: Z podziemia żydowskiego w Polsce* (New York: Association of Friends of *Our Tribune*, 1945); Michał Borwicz's poetry anthology *Pieśń ujdzie cało:* (The song will survive) *Antologia wierszy o Żydach pod okupacją niemiecką* (Warsaw: Centralna Żydowska Komisja Historyczna w Polsce, 1947); Leopold Buczkowski's novel *Czarny potok* (Black torrent) (Warsaw: Pax, 1954); and collections of stories by Zofia Nałkowska and Tadeusz Borowski; on the latter authors see p. 84 above.

40. Ironically, *Głosy w ciemności*, which launched Stryjkowski's career as the "Polish I. B. Singer," was written in Moscow in 1942, where the author, a dedicated Communist at the time, had fled as the war began. On Stryjkowski in English, see Stanisław Eile, "The Tragedy of the Chosen People: Jewish Themes in the Novels of Julian Stryjkowski," *Soviet Jewish Affairs* 13, no. 3 (1983): 27–43; Laura Quercioli-Mincer, "A Voice from the Diaspora: Julian Stryjkowski," in Antony Polonsky, ed., *From Shtetl to Socialism: Studies from Polin* (London: Littman Library of Jewish Civilization, 1993), 487–501. On Polish-language Jewish writers see Artur Sandauer, *O sytuacji pisarza polskiego pochodzenia żydowskiego w XX wieku (Rzecz, którą nie ja powinienem był napisać . . .)* (Warsaw: Czytlenik, 1982); Eugenia Prokop-Janiec, *Międzywojenna literatura polsko-żydowska* (Kraków: Universitas Kraków, 1992); Zygmunt Bauman, "The Literary Afterlife of Polish Jewry," *Polin: A Journal of Polish-Jewish Studies* 7 (1992): 273–99; Jan Błoński, "Autoportret żydowski, czyli o żydowskiej szkole w literaturze polskiej," in *Biedni Polacy patrzą na getto* (Kraków: Wydawnictwo Literackie, 1994), 57–113. For an English translation of an earlier version of the latter, see "Is There a Jewish School of Polish Lirature?" *Polin: A Journal of Polish-Jewish Studies* 1 (1986): 196–211. On Polish films, see Edward Rogerson, "Images of Jewish Poland in the Post-war Polish Cinema," *Polin: A Journal of Polish-Jewish Studies* 2 (1987): 359–71.

41. Wojdowksi's novel was first published in Warsaw (Państwowy Instytut Wydawniczy) in 1971; in English, see Madeleine G. Levine, "Two Warsaws: The Literary Representation of Catastrophe," *Eastern European Politics and Societies* 1 (1987), no. 3: 349–62. Wojdowski committed suicide in 1994; for an obituary, see Helena Zaworska, "Śmierć Hioba," *Gazeta Wyborcza*, Apr. 25, 1994. On Krall's works, see also p. 107 above. Grynberg's first novel, *Żydowska wojna* (The Jewish war), was first published in Warsaw (Czytelnik) in 1965, but not reprinted by the official press until 1989 (Warsaw: Czytelnik). Several of Grynberg's works have been translated into English, most recently his novel *Zwycięstwo* (Paris: Instytut Literacki, 1969), about the years 1944–48, as *The Victory* (Evanston, Ill.: Northwestern Univ. Press, 1993). On Grynberg, see Józef Wróbel, "Henryk Grynberg Calls Poland to Account," *Polin: A Journal of Polish-Jewish Studies* 7 (1992): 176–91.

42. Błoński, "Autoportret żydowski," 63, 76. There was also new Polish fiction about the Holocaust written by non-Jews, most notably Jarosław Marek Rymkiewicz's *Umschlagplatz*, the first Polish novel exclusively about the Holocaust written by a non-Jew. First published in Paris (Instytut Literacki) in 1988, it has been translated into English as *The Final Station: Umschlagplatz* (New York: Farrar

Straus Giroux, 1994). For other examples, see Józef Wróbel, *Tematy żydowskie w prozie polskiej, 1939–1987* (Kraków: Towarzystwo Autorówi Wydawców Prac Naukowych "Universitas," 1991).

43. *Literatura*, March 19, 1981.

44. *Grunwald: Biuletyn Informacyjny Zjednoczenia Patriotycznego "Grunwald"* (Warsaw, 1980s).

45. Wacław Poterański, *Warszawskie getto*, preface by Ryszard Nazarewicz (Warsaw: Książka i Wiedza, 1983); Józef Orlicki, *Szkice z dziejów stosunków polsko-żydowskich, 1918–1949* (Szczecin: Krajowa Agencja Wydawnicza, 1983), 251–63.

46. Hanna Krall, *Zdążyć przed Panem Bogiem* (Kraków: Wydawnictwo Literackie) has been translated as *Shielding the Flame: An Intimate Conversation with Dr. Marek Edelman, the Last Surviving Leader of the Warsaw Ghetto Uprising* (New York: Henry Holt, 1986); this translation has been reprinted under a new title, along with Krall's memoirs of the Holocaust (*Sublokatorka* [Paris: Libella, 1985]) in: *The Subtenant; to Outwit God* (Evanston, Ill.: Northwestern Univ. Press, 1992). On *Sublokatorka*, see the review by Michael C. Steinlauf, *Polin: A Journal of Polish-Jewish Studies* 2 (1987): 466–70.

47. *Zdążyć przed Panem Bogiem*, 15–16.

48. The full text is reprinted in Władysław Bartoszewski and Marek Edelman, *Żydzi Warszawy* (Lublin: Towarzystwo Naukowe Katolickiego Uniwersytetu Lubelskiego, 1993), 178.

49. As a Fulbright Fellow in Poland in 1983–84 and on numerous subsequent visits, I was privileged to witness these and related events.

50. On these new monuments, see Young, *The Texture of Memory*, 203–6.

51. "Letter from Lech Wałęsa to Marek Edelman, Apr. 17, 1988," *Tikkun* 3 (1988), no. 5: 27.

52. For an excellent example, see Kaufman, *Mad Dreams, Saving Graces*, 175–77.

53. "Antysemityzm, Patriotyzm, Chrześcijaństwo," *Znak* 35 (1983), nos. 2–3: 176, 171.

54. "Dwie ojczyzny—dwa patriotyzmy (Uwagi o megalomanii narodowej i ksenofobii Polaków)," xeroxed (Warsaw: Wydawnictwo CDN, 1982), 3–4, 6. The essay was reprinted in Lipski's *Dwie ojczyzny i inne szkice* ([Poland]: Myśl, 1985).

55. "Dwie ojczyzny," 25.

56. Shoshana Felman, "The Return of the Voice: Claude Lanzmann's *Shoah*," in Shoshana Felman and Dori Laub, *Testimony: Crises of Witnessing in Literature, Psychoanalysis, and History* (New York: Routledge, 1992), 208, 210; emphasis in the original. For the text of the film, see Claude Lanzmann, *Shoah: An Oral History of the Holocaust* (New York: Pantheon, 1985).

57. *Rzeczpospolita* (Warsaw), May 2, 1985.

58. *Rzeczpospolita*, May 2, 1985; Neal Ascherson, "The *Shoah* Controversy," *Soviet Jewish Affairs* 16, no. 1 (1986): 54–55.

59. Maciej Kozłowski, "Zrozumieć," *Ogniwo* (Wrocław), no. 25, Apr. (1986): 26.

60. *Tygodnik Mazowsze*, no. 145, Nov. 7, 1985.

61. See, for example: Stanisław Kostarski, "Film 'Shoah': Prawda i fałsze Claude Lanzmanna," *Życie Warszawy*, May 11–12, 1985; "Po Projekcji 'Shoah': Fałszywy

obraz," *Rzeczpospolita*, Nov. 4, 1985; Jerzy Turowicz, "'Shoah' w polskich oczach," *Tygodnik Powszechny*, Nov. 10, 1985; Teresa Pisarek, "'Shoah' i myśl niezależna," *Obecność* (Wrocław), 1986, no. 14:103–6; Andrzej Stanisławski, "'Shoah,' czy może 'romantyzm rewolucyjny'?" *Kurs*, 1986, no. 18:45–50.

62. A recent analysis of 150 letters written to the Polish television station TVP by viewers of the original broadcast reveals similar opinions along with numerous primarily hostile stereotypes of Jews. See Anna Sawisz, "Obraz Żydów i stosunków polsko-żydowskich w listach telewidzów po emisji filmu *Shoah*," in Aleksandra Jasińska-Kania, ed., *Bliscy i dalecy*, Studia nad postawami wobec innych narodów, ras i grup etnicznych, vol. 2 (Warsaw: Uniwersytet Warszawski, Instytut Socjologii, 1992), 137–65.

63. The essay has been reprinted in Błoński's collection of articles, *Biedni Polacy patrzą na getto*. For translations of Miłosz's poem, Błoński's essay, and selected responses, see Antony Polonsky, ed., *My Brother's Keeper? Recent Polish Debates on the Holocaust* (London: Routledge, 1990).

64. Czesław Miłosz, "Campo dei Fiore," in *My Brother's Keeper?* 50; the translation is by A. Gillon; first published in *Z otchłani*, reprinted in *Poezje ghetta: Z podziemia żydowskiego w Polsce*, 23–24; see p. 166n. 39 above.

65. Czesław Miłosz, "A Poor Christian Looks at the Ghetto," in *My Brother's Keeper?* 51; the translation is the poet's.

66. Jan Błoński, "The Poor Poles Look at the Ghetto," in *My Brother's Keeper?* 41–42.

67. Ibid., 35, 44.

68. Ibid., 45.

69. Ibid., 43, 45–46; emphasis in the original. Nearly a decade later, Błoński described the personal roots of these feelings when, as a boy, he watched two Jewish boys fleeing the burning Warsaw ghetto emerge from the sewers on the "Aryan side." For the moment there were no Germans in sight. Passersby tried to look away; the boys clearly did not know where to turn. Błoński recalls: "I was twelve and a half. I knew no one in this neighborhood. I could have given them some money, a piece of bread. But I had neither money nor bread. I couldn't help them with anything. I couldn't even smile or nod at them, for they would have interpreted it as derision or as a sign that I would turn them in. There was truly nothing I could do. I was justified [usprawiedliwiony]. What relief. Nearly joy. But after a moment—shame. I felt ashamed at my joy. And in some sense I still feel this shame today." ("I policzą nas między pomocników śmierci," *Gazeta Wyborcza*, Sept. 9–10, 1995.)

70. "Ethical Problems of the Holocaust in Poland: Discussion Held at the International Conference on the History and Culture of Polish Jewry in Jerusalem on Monday 1 February 1988," in *My Brother's Keeper?* 215.

71. Ibid., 216.

72. "Polsko-żydowskie rozrachunki wojenne: Wyzwania Holocaustu; Analiza listów do redakcji *Tygodnika Powszechnego*, nadesłanych w odpowiedzi na dyskusję Błoński–Siła-Nowicki" (Institute of Sociology, University of Warsaw, 1992).

73. "The Hidden Complex of the Polish Mind: Polish-Jewish Relations During the Holocaust," in *My Brother's Keeper?* 168, 171–72.

74. On the controversy see Carol Rittner and John K. Roth, eds., *Memory Offended: The Auschwitz Convent Controversy* (New York: Praeger, 1991); and Władysław Bartoszewski, *The Convent at Auschwitz* (New York: George Braziller, 1991). Bartoszewski is the son of the chronicler of Polish aid to the Jews during the Holocaust.

75. On Kolbe, see p. 96 above.

76. To multiply the ironies, it is useful to recall the origins of this distinction. Because the Polish town of Oświęcim lay just inside the so-called Wartheland, the western part of Poland annexed by the Nazis, it was renamed Auschwitz by them. Similarly Łódź was renamed Litzmannstadt.

77. Mary Jo Leddy, "Auschwitz: Where Only Silence Becomes Prayer," *Memory Offended*, 175.

78. Bartoszewski, *The Convent at Auschwitz*, 7.

79. *Newsweek*, July 31, 1989, cited in Bartoszewski, *The Convent at Auschwitz*, 87.

80. Bartoszewski, *The Convent at Auschwitz*, 87.

81. Ibid., 90–93.

82. Francis A. Winiarz, "We're Not Moving a Single Inch," *Polish Daily News*, Nov. 1, 1989, reprinted in *Memory Offended*, 260–61. Sister Teresa's reference invokes a hallowed myth of the Polish Church: the miraculous intervention of the Virgin Mother to break the seventeenth-century Swedish siege of Częstochowa. The shrine that houses the icon known as the Black Madonna of Częstochowa is the most revered site in Poland. And yet another irony: during the war, as a child, Sister Teresa had apparently taken food to Jews in hiding; see Bartoszewski, *The Convent at Auschwitz*, 102.

83. Translated in *Memory Offended*, 218; the statement was made August 8.

84. "We trust in the capital of wisdom," homily delivered at Jasna Góra, Częstochowa, Aug. 26, 1989, translated in *Memory Offended*, 220–24.

85. *Jerusalem Post*, Sept. 16, 1989, cited in *Memory Offended*, 24.

86. On Polish sentiment against the nuns' moving, see, for example, an interview with Bishop Tadeusz Pieronek published in *Polityka*, no. 16, Apr. 17, 1993. For the pope's letter to the nuns, see *Gazeta Wyborcza*, no. 88, Apr. 15, 1993.

7. Memory Regained?: 1989–1995

1. Konstanty Gebert, "Rola antysemityzmu," in Mirosława Grabowska and Ireneusz Krzemiński, eds., *Bitwa o Belweder* (Warsaw: Wydawnictwo Myśl, 1991). See also, for example, Aleksander Małachowski, "Antysemityzm," *Życie Warszawy*, March 16, 1992; this article also recalls Kazimierz Wyka's observations about Poles inheriting Jewish property. In English, see Jarosław Kurski, *Lech Wałęsa: Democrat or Dictator?* (Boulder, Colo.: Westview Press, 1993), 42–45.

2. J. O., "Tejkowski skazany: Lżył, wyszydzał, poniżał," *Rzeczpospolita*, Oct. 26, 1994.

3. For the polemic about the NSZ, see the articles and letters to the editor in *Gazeta Wyborcza*, March 6–7, 13–14, 20–21, 25, 26, 27–28, and Sept. 27, 1993; and the interview with Krystyna Kersten ("Oblicza prawdy") in *Plus-Minus* (weekly supplement to *Rzeczpospolita*), no. 16, May 8–9, 1993. See also the interesting article by Dariusz Fikus on the term *Żydokomuna* in *Rzeczpospolita*, Apr. 30, 1993. The Jewish

Historical Institute devoted an entire issue of its *Biuletyn* (no. 3–4, July–Dec. 1993) to recent studies of anti-Seminitism in Poland and abroad.

4. "Naukowy imprimatur dla *Mein Kampf,*" *Gazeta Wyborcza,* Jan. 25, 1992; Andrzej Szczypiorski, *"Mein Kampf*—łatwa pokusa," *Gazeta Wyborcza,* Jan. 28, 1992; Małgorzata Szpakowska, "Jedna z książek, które zabiały," *Gazeta Wyborcza,* Feb. 29, 1992.

5. Aleksandra Jasińska-Kania, "Zmiany postaw Polaków wobec różnych narodów i państw," in Aleksandra Jasińska-Kania, ed., *Bliscy i dalecy.* Studia nad postawami wobec innych narodów, ras i grup etnicznych, vol. 2 (Warsaw: Uniwersytet Warszawski, Instytut Socjologii, 1992), 224. In English, see the pamphlet published by the American Jewish Committee: Renae Cohen and Jennifer L. Golub, *Attitudes Toward Jews in Poland, Hungary, and Czechoslovakia: A Comparative Survey* (New York, 1991); the figures for Poland are based on polls conducted by the Demoskop Research Agency in 1991.

6. "Nie w jednej ławce," *Gazeta Wyborcza,* July 14, 1992.

7. Alina Cała, "Autostereotyp i stereotypy narodowe," *Biuletyn Żydowskiego Instytutu Historycznego,* no. 3–4, July–Dec. 1993, 142.

8. The questionnaire was administered by the Office for Sociological Research [Pracownia Badań Socjologicznych] in Sopot; the ŻIH team consisted of Alina Cała, Helena Datner-Śpiewak, Ewa Koźmińska-Frejlak, Ireneusz Krzemiński (director), and Andrzej Żbikowski. The resulting study, a volume entitled *Czy Polacy są antysemitami?* (Are Poles anti-Semites?), is currently scheduled for publication. I am indebted to the Committee on Scholarly Research [Komitet Badań Naukowych] and the Jewish Historical Institute for furnishing me with a typescript and permitting me to quote from it. In the following notes, page numbers refer to chapters that are separately paginated in the typescript.

9. Helena Datner-Śpiewak, "Struktura i wyznaczniki postaw antysemickich," in *Czy Polacy są antysemitami?*

10. Ireneusz Krzemiński, "Wprowadzenie: Polacy i Żydzi w świetle socjologicznego badania," in *Czy Polacy są antysemitami?* 3, 5.

11. Ibid., 16.

12. Ireneusz Krzemiński, "Czy Polacy są antysemitami? Zjawisko i znaczenie antysemityzmu w Polsce w oczach badanych," in *Czy Polacy są antysemitami?* 29–30.

13. Krzemiński, "Wprowadzenie: Polacy i Żydzi w świetle socjologicznego badania," in *Czy Polacy są antysemitami?* 6.

14. Compare the somewhat different responses to a similar question on p. 173n. 55 below.

15. Andrzej Żbikowski, "Źródła wiedzy Polaków o Żydach: Socjalizacja postaw," in *Czy Polacy są antysemitami?* 16.

16. On this phenomenon, see Monika Adamczyk-Garbowska, *Polska Isaaca Bashevisa Singera: Rozstanie i Powrót* (Lublin: Wydawnictwo Uniwersytetu Marii Curie-Skłodkowskiej, 1994). The author, who is also the first to have published Polish translations of Singer directly from the Yiddish, appends useful bibliographies of works by and about Singer in Polish (181–94).

17. On the conferences, see, respectively: Helena Balicka-Kozłowska, "Nie wolno

uogólniać: Na marginesie konferencji 'Czy obojętność może zabić,'" *Więź*, Apr. 1994:68–82; Michael C. Steinlauf, "International Conference on Jewish Theater Held in Poland," *Slavic and East European Performance* 14 (1994), no. 1: 44–48.

18. According to *Rocznik Statystyczny* (Warsaw) for 1994, in 1993 there were 1,170 members of the Związek Religijny Wyznania Mojżeszowego (Union of Congregations of the Mosaic Faith) and 3,245 members of the secular Towarzystwo Społeczno-Kulturalne Żydów w Polsce (Social-Cultural Society of the Jews of Poland). There may be some overlap in these figures. A key problem, as usual, is how to define who is a Jew. Some have estimated the number of Poles of Jewish descent at 40,000. In public opinion surveys, Poles greatly overestimate the number of Jews in Poland. According to a survey published in November 1992, one in ten Poles believe that 10 to 20 percent of the Polish population is Jewish; see *Spotkania*, Apr. 15–21, 1993:28.

19. Gregorz Polak, "Lekcja prawdy," *Gazeta Wyborcza*, Oct. 26, 1993. In 1991 and 1992 the Polish-Israeli Friendship Society and the Jewish Historical Institute organized competitions for Polish master's theses and doctoral dissertations on Jewish topics. See Alina Cała, "The Second Competition of Scholarly Works on Polish Jewish Themes," *Polin: Studies in Polish Jewry* (London) 9 (1996): 232–43. The author appends a list of all the works submitted to these competitions.

20. Jacek E. Wilczur, "Sobibór—fałsz i prawda," *Życie Warszawy*, Dec. 13, 1991; "Śladami 'marszu śmierci,'" *Życie Warszawy*, Aug. 24, 1992.

21. Marcin Piasecki, "Odwaga sumienia," *Gazeta Wyborcza*, Feb. 10, 1995.

22. Barbara Engelking, *Zagłada i pamięć* (Annihilation and memory) (Warsaw: Wydawnictwo IFiS PAN, 1994); Piotr Matywiecki, *Kamień Graniczny* (Border stone) (Warsaw: Oficyna Wydawnicza Latona, 1994); Calel Perechodnik, *Czy ja jestem mordercą?* ed. Paweł Szapiro (Warsaw: Karta, 1993), trans. Frank Fox as *Am I a Murderer? Testament of a Jewish Ghetto Policeman* (Boulder, Colo.: Westview Press, 1996).

23. Katarzyna Bielas, "Miejsce dochodzenia," *Gazeta Wyborcza*, Oct. 21, 1993.

24. Andrzej Żbikowski, "Źródła wiedzy Polaków o Żydach: Socjalizacja postaw," 11.

25. *Czarny Ptasior* (Gdańsk: Wydawnictwo Marabut, 1994); and see James Park Sloan, "Kosinski's War," *The New Yorker*, Oct. 10, 1994:46–53.

26. *Czarny Ptasior*, 155.

27. "Scena, której nie mogę zapomnieć," *Polityka*, no. 16, Apr. 17, 1993; no. 17, Apr. 23, 1994.

28. "Pastoral on Jewish-Catholic Relations," issued Nov. 30, 1990, translated in Carol Rittner and John K. Roth, eds., *Memory Offended: The Auschwitz Convent Controversy* (New York: Praeger, 1991), 265–66.

29. "Wspomnienia umarłego," *Gazeta o książkach* (monthly literary supplement to *Gazeta Wyborcza*), no. 11, 1993.

30. Ryszard Siciński, letter to the editor; and Światowy Związek Żołnierzy Armii Krajowej, Zarząd Okręgu "Warszawa," letter to the editor, *Gazeta Wyborcza*, Jan. 29–30, 1994.

31. *Gazeta Wyborcza*, Jan. 29–30, 1994:12–13 (headline).

32. "Polacy-Żydzi: Czarne karty powstania," *Gazeta Wyborcza*, Jan. 29–30, 1994: 12–16. Cichy's article mentions that the insurrectionists also freed hundreds of Jews

from a Nazi prison and that an estimated one thousand Jews, half of whom fell in battle, emerged from hiding to join the fight against the Nazis.

33. *Gazeta Wyborcza,* Feb. 5–6, 1994:10–11 (headline).

34. The entire Polish press joined in the fray; the following year a book-length attack on Michnik and Cichy appeared: Leszek Żebrowski, *Paszkwil Wyborczej (Michnik i Cichy o Powstaniu Warszawskim)* (Warsaw: Burchard Editions, 1995).

35. Tadeusz Filipkowski, letter to the editor, *Gazeta Wyborcza,* Feb. 11, 1994.

36. Ewa L., letter to the editor, *Gazeta Wyborcza,* Feb. 11, 1994.

37. Witold Zalewski, "Pod maską prawdy," *Rzeczpospolita,* Dec. 19, 1994.

38. Wojciech Adamiecki, "Dziedzictwo," *Rzeczpospolita,* Jan. 26, 1995. See also Joanna Podgórska, "Kiedy się już tu jest . . ." *Polityka,* Jan. 28, 1995.

39. Besides the organization of a permanent International Auschwitz Advisory Council, there have been two Symposiums of Jewish Intellectuals on the Future of Auschwitz, one in Oxford in 1990 and another in Kraków in 1992. These gatherings have also addressed the problem of the progressive deterioration of the grounds and exhibits at Auschwitz. On this issue see Timothy W. Ryback, "A Reporter at Large: Evidence of Evil," *The New Yorker,* Nov. 15, 1993:68–81; Jane Perlez, "Decay of a 20th Century Relic: What's the Future of Auschwitz?" *New York Times,* Jan. 5, 1994; and see p. 143 above.

40. Franciszek Piper, "Estimating the Number of Deportees to and Victims of the Auschwitz-Birkenau Camp," *Yad Vashem Studies* 21 (1991): 49–103; see pp. 69–70 above.

41. *New York Times,* June 17, 1992.

42. Aleksander Klugman, "Arafat zaproszony do Oświęcimia: Oburzenie w Izraelu," *Rzeczpospolita,* Nov. 3, 1994. On several occasions in the 1980s, the PLO had participated in commemorations of the Warsaw Ghetto Uprising, with an explicitly ideological rationale: Palestinians today were the "new Jews." See Young, *The Texture of Memory,* 180–82. For a brief summary of the controversies around the meaning of Auschwitz, see Andrew Nagorski, "A Tortured Legacy," *Newsweek,* Jan. 16, 1995.

43. Paweł Wroński, "Jak się modlić w Oświęcimiu," *Gazeta Wyborcza,* Jan. 17, 1995; "Przed 50. rocznicą wyzwolenia obozu w Oświęcimiu: Atmosfera nie taka zła," *Rzeczpospolita,* Jan. 18, 1995.

44. (pw), "Kto przyjedzie do Oświęcimia: Wyzwolicieli nie będzie," *Gazeta Wyborcza,* Jan. 17, 1995; B. M., "Przed 50. rocznicą wyzwolenia obozu w Oświęcimiu: Armia Czerwona nie przyjedzie," *Rzcezpospolita,* Jan. 17, 1995; "Weiss zaprotestuje w Oświęcimiu," *Gazeta Wyborcza,* Jan. 20, 1995; B. M., "Rabin Weiss protestuje w Warszawie," *Rzeczpospolita,* Jan. 25, 1995.

45. "Auschwitz po 50 latach: Dlaczego dwa?" February 5, 1995. The Polish "retreat" had been contrasted with the historic initiative of Cardinal Wyszyński and Polish bishops to their German counterparts in 1965; on the latter see Andrzej Micewski, *Cardinal Wyszynski: A Biography* (San Diego, Calif.: Harcourt Brace Jovanovich, 1984), 255–57.

46. "Słowo biskupów niemieckich z okazji 50. rocznicy wyzwolenia obozu zagłady Auschwitz 27 stycznia 1995 r.: Kościół szanuje niezależność narodu żydowskiego," *Gazeta Wyborcza,* Jan. 25, 1995. A summary appears in Stephen Kinzer,

"German Bishops Cite Catholic 'Denial and Guilt' at Holocaust," *New York Times,* Jan. 27, 1995.

47. Kinzer, "German Bishops."

48. "Oświadczenie Komisji Episkopatu Polski do Dialogu z Judaizmem na 50. rocznicę? wyzwolenia obozu zagłady Auschwitz-Birkenau w Oświęcimiu 27 stycznia 1995 r.: Sprawiedliwi i niegodni," *Gazeta Wyborcza,* Jan. 24, 1995.

49. For an account in English, see Jane Perlez, "Separate Auschwitz Services Highlight Jewish-Polish Dispute," *New York Times,* Jan. 26, 1995; "Survivors Pray at the Crematories of Auschwitz," *New York Times,* Jan. 27, 1995.

50. Jane Perlez, "In Auschwitz, Snow Faintly Falls on the Living and Dead," *New York Times,* Jan. 28, 1995.

51. Klaus Bachman, "Dwa mity Auschwitz," *Rzeczpospolita,* Feb. 7, 1995.

52. B. M., "Rabin Weiss protestuje," *Rzeczpospolita,* Jan. 25, 1995; Beata Modrzejewska, Piotr Kościński, "Nie każdy chce się narażać: Rozmowa z rabinem Avi Weissem," in ibid.; Jerzy Sadecki and Beata Modrzejewska, "Rabin Weiss pikietował kościół w Brzezince," *Rzeczpospolita,* Jan. 26, 1995; "'Przeciw chrystianizacji cierpień żydowskich,'" *Gazeta Krakowska,* Jan. 27, 1995; "Hołd ofiarom Holocaustu," *Echo Krakowy,* Jan. 27–29, 1995; *Berliner Zeitung,* Jan. 28–29, 1995:4; Zbigniew Bartuś and Bogdan Wasztyl, "Rocznica," *Dziennik Polski,* Jan. 30, 1995. The building that housed the nuns has apparently been leased by an anti-Semitic Polish group.

53. Bartuś and Wasztyl, "Rocznica."

54. Beata Modrzejewska, "Gospodarze obozu," *Rzeczpospolita,* Jan. 30, 1995.

55. A. W., "Oświęcim dla Polaków: Symbol męczeństwa narodu polskiego," *Rzeczpospolita,* Jan. 26, 1995; see also Leszek Michno, "Będzie kadisz w Oświęcimiu," *Gazeta Wyborcza,* Jan. 24, 1995. The poll, entitled "Oświęcim in the Polish Collective Memory," was commissioned by the presidential chancellery and undertaken by the CBOS organization; it questioned 1,011 subjects from Jan. 13 to 16, 1995. Another, more general survey, taken by the Demoskop organization between Dec. 29, 1994, and Jan. 5, 1995, revealed that 29 percent of Poles believed that Jews "suffered more from Nazi persecution during the Second World War," 28 percent believed Poles suffered more, and 40 percent believed "both groups suffered about the same." See Jennifer Golub and Renae Cohen, *Knowledge and Remembrance of the Holocaust in Poland* (New York: American Jewish Committee, 1995), 1–2, 28. This survey also establishes that Poles, compared to other nationalities, are the least likely to have heard the claims of Holocaust "revisionists" that the Holocaust never happened (7, 32).

56. "Wiesel chwali," *Gazeta Wyborcza,* Feb. 4–5, 1995.

57. Serge Klarsfeld, "Slaughter of the Innocents," *New York Times,* Jan. 25, 1995; Jarosław Kurek, letter to the editor, *New York Times,* Feb. 2, 1995; Jacek Kalabiński, "NYT o 'polskim Auschwitz,'" *Gazeta Wyborcza,* Jan. 27, 1995; Maria Graczyk, "Rachunek sumień," *Wprost,* Feb. 12, 1995.

58. Jacek Maziarski, "Spór o Auschwitz," *Ład* (Warsaw), Feb. 12, 1995.

59. "Wywiad Adama Michnika," *Gazeta Wyborcza,* Mar. 10, 1995; the interview first appeared in *Le Monde* on Feb. 10.

60. "Pierre Weil i Jean Kahn odpowiadają Michnikowi"; "List barona Maurice'a

Goldsteina do Adama Michnika"; Adam Michnik, "Uogólnienie—przekleństwo XX wieku," *Gazeta Wyborcza*, Mar. 10, 1995.

61. *Gazeta Wyborcza*, Mar. 10, 1995.

62. Katarzyna Janowska, "Tydzień po obchodach 50. rocznicy wyzwolenia obozu w Oświęcimiu: Zła pamięć pozostanie," *Gazeta Krakowska*, Feb. 2, 1995; Bartuś and Wasztyl, "Rocznica."

63. "Pytania o Auschwitz," Feb. 5, 1995.

64. Ibid. For a disturbing fictional account of a visit to Auschwitz written thirty years earlier, see Tadeusz Róziewicz's story "Wycieczka do muzeum" (A trip to a museum) in *Wycieczka do muzeum* (Warsaw: Czytelnik, 1966); on this story, see David H. Hirsch, "Tadeusz Róziewicz Faces the Holocaust Past," in Jacob Neusner, Ernest S. Frerichs, and Nahum M. Sarna, eds., *From Ancient Israel to Modern Judaism: Intellect in Quest of Understand—Essays in Honor of Marvin Fox* (Atlanta, Ga.: Scholars Press, 1991), vol. 4, 137–51.

65. *The Communist Manifesto* (New York: Bantam Books, 1992), 21; the phrase has been used by Marshall Berman in the title of his book of cultural criticism, *All That Is Solid Melts into Air: The Experience of Modernity* (New York: Simon and Schuster, 1982).

Index

Other books in the Modern Jewish History series

Bearing Witness: How America and Its Jews Responded to the Holocaust.
    Henry L. Feingold

The Golden Tradition: Jewish Life and Thought in Eastern Europe.
    Lucy S. Davidowicz

Lest Memory Cease: Finding Meaning in the American Jewish Past.
    Henry L. Feingold